LIBRARY OF HEBREW BIBLE/ OLD TESTAMENT STUDIES

391

Formerly Journal for the Study of the Old Testament Supplement Series

LAND AND CALENDAR

The Priestly Document from Genesis 1 to Joshua 18

Philippe Guillaume

t&t clark

NEW YORK • LONDON

T & T Clark International, 80 Maiden Lane, New York, NY 10038

T & T Clark International, The Tower Building, 11 York Road, London SE1 7NX

T & T Clark International is a Continuum imprint.

Visit the T & T Clark blog at www.tandtclarkblog.com

A catalog record for this book is available from the Library of Congress.

ISBN-13: 978-0-567-32200-5
ISBN-10: 0-567-32200-9

06 07 08 09 10   10 9 8 7 6 5 4 3 2 1

CONTENTS

Part I
THE SABBATICAL CALENDAR AS BASIS
OF THE PRIESTLY DOCUMENT

Part II
LAND AS A MAJOR THEME OF THE PRIESTLY DOCUMENT

FOREWORD

The aim of this study is to save the Priestly document from the debacle of the Graf–Wellhausen system of Pentateuch sources. Thanks to the use of a new criterion provided by the sabbatical calendar, the existence of the *Priesterschrift Grundschicht* (Pg or Priestly Document) can be demonstrated and its delimitation can be fine-tuned. Recent advances on calendar studies in the Dead Sea Scrolls provide new tools for studying Pg since chronology is one of Pg's distinctive marks.

Part I of this study demonstrates that the 364-day or sabbatical calendar known from the books of *Enoch*, *Jubilees* and some Dead Sea Scrolls is already at work in Pg, the narrative base of the Torah. This calendar constitutes the main focus of Gen 1 which introduces Pg with the creation of the week. The other components of the calendar are delineated further on in the Pg narrative, which is structured by the constant interaction between narrative and calendar. Pg appears as a charter for calendar reform. The sabbatical calendar is presented as the basic structure of creation and as the calendar used by the patriarchs and the sons of Israel when they entered the land of Canaan. The calendar thus constitutes the first theme of the present study.

Part II focuses on the delimitation of Pg. Being less easily manipulated than redactors postulated by exegetes, the simple mathematics of the sabbatical calendar establish a firm basis with which to check previous delimitations of Pg, in particular its conclusion, which is a most contentious issue in recent research. Convinced that Pg is the product of priests interested in purity and sacrifice, Pg studies have been oblivious to the constant reference to land. Therefore, the importance of the land in Pg constitutes the second theme to demonstrate Pg's theological and chronological coherence from Creation to Canaan. Anthropological studies of the Levant are introduced into the discussion in order to present a new understanding of the sabbatical year and of the Jubilee which are integrated into Pg.

Originally submitted to the Christkatholischen und Evangelischen Theologischen Fakultät of Berne as *Habilitationsschrift*, the present study focuses upon two themes, land and calendar, leaving a verse by verse commentary of the entire Pg for a later publication. This monograph intends to demonstrate that Pg is more coherent and substantial than current studies suggest.

At this point, I wish to express special thanks to Helen Jacobus (presently writing a dissertation on the lunar zodiac in the Dead Sea Scrolls at the University of Manchester), Peter Nockolds (London) and Meir Bar-Ilan (Bar Ilan University) for enlightening discussions on biblical chronologies and calendars. George Mills (Geneva) was a great help on matters related to Lev 25. Michael Schunck (Bangkok) has made the text much more readable. The editors of the series, Claudia Camp and Andrew Mein, also played a crucial part in the genesis of the book.

ABBREVIATIONS

AB	Anchor Bible
ABD	*Anchor Bible Dictionary*. Edited by D. N. Freedman. 6 vols. New York, 1992
AfOB	Archiv für Orientforschung Beiheft
ANET	*Ancient Near Eastern Texts Relating to the Old Testament*. Edited by J. B. Pritchard. 3d ed. Princeton, 1969
AOAT	Alter Orient und Altes Testament
ARM	Archives royales de Mari
BBB	Bonner biblische Beiträge
BBR	*Bulletin for Biblical Research*
BETL	Bibliotheca ephemeridum theologicarum lovaniensium
BHS	*Biblia hebraica stuttgartensia*
BibInt	*Biblical Interpretation*
BIOSCS	*Bulletin of the International Organization for Septuagint and Cognate Studies*
BK	*Bibel und Kirche*
BKAT	Biblischer Kommentar, Altes Testament. Edited by M. Noth and H. W. Wolff
BN	*Biblische Notizen*
BSO(A)S	*Bulletin of the School of Oriental (and African) Studies*
BWANT	Beiträge zur Wissenschaft vom Alten und Neuen Testament
BZ	*Biblische Zeitschrift*
BZABR	Beihefte zur *ZABR*
BZAW	Beihefte zur *ZAW*
CAD	*The Assyrian Dictionary of the Oriental Institute of the University of Chicago*. Chicago, 1956–
CBET	Contributions to biblical exegesis and theology
CBQ	*Catholic Biblical Quarterly*
CHANE	Culture and History of the Ancient Near East
CoS	*The Context of Scripture*. Edited by W. W. Hallo. 3 vols. Leiden, 1997–
CP	*Classical Philology*
CPJ	*Corpus papyrorum judaicorum*. Edited by V. Tcherikover. 3 vols. Cambridge, 1957–64

DDD	*Dictionary of Deities and Demons in the Bible*. Edited by K. van der Toorn, B. Becking, and P. W. van der Horst. Leiden, 1995
DJD	Discoveries in the Judaean Desert
DK	Diels, H. *Die Fragmente der Vorsokratiker*. Rev. W. Kranz. Berlin, 1952
DSD	*Dead Sea Discoveries*
DSS	Dead Sea Scrolls
ETR	*Etudes théologiques et religieuses*
FAT	Forschungen zum Alten Testament
FRLANT	Forschungen zur Religion und Literatur des Alten und Neuen Testaments
HALOT	Koehler, L., W. Baumgartner, and J. J. Stamm, *The Hebrew and Aramaic Lexicon of the Old Testament*. Translated and edited under the supervision of M. E. J. Richardson. 4 vols. Leiden, 1994–99
HbS	Herders biblische Studien
HdO	Handbuch der Orientalistik
HTR	*Harvard Theological Review*
HUCA	*Hebrew Union College Annual*
IEJ	*Israel Exploration Journal*
JA	*Journal asiatique*
JANES	*Journal of the Ancient Near Eastern Society*
JAOS	*Journal of the American Oriental Society*
JBL	*Journal of Biblical Literature*
JCS	*Journal of Cuneiform Studies*
JESHO	*Journal of the Economic and Social History of the Orient*
JHS	*Journal of Hebrew Scriptures*
JJS	*Journal of Jewish Studies*
JNES	*Journal of Near Eastern Studies*
JQR	*Jewish Quarterly Review*
JSJ	*Journal for the study of Judaism in the Persian, Hellenistic and Roman Period*
JSOT	*Journal for the Study of the Old Testament*
JSOTSup	Journal for the Study of the Old Testament, Supplement Series
JS	*Journal for Semitics / Tydskrif vir Semitistiek*
JTS	*Journal of Theological Studies*
LHBOTS	Library of Hebrew Bible Old Testament Studies
LSTS	Library of Second Temple Studies
LTK	*Lexikon für Theologie und Kirche*
LTP	*Laval théologique et philosophique*
LXX	Septuagint
MT	Masoretic text
NABU	*Nouvelles archéologiques brèves et utilitaires*
NTR	*New Theological Review*
OBO	Orbis biblicus et orientalis

OTS	Oudtestamentische Studiën
PCZ	Edgar, C. C., *Catalogue général des antiquités égyptiennes du Musée du Caire; Zenon Papyri*. Cairo, 1925–40
PEQ	*Palestine Exploration Quarterly*
RA	*Revue d'assyriologie et d'archéologie orientale*
RB	*Revue biblique*
RQ	*Revue de Qumran*
RSB	*Ricerche Storico Bibliche*
SBL	Society of Biblical Literature
SBLSS	SBL Semeia Studies
SJOT	*Scandinavian Journal of the Old Testament*
SJSJ	Supplements to the Journal for the Study of Judaism
SP	Samaritan Pentateuch
TBR	D. Arnaud, *Textes syriens de l'âge du bronze recent*. Barcelona, 1991
TCS	Texts from Cuneiform Sources
TQ	*Theologische Quartalschrift*
TRu	*Theologische Rundschau*
TZ	*Theologische Zeitschrift*
UF	*Ugarit Forschungen*
VT	*Vetus Testamentum*
VTSup	Supplements to Vetus Testamentum
VWGT	Veröffentlichungen der Wissenschaftlichen Gesellschaft für Theologie
Wehr	H. Wehr, *A Dictionary of Modern Written Arabic*. 4th ed. Wiesbaden, 1979
WMANT	Wissenschaftliche Monographien zum Alten und Neuen Testament
ZA	*Zeitschrift für Assyriologie*
ZABR	*Zeitschrift für altorientalische und biblische Rechtsgeschichte*
ZAW	*Zeitschrift für die alttestamentliche Wissenschaft*
ZPE	*Zeitschrift für Papyrologie und Epigraphik*
ZTK	*Zeitschrift für Theologie und Kirche*

INTRODUCTION

"If it ain't broken, don't fix it" is a good piece of advice given in the introduction to a recent proposal to do away with the sources of the Documentary Hypothesis.[1] If most scholars agree today that the so-called Graf–Wellhausen hypothesis of Pentateuch sources is broken,[2] the question is what should be done next. Is it broken beyond repair, and if so, how can it be replaced? The only certainty at this point is that it has not been replaced and it is uncertain whether it ever will be, since the post-modern situation is characterized by a healthy distrust in meta-narratives.[3] If the rise of an all-encompassing hypothesis to replace the Documentary Hypothesis is unlikely, the scholarly discussion faces the grave danger of turning into a "cacophony of voices, each asserting that their convictions are by definition preferred because they are their convictions."[4] The very nature of the Pentateuch requires taking into account its composite nature and the ability to plot the various elements and outright contradictions onto a chronological sequence, however imprecise these may be. Present scholarship is caught on the horns of a dilemma. The Wellhausen categories are either avoided altogether by focusing exclusively upon the final text, or the old system is saved by means of qualifying positions concerning the nature and the date of the E, J and P phases of textual development, thus hoping for a safe middle ground.[5] Such middle ground does not exist anymore. Since it precon-ditions the entire hermeneutical process, the price of avoiding the issue is

---

1. A. F. Campbell and M. A. O'Brien, *Rethinking the Pentateuch* (Louisville: Westminster John Knox, 2005), 1.

2. J. D. Levenson, "The Hebrew Bible, the Old Testament, and Historical Criti-cism," in *The Future of Biblical Studies: The Hebrew Scriptures* (ed. R. E. Friedman and H. G. M. Williamson; Atlanta: Scholars Press, 1987), 19–59; E. W. Nicholson, *The Pentateuch in the Twentieth Century: The Legacy of Julius Wellhausen* (Oxford: Clarendon, 1998).

3. J.-F. Lyotard, *The Postmodern Condition* (Manchester: Manchester University Press, 1984).

4. J. J. Collins, *The Bible After Babel* (Grand Rapids: Eerdmans, 2005), 161.

5. See, for instance, J. F. Gomes, *The Sanctuary of Bethel and the Configura-tion of Israelite Religion* (BZAW 368; Berlin: de Gruyter, 2006), 21–22, 62–65, 93–97.

high. Synchronistic studies are more successful with books from the canon of the Writings, which are characterized by a simpler redactional history, but they are unable to deal adequately with the complexities of the text of the Pentateuch. Judging from recent publications on the market, synchrony has not rendered diachrony obsolete. The English title of an edited volume dealing with the phasing out of the Yahwist adds a question mark to the German title, indicating that the English-reading world is less ready to abandon a system that has been deemed obsolete for the last 30 years on the "continent."[6] Yet, the gravity of the post-Wellhausen situation is felt even in the English-reading world and the LHBOTS series includes one or two volumes per year pertaining directly to the issue.

In 2004, an analysis of the use of the Tetrateuch in Deuteronomistic texts concluded that the Deuteronomistic historian was dealing with a unified Tetrateuch rather than with disparate accounts because Priestly (P) texts are used in Deuteronomy, 1 Samuel and 1 Kings.[7] Such findings will have major consequences when the categories upon which they are based are more sharply defined. However, positing the existence of a sixth-century B.C.E. Deuteronomistic historian and a body of texts traditionally attributed to P have become hypotheses needing to be tested rather than solid premises. It is nevertheless highly significant that most of the Priestly texts discussed by John Harvey correspond to Post-P texts according to the delimitation of the *Priesterschrift Grundschicht* (Pg) offered here.[8] I interpret it as supporting the Pg / *Priesterschrift Supplements* (Ps) division, indicating that Ps texts have "Deuteronomistic" traits.

In 2005, a 200-page study defended the pre-exilic date of the Yahwistic source, although the author states at the outset that he is not "convinced personally of the existence of a 'J' source."[9] It is highly debatable whether linguistic analysis can provide a solid basis to argue that J originated from a period earlier than the late pre-exilic period,[10] yet the

6. J. C. Gertz, K. Schmid and M. Witte (eds.), *Abschied vom Jahwisten* (BZAW 315; Berlin: de Gruyter, 2002), becomes T. B. Dozeman and K. Schmid, *A Farewell to the Yahwist?* (SBLSS 34; Atlanta: SBL, 2006).

7. J. E. Harvey, *Retelling the Torah: The Deuteronomistic Historian's Use of Tetrateuchal Narratives* (JSOTSup 403; London: T&T Clark International, 2004), 99–100.

8. Out of the direct quotations, only Num 13:26 (quoted in Deut 1:25) and Exod 2:23 (quoted in 1 Sam 5:12) correspond to my delimitation of Pg.

9. R. M. Wright, *Linguistic Evidence for the Pre-exilic Date of the Yahwistic Source* (LHBOTS 419; London: T&T Clark International, 2005), 4.

10. Ibid., 164.

study has the merit of showing how little evidence there is for a post-exilic date of J. The very existence of J is debated and present scholarship is a long way from reaching a new consensus.

In 2006, a study in the same collection argues in a radically opposite direction. The Hebrew Pentateuch, J included, would have been composed in its entirety at Alexandria shortly before its translation into Greek and using literary sources found in the famous library, in particular Berossus and Manetho.[11] No scholarly exegesis pertaining to the Pentateuch can afford to overlook the debate, which has far-reaching consequences.

To deal with the confusion generated by the collapse of the Graf–Wellhausen system, the English translation of Reinhard Kratz's introduction to the composition of Old Testament narratives was published in 2005.[12] Seeking undisputed fundamental assumptions, Kratz works with a minimal hypothesis, only presupposing the distinction between Priestly and non-Priestly texts and the special position of Deuteronomy.[13] The same year, Antony Campbell and Mark O'Brien ventured further out, considering tensions and contradictions within the Pentateuch as the result of the compilation of variant versions of the same basic narrative. End users such as story-tellers, preachers or political advisors would pick and choose a particular interpretation that suited their present purpose.[14] This is a useful way to depict of the Pentateuch, which appears more as a repository of a number of contradicting interpretations than as a script aligned upon one single ideology. Yet, exposing the Pentateuch as an internally incoherent collection of narratives merely displaces the obvious question of the origin of such competing interpretations and why they were recorded.

Campbell and O'Brien call for more space to be given to the possibility that the text was used for entertainment or diversion purposes.[15] The authors suggest a *Sitz im Leben* for the story-teller, but bards hardly need the elaborate recording and transmission process of the Pentateuch to practice their art. As for religious and political preaching, partisans tend to destroy rather than transmit their opponents' opinions. The careful

11. R. E. Gmirkin, *Berossus and Genesis, Manetho and Exodus* (LHBOTS 433; London: T&T Clark International, 2006).

12. R. G. Kratz, *Die Komposition der erzählenden Bücher des Alten Testaments* (Göttingen: Vandenhoeck & Ruprecht, 2000); ET *The Composition of the Narrative Books of the Old Testament* (trans. J. Bowden. London: T&T Clark International, 2005).

13. Ibid., ix.

14. Campbell and O'Brien, *Rethinking*, 4–8.

15. Ibid., 6.

recording and transmission of these texts is the consequence of processes further down their history. Yet, it is significant that Campbell and O'Brien bring the brunt of the argument to bear against P, setting out to overthrow the last standing pillar of the Wellhausen system. They claim that there is no P text in Gen 1–11, nor in Genesis at all. The main evidence consists of a list of 25 terms used in Gen 1. Each term receives a very short discussion noting occurrences of the term outside P. Campbell and O'Brien conclude that "the evidence of vocabulary indicating that P *must* have composed Genesis One is certainly *not* there" although it is conceded that "P *may* have composed Genesis One. The language of Genesis One is not restricted to a small or exclusive group within the Hebrew-language community."[16] Since the study is limited to the occurrence of individual terms and avoids concepts developed through particular word clusters, Campbell and O'Brien's conclusion can hardly be more specific than stating that P may or may not have composed Gen 1.

Campbell and O'Brien then argue that the juxtaposition of the Toldot formula in Gen 2:4 and 5:1 and the difference in the depiction of Adam in the two passages indicate that Gen 5:1–2 is not an obvious continuation of Gen 1, although they admit that "the juxtaposition of two previously independent texts to form a single composition is always a possibility. The discontinuity is minor enough to be overlooked, but evident enough that is should not be ignored."[17] Differences of vocabulary between Gen 1 and the Flood narrative are used to silence the coherence, although the authors admit that Creation and P's Flood narrative have more in common with each other than with the alternative J traditions of the Flood.[18] Campbell and O'Brien conclude that it is possible that Gen 1 was written by the Priestly Writer and equally possible that it was written by someone else. Yet the unity of authorship for Gen 1, Gen 5:1–2 and the P Flood narrative must, according to Campbell and O'Brien, be considered highly unlikely.[19] While they recognize that the key to the existence of a Priestly narrative is found in the first chapters of Genesis, the demonstration by Campbell and O'Brien reveals the inconclusiveness of studies based solely on lexicography. Individual words are too narrow to serve as reliable criteria to identify redactors; studies must embrace ideas and notions conveyed by word clusters. Moreover, authorship is a flawed category since it is not relevant to the existence or inexistence of a Priestly narrative. Pg could have been written by several hands and still

16. Ibid., 105–11.
17. Ibid., 111–12.
18. Ibid., 113–14.
19. Ibid., 115.

retain the theological coherence that would prove its existence as an independent and self-contained document.

In conclusion, while current studies are conscious of the inadequacy of the Graf–Wellhausen system, they often continue to function within its framework because there is no viable alternative. The intent of the present work is to repair one component of the broken system, namely, P.[20] Contrary to Van Seters, who saves the Yahwist (J) by transferring it from the reign of Solomon to after the destruction of Jerusalem,[21] I claim that Pg rather than J is the earliest narrative providing the backbone of the Pentateuch. The consequence is that Pg absorbs some elements traditionally attributed to J, while other J elements become post-Pg, as parts of Ps, that is, major editing phases of Pg.

At this point in time, the loss of consensus on how to replace the Graf–Wellhausen system with a systematic chronological sequence of textual phases is daunting, leading to an exclusive focus on the canonical form of the text. Yet, the loss of historical focus for critical exegesis leads to the loss of otherness. One benefit of a historical focus renders the confessional identity of the exegete irrelevant and allows scholars of different horizons to enter a discussion in which each tries to persuade the others by appeal to evidence and criteria acceptable to the other participants.[22] Those advantages of a historical approach are no small achievements and for this reason it is worth the effort to maintain a viable platform to enable continued dialogue. At the moment, the platform is reduced to the fact that the Documentary Hypothesis is unsustainable. Great is the temptation to withdraw within the walls of fortresses where a broader platform is shared by a smaller audience. The alternative is to salvage academic debate by setting new paradigms. A new consensus will somehow be founded upon P because P remains the least contested pillar of the Wellhausen system. Abandoning P alongside E and J, as Campbell and O'Brien suggest, is like tossing the last available compass overboard upon learning about the drift of the Magnetic North Pole.

The outlines of P identified by Theodor Nöldeke in 1869 have somehow survived the turmoil which swept J away.[23] The identification of the *Priesterschrift* primarily on the basis of language has held its ground,

20. Since D pertains mainly to Deuteronomy, it constitutes a particular case within the Pentateuch which will not be discussed here.

21. J. Van Seters, *Prologue to History: The Yahwist as Historian in Genesis* (Zurich: Theologischer Verlag, 1992).

22. Collins, *Bible*, 10.

23. T. Nöldeke, "Die sogennante Grundschicht des Pentateuch," in *Untersuchungen zur Kritik des Alten Testaments* (Kiel, 1869), 1–144 (94–95).

thanks to a propensity for numbers and formula, strikingly different theological concepts and a consistent chronology.[24] Pg's style was often deemed stiff and pedantic,[25] which helps to make it easy to recognize. Hence Pg is so peculiar that its identification is much more objective than is the case with other potential layers. Of course, style can be imitated, but theological content often unmasks imitation. Therefore, it is my contention that the Pg hypothesis remains valid, although it needs to be reviewed in the light of recent advances. Kratz's distinction between Priestly and non-Priestly texts is a promising avenue in the move towards a post-Wellhausen consensus, although the priestly category needs serious redefinition. An updated Pg can provide a reliable base for exploring the formation of the Pentateuch and Hexateuch. We desperately need a stepping-stone, an intermediary stage between the final text and individual old traditions that were integrated into it.

Current Rival Hypotheses

Updating Pg faces several challenges, the first one being the definition of the P siglum. Considerable confusion exists in present scholarship since P designates two different but partially overlapping entities. The Kaufmann School opposes a vaguely circumscribed Priestly Code named P, to a Holiness Code (H) which comprising of Lev 17–26.[26] Although this understanding of P derives from the Graf–Wellhausen system, it is resolutely attributed an earlier date, at least during the "first" temple because the period is seen as foundational for Judaism. The focus on the first temple period represents a reaction to nineteenth-century Protestantism, which saw Prophetism as the unaltered fountainhead. The Kaufmann School focuses mainly on the legal parts of Leviticus and Numbers. The problem is that this approach downplays the fact that P and H are the

24. S. R. Driver, *Introduction to the Literature of the Old Testament* (Edinburgh: T. & T. Clark, 1894), 118–50. M. Weinfeld, *Deuteronomy and the Deuteronomist School* (Oxford: Clarendon, 1972), 320–65; J. Blenkinsopp, "The Structure of P," *CBQ* 38 (1976): 276–92; N. Lohfink, "Die Priesterschrift und die Geschichte," in his *Studien zum Pentateuch* (Stuttgart: Katholisches Bibelwerk, 1988), 222–23 n. 29 (published in English as "The Priestly Narrative and History," in Lohfink, *Theology of the Old Testament* [Minneapolis: Fortress, 1994], 136–72).

25. J. Wellhausen, *Prolegomena to the History of Ancient Israel* (trans. J. S. Black and A. Menzies; Cleveland: Meridian, 1957), 6; S. McEvenue, "Word and Fulfilment," *Semitics* 1 (1970): 104–10.

26. Y. Kaufmann, *The Religion of Israel* (Chicago: University of Chicago Press, 1960); J. Milgrom, "Priestly 'P' Source," *ABD* 5:454–61; M. Haran, "Ezekiel, P, and the Priestly School," *VT* 58 (2008): 211–18.

products of a literary process and that it has been impossible to establish
the chronological primacy of P or H over the other, for the simple reason
that neither P nor H is homogeneous. The other approach to P distinguishes between Pg and various Ps redactions. Pg is restricted to the
narrative parts while Ps designates legislative and ritual texts inserted
into Pg.[27] Pg is dated to the Persian period and is seen either as the
backbone of the Pentateuch, a kind of Gospel before the Law, or as one
of the final redactions of the Torah. Pg is the object of the present study
and for this reason "Pg" will be used throughout this text to differentiate
it from the P of the Kaufmann School. Under the general designation of
Ps, I refer to any material that I exclude from my delimitation of Pg,
whether this material is pre-Pg, post-Pg, or displaying Deuteronomistic
traits.

The second challenge facing the study of Pg is that its extent is
disputed. Everyone agrees that Pg starts with Gen 1, but where does it
end? For the last fifty years, the trend has been to shift gradually the end
of Pg back from the Historical books to the Pentateuch. The most
extreme shrinking is that proposed by Eckart Otto, who sees Pg ending at
Exod 29:42 with YHWH ordering a perpetual holocaust.[28] The work of
Thomas Pola has gained a wider recognition. Pola argues that Pg ends at
Exod 40:33b and the erection of the cultic structure (the Residence,
mishkan) in the wilderness. The Tent of Meeting (or Tabernacle), its
sacrificial apparatus and the infilling of the Residence with YHWH's
glory are all excluded from Pg.[29] Such an abrupt end of Pg is problematic. There are indeed elements in the narration of the completion of the
Residence that connect it back to Gen 1, but this is not enough to support
the claim that the narrative closes there and then, since linkages with
Priestly elements are also found in Joshua. Pola shores up his claim with
parallels from Ezekiel. He equates Pg's Sinai with Ezekiel's Zion to
establish that the land promises (Gen 17:8; 35:12; Exod 6:8) are fulfilled
when YHWH announces that "They will know that I am YHWH their God,
who brought them out from the land of Egypt for my Residence is among

---

27. M. Noth, *Überlieferungsgeschichte des Pentateuch* (Stuttgart: Kohlhammer, 1948), 48; K. Elliger, "Sinn und Ursprung der priesterlichen Geschichtserzählung," *ZTK* 49 (1952): 121–42.

28. E. Otto, "Forschungen zur Priesterschrift," *TRu* 62 (1997): 1–50, and "Die nachpriesterschriftliche Pentateuch Redaktion," in *Studies in the Book of Exodus* (ed. M. Vervenne; BETL 126; Leuven: Leuven University Press, 1996), 63–111 (83).

29. T. Pola, *Die ursprüngliche Priesterschrift* (WMANT 70; Neukirchen–Vluyn: Neukirchener Verlag, 1995).

them" (Exod 29:46). For Pola, the original sanctuary built at Sinai was not transportable (Exod 25:8–9).[30] Hence, he claims that Sinai in Pg means nothing but Zion. The problem is that the relevant passages (Ezek 20; 37:26–28; 40–48) do not mention Jerusalem, while Zion never occurs in Ezekiel at all. Pola has to infer Zion theology from the book of Ezekiel as a whole.[31] His mini-Pg relies heavily on a problematic reading of Ezekiel. In spite of this overinvestment on Sinai, Pola does not integrate the Sinai covenant into Pg and even removes all the cultic material between Exod 29:45–46 and 40:16.[32] After crossing the Reed Sea, the sons of Israel enter the wilderness of Sinai; Moses climbs the mountain to receive the order to build a sanctuary.[33] This sanctuary is a residence which allows YHWH to dwell among his people. For Pola, Pg closes with the completion of the Residence.

Despite such a constrained delimitation of Pg, Pola's study marks a major advance in Pg studies since it drives a wedge between the Residence (משכן) and the Tabernacle (אהל). It offers a new criterion to identify two separate Priestly strands in the wilderness material. When the Tabernacle and all its sacrificial gear are treated as secondary, the Residence becomes the red thread that allows the tracing of the Pg narrative through Leviticus and Numbers, precisely where it is blurred by the huge amount of secondary material added to it. Therefore, Pola has unwittingly opened the way for a much longer version of Pg with a sharper theological profile.

After Otto and Pola, further shrinkage would be fatal to the Pg hypothesis, the existence of which is now at stake in present scholarship. For instance, a recent study claims that Abraham, one the traditional

---

30. Ibid., 273.

31. Ezek 20:40 may or may not refer to Jerusalem; see ibid., 211.

32. See also J. Blenkinsopp, "Structure and Meaning in the Sinai–Horeb Narrative," in *A Biblical Itinerary in Search of Method, Form and Content* (ed. E. E. Carpenter; JSOTSup 240; Sheffield: Sheffield Academic Press, 1997), 109–25 (113–14): "The most notable feature of P's Sinai narrative is not, however, what it says but what it omits: it has nothing to say about the *making of a covenant*… [T]he absence of any distinct or conflated P version of covenant-making at Sinai signals a distinctive feature of Priestly theology." One of the most cogent indicators for the lateness of the Sinai covenant is that Lev 26:42–45 does not mention it, although it is later than Pg; see J. Hughes, *Secrets of the Times* (JSOTSup 66; Sheffield: JSOT Press, 1990), 49. After an in-depth examination of the murmuring episodes, D. Frankel, *The Murmuring Stories of the Priestly School* (VTSup 89; Leiden: Brill, 2002), 316, concludes that none of those stories betray the slightest awareness of a Sinai covenant.

33. Refer to the Appendix to the present study for Pola's exact delimitation.

pillars of Pg, has nothing to do with Pg.[34] Conscious of the dangerous consequences of the current reductions of Pg, Christian Frevel argues in favour of a return to the traditional conclusion of Pg at Moses' death in a conscious attempt to save Martin Noth's heritage.[35] However, the import of Frevel's study is limited by its focus, which is restricted to the second part of Pg only (Exod 19:1–Deut 34:8). Christophe Nihan also seeks to overcome Pola's minimal delimitation by extending Pg to Lev 16. Nihan rejects Pola's exclusion of the Tabernacle and integrates the sacrificial cult described in Exod 25–Lev 16*, accepting the traditional distinction between P (Lev 1–16) and H (Lev 17–21).[36] Nihan's argument is built upon ancient Near Eastern parallels, in particular *Enuma eliš* where Marduk's sanctuary is completed exactly one year after the victory over Tiamat. Because YHWH's temple is "achieved one year after the *exodus*," Nihan considers that Pg's account of the Exodus must continue with the setting up of a sacrificial cult.[37] There are two problems here. With all its sacrificial gear, the Tent is no temple, although Nihan insists that the P composition was supposed to legitimate the Second Temple cult at Jerusalem.[38] The second problem is that, contrary to Marduk's temple, the Residence (not the Tent) was not set up exactly one year after the Exodus, unless one discusses the significance of the period between the night following the fourteenth day of first month (14 I) and the first day of the first month a year later. The parallel must be weighted in the light of the chronology, a conspicuous element in Pg which implies a discussion of calendars. For this reason, I agree with Nihan that Pola's ending in Exod 40 is too restrictive; I, however, take the opposite path to compensate it. I accept Pola's rejection of the Tabernacle and of the sacrificial cult it entails while I reject the traditional distinction between P and H in Leviticus. On the basis of Pg's chronology and calendar, I integrate elements of H which are congruent with the sabbatical calendar and set the end of Pg in Joshua.

34. B. Ziemer, *Abram–Abraham* (BZAW 350; Berlin: de Gruyter, 2005), 280–90, and "Erklärung der Zahlen von Gen 5 aus ihrem kompositionellen Zusammenhang," *ZAW* 121 (2009): 1–18.

35. C. Frevel, *Mit Blick auf das Land die Schöpfung erinnern. Zum Ende der Priestergrundschrift* (HbS 23; Freiburg: Herder, 2000).

36. C. Nihan, *From Priestly Torah to Pentateuch* (Tübingen: Mohr Siebeck, 2007).

37. Ibid., 55.

38. Ibid., 383–94.

Method and Presentation

The sabbatical calendar provides the external criterion needed for the recovery of Pg. The significant advantage of a calendar is that mathematics is less easily manipulated than redactional layers. Being less subjective, it is a better guide for identifying Pg from the mass of secondary material. Internal criteria are used in complement as Pg provides highly distinctive theological points in the course of the narrative. The amount of circularity is reduced since most of the internal criteria are drawn from the beginning of Genesis which remains the least contentious part of the narrative in contemporary exegesis. Besides the guidelines provided by the sabbatical calendar, the Pg thread can be followed throughout Genesis by simply applying the principles established in the first ten chapters of the book. Then, using the Residence as a characteristic of Pg greatly facilitates the isolation of Pg throughout the wilderness narratives, beyond the end of the book of Exodus where Pola placed the end of Pg. Treating the Tabernacle and all its sacrificial gear as secondary, Pg becomes a lot easier to identify in Exodus, Leviticus and Numbers, precisely where its traces have always been felt to fade away. The implications of the identification of such a long Pg unconcerned with priestly matters are discussed in the concluding chapter of the present study, where Pg is put in historical perspective.

For reasons of size, a verse to verse analysis of the delimitation of Pg with extensive bibliographic references has to be postponed for another publication. To compensate for the lack of a detailed discussion of the delimitation of Pg, the next section provides a translation of the entire Pg document as I delimitate its contents. The aim is to enable the reader to know what I include in Pg. Campbell and O'Brien have already published an English translation of Pg, which demarcates the J, E and non-source material.[39] This edition, however, reproduces Noth's delimitation of Pg, a delimitation which took the validity of the Graf–Wellhausen system of sources for granted. Moreover, Noth's interest in Pg was peripheral. Not only did he not question the existence of J (which I do), he also downplayed the significance of Pg in Joshua to shore up his hypothesis of the Deuteronomistic History.[40] For these reasons, the

---

39. A. F. Campbell and M. A. O'Brien, *Sources of the Pentateuch* (Minneapolis: Fortress, 1993).

40. See M. Noth, *Überlieferungsgeschichtliche Studien* (Tübingen: Niemeyer, 1967), 180–90, for a brazenly biased discussion of Joshua material "in Pg style" or "remembering Pg."

appendix supplies a synoptic list of chapters and verses which compares my delimitation of Pg with other recent ones.

Some sections of the translation are reproduced and their delimitation discussed at relevant points of the study.[41] Otherwise readers are referred to the overall translation. Readers unfamiliar with Pg are advised to take the time to read through the translation to get a feel for the entire document in one go. The ultimate aim of this work is to produce a full-fledged commentary of Pg which would overcome the problems resulting from the artificial division of commentaries of the Pentateuch to individual biblical books. The division by biblical books is justified from an editorial point of view, but since Pg runs across six of these books, Pg's impressive coherence is lost and claims that Pg is an incoherent and fragmentary redaction layer become a self-fulfilling prophecy. I thus hope to demonstrate that Pg is more coherent and substantial than current studies suggest.

---

41. Throughout the present work an asterisk attached to a biblical reference signifies a partial form of the given verse or chapter.

THE PRIESTLY DOCUMENT TRANSLATED

The following translation reflects a new delimitation of Pg according to the results of my enquiry, which are partially presented in this study. Since the target reader is familiar with the biblical text, it seemed preferable to pursue adequacy rather than acceptability, to bring the original to the reader rather than the reader to the original.[1] The requirements of idiomatic English have been subordinated to the need to remain close to the original and to limit interpretative smoothing as much as possible. The importance of retaining closeness to the Hebrew led to the attempted rendering of a Hebrew term by one English word or expression. Notable exceptions to this rule are the very frequent occurrences of אמר√, rendered here as "to order, say, talk, speak" according to context. Repetitions have been mostly retained. The basic clause structure of Pg's Hebrew has not been improved. As much as possible, adjectives and participles are rendered as such, except in Lev 25, which represents a particular challenge. Couched in legal jargon that is not fully understood today, literality had to give way to a more interpretative translation for the sake of readability since the literal rendering adopted for the rest of Pg produced a totally unintelligible text.

Since this study aims at demonstrating the coherence of Pg, all indications of intervening non-Pg material have been deliberately removed to ensure a smooth reading and help the reader picture Pg as a narrative whole rather than as a fragmentary redactional layer. Only book title and chapters are indicated at the head of each section. The breakdown in verses is given in the appendix. Readers are offered here what biblical commentaries or standard studies of Pg cannot offer: a reading of Pg as the hypothesis claims it once stood, as an independent document presenting Israelite antiquity from Creation to Canaan. Access comes at a price. Native English speakers are kindly requested to allow some oddness as reflection of the original. It important to note at this point that it was not necessary to add a single postulated Hebrew word to obtain a continuous

---

1. See B. G. Wright III, "The Letter of Aristeas and the Reception History of the Septuagint," *BIOSCS* 39 (2006): 47–67 (63).

text. This means that subsequent redactors carefully inserted additions without removing any parts of the original narrative, which stands intact in the final form of the Torah.

* * *

Genesis 1–2

Once upon a time, Elohim created the skies and the land, the land had been a hodgepodge: darkness on the surface of Deep and the wind of Elohim hovering on the surface of the waters. Elohim ordered: "Let there be light!" There was light. Elohim saw the light was good. Elohim separated the light from the darkness. Elohim called the light "day," and the darkness he called "night." There was evening. There was morning, day one.

Elohim ordered: "Let there be a dome inside the waters and let it separate waters from waters!" Elohim made the dome. He separated the waters under the dome from the waters above the dome. It was so. Elohim called the dome "skies." There was evening; there was morning, day two.

Elohim ordered: "Let the waters under the skies be gathered to a single place, and let the dry be seen!" The waters were assembled under the skies to their place. The dry was seen. It was so. Elohim called the dry "land" and the gathered waters "seas." Elohim saw it was good. Elohim ordered: "Let the land sprout grass and trees bearing fruits and seeds each according to its own kind on the land!" It was so. The land brought out grass and trees bearing fruit and seed according to its kind. Elohim saw it was good. There was evening. There was morning, day three.

Elohim ordered: "Let there be lights on the dome of the skies to separate the day and the night. They will serve as signs for festivals, for days and years. They will be luminaries on the dome of the skies to lighten the land!" It was so. Elohim made the two great lights—the great one to rule the day and the small one to rule the night, and the stars. Elohim put them in the expanse of the sky to lighten the land, to rule the day and the night and to separate light and darkness. Elohim saw it was good. There was evening. There was morning, day four.

Elohim ordered: "Let the waters teem with living creatures, and let fowl fly over the land in front of the dome of the skies!" It was so. Elohim created the great monsters and every living creature: the crawlers teeming in waters according to their kinds, and every winged fowl according to its kind. Elohim saw it was good. Elohim blessed them: "Fructify, multiply and fill the waters in the seas, let the bird multiply in the land." There was evening. There was morning, day five.

Elohim ordered: "Let the land bring out living creatures according to their kind: livestock, crawler and wild animal each according to its kind!" It was so. Elohim made the wild animals according to their kind, the livestock according to its kind, and all crawlers of the soil according to their kinds. Elohim saw it was good. Elohim ordered: "Let us make humankind in our image, in our similitude, and let them tame the fish of the sea, the fowl of the skies and the livestock and all the land and all the crawlers over the land!" Elohim created the humankind in his image, in the image of Elohim he created it; male and female he created them. Elohim blessed them. Elohim ordered them: "Fructify and multiply and fill the land and domesticate it and exploit the fish of the sea and the fowl of the skies and every life that is crawling on the land!" Elohim ordered: "Look,[2] I gave you every seed-bearing grass that is on the face of the whole land and every fruit tree; it will be food for you and for the wild animal and for every fowl of the skies and for every crawler on the land with a breath of life in it, every green plant for food!" It was so. Elohim saw all he had made, and look, it was very good. There was evening. There was morning, day six.

The skies, the land and all their armies were completed. In the seventh day Elohim completed his work that he had done. He stopped on the seventh day from all his work that he had done. Elohim blessed the seventh day. He sanctified it because on it he stopped from all the work which Elohim had created in order to continue making it. This is the genesis of the skies and the land when they were created.

Genesis 5

This is the book of humankind's genesis in the day Elohim created Humankind.[3] In the similitude of Elohim he made it, male and female he created them. He blessed them. He called their names humankind on the day of their creation. Adam Humankind had lived 130 years. He fathered a son in his similitude, according to his own image. He called his name Seth Foundation. The days of Adam Humankind after his fathering Seth Foundation were 800 years. He fathered sons and daughters. All the days of Adam Humankind which he lived were 930 years. He died.

Seth Foundation lived 105 years. He fathered Enosh Man. Seth Foundation lived 807 years after his fathering of Enosh Man. He fathered sons and daughters. All the days of Seth Foundation: 912 years. He died.

Enosh Man lived 90 years. He fathered Kenan Blacksmithy. Enosh Man lived 815 years after his fathering of Kenan Blacksmithy. He fathered sons and daughters. All the days of Enosh Man were 905 years. He died.

Kenan Blacksmithy lived 70 years. He fathered Mahalel Maddened-God. Kenan Blacksmithy lived 840 years after his fathering of Mahalel Maddened-God. He fathered sons and daughters. All the days of Kenan Blacksmithy were 910 years. He died.

Mahalel Maddened-God lived 65 years. He fathered Jared Going-Down. Mahalel Maddened-God lived 830 years after he fathered Jared Going-Down. He fathered sons and daughters. All the days of Mahalel Maddened-God were 895 years. He died.

Jared Going-Down lived 162 years. He fathered Enoch Initiated. Jared Going-Down lived 800 years after his fathering of Enoch Initiated. He fathered sons and daughters. All the days of Jared Going-Down were 962 years. He died.

Enoch Initiated lived 65 years. He fathered Methuselah Man-at-Arms. Enoch Initiated behaved himself with the Elohim 300 years after his fathering of

---

2. On הנה, see Y. Sadka, "*Hinne* in Biblical Hebrew," *UF* 33 (2001): 479–93.

3. In this verse, Pg purposefully mingles Adam, as humankind, both male and female, as in Gen 1, and Adam as a male ancestor, as in the genealogical list that follows in Gen 5. Since the names of the ancestors in this chapter are significant, I juxtapose their traditional rendering with their meaning. See also D. J. A. Clines, "אדם, the Hebrew for Human, Humanity," *VT* 53 (2003): 297–310.

Methuselah Man-at-Arms. He fathered sons and daughters. All the days of Enoch Initiated *was*[4] 365 years. Enoch Initiated behaved himself with the Elohim; then he was no more because Elohim took him.

Methuselah Man-at-Arms lived 187 years. He fathered Lamech Sword. Methuselah Man-at-Arms lived 782 years after he fathered Lamech Sword. He fathered sons and daughters. All the days of Methuselah Man-at-Arms were 969 years. He died.

Lamech Sword lived 182 years. He fathered Noah Comfort. Lamech Sword lived 595 years after his fathering of Noah Comfort. He fathered sons and daughters. All the days of Lamech Sword were 753 years. He died.

Noah Comfort was 500 years old. He fathered Shem Us, Ham Cousin and Japheth Westman.

Genesis 6–9

This is Noah's genesis:

Noah was a whole and righteous man among his generations; with the Elohim Noah behaved himself. Noah fathered three sons: Shem, Ham and Japheth. The land was decayed in front of the Elohim. The land was filled with violence. Elohim saw the land, and look, it was decayed because all flesh had made it decay by its behaviour on the land. Elohim ordered Noah: "As far as I am concerned, the end to all flesh has arrived because the land is filled with their violence and look, I am going to let them decay along with the land. Make yourself a box of cypress wood; make compartments in the box and cover it with pitch inside and outside. This is how you will make it: 300 cubits long, 50 cubits wide and 30 cubits high. Make a top for the box and complete it to a cubit from the top. Put the door of the box in its side. Make lower, second and third decks! Look, I am bringing the flood's waters on the land to destroy from under the skies every flesh that has a breath of life; everything on the land will perish but I will set up my treaty with you. You should enter the box—you and your sons and your wife and your sons' wives with you. From every animal, from every flesh, two of each you will bring into the box to be with you: male and female shall they be from the fowl according to their kind and from the livestock according to their kind, from every crawler of the soil according to their kind, two of each will come to you to be kept alive. Take from every food that will be eaten and store it with you, it will be food for you and for them!" Noah did everything according to what Elohim commanded him, so he did. In the six-hundredth year of Noah's lifespan, in the second month, on the seventeenth day of the month—on that day all the springs of the great Deep split and the hatches of the skies were opened. The rain was on the land 40 days and 40 nights.[5] On that very day, Noah entered the box with Shem, Ham and Japheth, Noah's sons, and Noah's wife and his sons' three wives with them, them and every wild animal according to its kind and every livestock according to its kind and every crawler that crawls on

---

4. Though ungrammatical in English, the Masoretic text uses the singular to underline the importance of number 365 as a unit (see Chapter 2).

5. This phrase is usually attributed to J. For the reasons why I ascribe it to Pg, see Chapter 3.

the land according to its kind and every fowl according to its kind, every bird, every wing. Two of every flesh that has a living breath arrived to Noah in the box. Those entering were a male and a female of every flesh. They entered according to what Elohim had commanded him. The flood was on the land 40 days and 40 nights. The waters multiplied. They lifted the box. It rose above the land. The waters were strong. They multiplied greatly on the land. The box went on the surface of the waters and the waters were extremely strong on the land. All the high mountains that were under all the skies were covered. The waters went strong fifteen cubits above the top. The mountains were covered. Every flesh crawling on the land perished: fowl, livestock, wild animals, insects teeming on the land, and all humankind. Elohim remembered Noah and all the wild animals and all the livestock that were with him in the box. Elohim caused a wind to pass on the land. The waters receded. The springs of the Deep and the hatches of the skies were closed. The rain was restrained from the skies. The waters returned. The box rested in the seventh month, on the twenty-seventh day of the month on the mountains of Urartu and the waters were going on and receding until the tenth month. In the eleventh month, on day one of the month, the heads of the mountains became visible. In year 601, at first on day one of the month, the waters were wasted from over the land. Noah removed the covering of the box. He saw, and look, the face of the soil was devastated but on the second month, on the twenty-seventh day of the month, the land was dry. Elohim said to Noah: "Come out of the box, you and your wife and your sons and your sons' wives with you, all the animals that are with you—every flesh, fowl, livestock and all the insects that crawls on the land—make them come out with you so they will teem in the land and fructify and multiply on the land!" Noah came out with his sons and his wife and his sons' wives with him, all the animals, all insects, fowl, and crawlers on the land according to their families they came out of the box. Elohim blessed Noah and his sons. He ordered them: "Fructify and multiply and fill the land, fear and dread of you will be upon all the animals of the land and upon all the fowl of the skies; among all that crawls on the soil and among all the fish of the sea. Into your hands they are given, every crawler that has life will be food for you like green grass. I have given you all except your blood representing your life. I will request it from the hand of every animal. I will request it from the hand of humankind. From the hand of each one I will request the life of humankind. Whoever sheds the blood of humankind, by humankind his blood will be shed; for in the image of Elohim he made humankind and you, fructify and multiply, teem in the land and multiply upon it!" Elohim ordered Noah and to his sons with him: "Look, I am validating my treaty with you and with your seed after you and with every living creature that is with you—fowl, livestock and every wild animal which came out of the box with you— every living creature of the land and I validate my treaty with you so that no flesh will ever be cut off again by the waters of the flood. Never again will there be a flood to destroy the land!" Elohim ordered: "This is the sign of the treaty I am establishing between me and you and every living creature with you, for everlasting generations herewith I give my bow in the cloud. It will be the sign of the treaty between me and the land. Whenever clouds are on the land the bow will be seen in the cloud and I will remember my treaty between me and you and all living creatures among all flesh. Never again will the waters flood to destroy all flesh. Whenever the bow will be in the clouds I will see it to remember the everlasting treaty between Elohim and all living creatures among all flesh on the land!" Elohim ordered Noah: "This is the sign of the treaty I validated between me and all flesh on the land!" Noah lived 350 years after the flood. All the days of Noah were 950 years. He died.

Genesis 10

This is the genesis of Noah's sons, Shem, Ham and Japheth. Sons were born to them after the flood:

Sons of Japheth: Gomer, Magog, Madai, Javan, Tubal, Meshech and Tiras.

Sons of Gomer: Ashkenaz, Riphath and Togarmah.

Sons of Javan: Elishah, Tarshish, the Kittim and the Rodanim from these the island of the folks[6] were organized according to their lands, each with its own language, their clans within their folks.

Sons of Ham: Cush, Mizraim, Put and Canaan.

Sons of Cush: Seba, Havilah, Sabtah, Raamah and Sabteca.

Sons of Raamah: Sheba and Dedan. These are the sons of Ham by their families and languages, in their lands and folks.

Sons of Shem: Arpachshad, Lud and Aram.

Sons of Aram: Uz, Hul, Gether and Mash. These are the sons of Shem by their families and languages, in their lands and folks.

Those are the families of Noah's sons, according to their genesis, within their folks; and from these the folks were organized in the land after the flood.

Genesis 11

This is Shem's genesis:

Shem was 100 years old. He fathered Arpachshad 2 years after the flood. Shem lived 500 years after his fathering of Arpachshad. He fathered sons and daughters. He died.

Arpachshad lived 35 years, he fathered Kainan. Arpachshad lived 430 years after his fathering Kainan. He fathered sons and daughters and he died.

Kainan lived 130 years and he fathered Shelah. And after he engendered Shelah, Kainan lived 330 years and had other sons and daughters and he died.

Shelah lived 30 years. He fathered Heber. Shelah lived 403 years after his fathering of Heber. He fathered sons and daughters. He died.

Heber lived 34 years. He fathered Peleg. Heber lived 430 years after his fathering of Peleg. He fathered sons and daughters. He died.

Peleg lived 30 years. He fathered Reu. Peleg lived 209 years after his fathering of Reu. He fathered sons and daughters. He died.

Reu lived 32 years. He fathered Serug. Reu lived 207 years after his fathering of Serug. He fathered sons and daughters. He died.

Serug lived 30 years. He fathered Nahor. Serug lived 200 years after his fathering of Nahor. He fathered sons and daughters. He died.

6.   The rendering of גוים as "nations" and "peoples" (NRSV) is inadequate since it mixes ancient and modern ethnographic categories. Although outdated, "folk" avoids the confusion with עם.

Nahor lived 29 years. He fathered Terah. Nahor lived 119 years after his fathering of Terah. He fathered sons and daughters. He died.

Terah lived 70 years. He fathered Abram, Nahor and Haran.

Genesis 11–13; 16–17; 21; 23; 25

This is Terah's genesis:

Terah fathered Abram, Nahor and Haran and Haran fathered Lot. Haran died before Terah his father in the land of his birth, in Ur of the Chaldeans. Abram and Nahor took wives; the name of Abram's wife was Sarai, and the name of Nahor's wife was Milcah daughter of Haran, the father of Milcah and Iscah. Sarai was barren; there was no child for her. Terah took Abram his son, and Lot son of Haran son of his son, and Sarai his daughter-in-law wife of Abram his son. They went out with them from Ur of the Chaldeans to go to the land of Canaan. They went as far as Haran. They settled there. The days of Terah were 205 years. Terah died in Haran. Abram was 75 years old when he set out from Haran. Abram took Sarai his wife, Lot his brother's son, all the possessions and souls they got in Haran. They set out to go to the land of Canaan. They arrived in the land of Canaan, but the land could not support them together, for their possessions had multiplied and they could not stay together. They went their separate ways. Abram lived in the land of Canaan but Lot lived in the cities of the Kikar. Yet, Sarai Abram's wife had not borne for him. She had an Egyptian maid, her name was Hagar. Sarai, Abram's wife took Hagar her Egyptian maid at the end of 10 years of Abram's presence in the land of Canaan. She gave her to Abram her husband as wife. Hagar bore a son for Abram. Abram called the son Hagar bore Ishmael. Abram was 86 years old when Hagar bore Ishmael for Abram. Then, Abram was 99 years old. YHWH presented himself to Abram. He ordered him: "I am El Shaddai, behave yourself in front of me and be whole, and I will set my treaty between me and you, and you will multiply yourself very very much!" Abram fell on his face. Elohim said to him: "As for me, look, my treaty with you: you will be a father of a crowd of folks, therefore your name is no longer Abram. It will be Abraham for I have made you father of a crowd of folks, I will make you fructify very very much. I will turn you into folks. Kings will come from you. I will validate my treaty between me and you and your seed after you for generations as an everlasting treaty. I will be your Elohim and the one of your seed after you. I will give you and your seed after you the land of your sojourns, all the land of Canaan as everlasting tenure to you and your seed after you. I will be their Elohim." Elohim ordered Abraham, "As for you, keep my treaty, you and your seed after you and their generations. This is my treaty which you will keep between me and you and your seed after you. Make sure that every male is circumcised. You will circumcise your foreskins. It will be the sign of the treaty between me and you: at eight days old every male of your generations will be circumcised. House-born or bought from any foreigner that is not from your seed, they will be circumcised irrespective whether born of your household or bought with your money. It will be my treaty in your flesh as everlasting treaty. But any uncircumcised male whose foreskin has not been circumcised, his life will be cut off from his people!" Elohim ordered Abraham: "Sarai your wife, don't call her Sarai any more for her name will be Sarah, I will bless her. I will even give for you a son from her and I will bless her. She will turn into folks; there will be kings of people from her." Abraham fell on his face. He laughed. He said in his heart: "Will I really—a 100 year old man—father? Will Sarah—this 90 year old woman—bear?" Abraham argued with the Elohim, "May Ishmael live in front of you!" Elohim ordered "Certainly, yet Sarah your woman is bearing you a son and you will call his name Isaac; and I will set up my treaty with him as an everlasting treaty for his seed after him. As for Ishmael, I have heard you. Look, I have blessed him and I will make him fructify and I will multiply him very very much; twelve rulers he will father, and I will turn him into a great folk, although I will validate my treaty with Isaac whom Sarah will bear for you by this season next year." He finished speaking with him. Elohim went away from Abraham.

Abraham took Ishmael his son and all those born of his house and all those bought with his money, every male among the men of Abraham's house. He circumcised the flesh of their foreskin on this very day according to what Elohim had told him. Abraham was 99 years old when the flesh of his foreskin was circumcised. Ishmael his son was 13 years old when the flesh of his foreskin was circumcised. On that very day Abraham was circumcised and his son Ishmael and every man of his house, house-born or bought with silver from a foreigner's son, they were circumcised with him. Sarah bore a son for Abraham in his old age, at the season Elohim had spoken to him. Abraham called the name of the son Sarah bore for him Isaac. Abraham circumcised Isaac his son when he was eight days old, according to what Elohim commanded him and Abraham was 100 years old when Isaac his son was born to him. The lifespan of Sarah was 127 years, the years of Sarah's lifespan. Sarah died at Kiriath-arba—Hebron—in the land of Canaan. Abraham came to mourn Sarah and to weep over her.

Abraham rose from beside his dead. He said to the sons of Heth: "I am a migrant and resident among you; give me a burial tenure among you so that I can bury my dead away from me." The sons of Heth replied to Abraham: "Please listen to us, my lord! You are a ruler of Elohim among us, bury your dead in the choicest of our tombs, none of us will refuse you his tomb for burying your dead!" Abraham rose. He bowed down before the people of the land, the sons of Heth. He said to them: "If you are set to let me bury my dead away from me, listen to me and plead with Ephron son of Zohar on my behalf so that he may sell the cave of Machpelah to me, which belongs to him. It is at the end of his field. For a full price may he sell it to me as burial tenure among you." Ephron was sitting among the sons of Heth. Ephron the Hittite replied to Abraham in the hearing of all the sons of Heth who had come to the gate of his city: "No, my lord, listen to me; I would give you the field, and the cave that is in it I would give it to you, in the eyes of the sons of my people I would give it to you. Bury your dead!" Abraham bowed down before the people of the land. He said to Ephron in the hearing of the people of the land: "If only you would listen to me I would give the price of the field. Take from me and I will bury my dead there!" Ephron answered Abraham, "If only my lord would listen to me! A land of four hundred shekels of silver, what's that between me and you? Bury your dead!" Abraham listened to Ephron. Abraham weighed for Ephron the silver that he had said in the hearing of the sons of Heth: four hundred shekels of silver current among the merchants. Ephron's field in Machpelah near Mamre—both the field and the cave in it, and all the trees within the borders of the field—were validated for Abraham as property in the eyes of all the sons of Heth who had come to the gate of his city. Afterwards, Abraham buried Sarah his wife in the cave in the field of Machpelah near Mamre which is at Hebron in the land of Canaan. The field and the cave that is in it were validated for Abraham as burial tenure from the sons of Heth. And these are the days of the years of the lifespan of Abraham which he lived: 175 years. He expired. Abraham died in a good old age, elderly and sated of days. He was added[7] to his people. Isaac and Ishmael his sons buried him in the cave of Machpelah near Mamre, in the field of Ephron son of Zohar the Hittite, the field Abraham bought from the sons of Heth, there were buried Abraham and Sarah his woman.

Genesis 25

And this is the genesis of Ishmael son of Abraham whom Hagar the Egyptian Sarah's maid bore to Abraham and these are the names of the sons of Ishmael, according to their genesis:

Nebaioth the firstborn of Ishmael, Kedar, Adbeel, Mibsam, Mishma, Dumah, Massa, Hadad, Tema, Jetur, Naphish and Kedemah. They are the sons of Ishmael, and these are their names according to their villages and enclosures, twelve rulers by their ethnic groups and these are the years of the lifespan of Ishmael: 137 years. He expired. He died. He was added to his people.

Genesis 25–31; 33; 35

And this is the genesis of Isaac son of Abraham:

Abraham fathered Isaac. Isaac was 40 years old when he married Rebekah daughter of Bethuel the Aramean from Paddan Aram and sister of Laban the Aramean. Rebekah his woman conceived. Her days were full to give birth and look, there were twins in her womb but Isaac was 60 years old when Rebekah gave birth to them. Esau was 40 years old. Esau took Judith daughter of Beeri the Hittite, and Basemath daughter of Elon the Hittite. They were a bitter spirit to Isaac and Rebekah. Rebekah ordered Isaac, "I'm sick of life because of the daughters of Heth. If Jacob takes a woman from the daughters of Heth like these women of the land, what's the point of living?" Isaac called for Jacob. He blessed him. He commanded him. He ordered him "Do not take a woman from the daughters of Canaan. Get up! Go to Paddan Aram to the house of Bethuel your mother's father and marry a woman from the daughters of Laban your mother's brother. El Shaddai will bless you and make you fructify and multiply and you will be an assembly of people and he will give you the blessing of Abraham, for you and for your seed with you so that you will inherit the land of your sojourns which Elohim has given to Abraham!" Isaac sent Jacob. He went to Paddan Aram to Laban son of Bethuel the Aramean the brother of Rebekah the mother of Jacob and Esau. Esau saw that Isaac had blessed Jacob and had sent him to Paddan Aram to marry a woman from there, that while blessing him he had commanded him not to marry a woman from the daughters of Canaan, and that Jacob had listened to his father and to his mother and that he had gone to Paddan Aram. Esau saw that the daughters of Canaan were bad in the eyes

---

7. Since he is not buried at Machpelah, Aaron is not "added" to his fathers (compare Gen 25:8, 17; 49:29, 33).

of Isaac his father. Esau went to Ishmael. He took Mahalath, daughter of Ishmael son of Abraham, the sister of Nebaioth in addition to the women he had.

As soon as Laban heard about Jacob, his sister's son, he ran to meet him. He embraced him. He kissed him. He made him enter his house. Laban proclaimed: "You are my bone and my flesh!" He stayed with him. The man prospered very very much. Jacob got up. He drove all his herds and possessions, all his fortune he made in Paddan Aram, to go back to Isaac his father in the land of Canaan. Jacob arrived safely at the city of Shechem in the land of Canaan on his way back from Paddan Aram. Then Jacob entered Luz in the land of Canaan—it is Bethel. Elohim was again shown to Jacob upon his arrival from Paddan Aram. He blessed him. Elohim ordered him: "Your name is Jacob; your name will no longer be Jacob because Israel will be your name!" He called his name Israel. Elohim ordered him: "I am El Shaddai, fructify and multiply, there will be a folk and an assembly of folks from you, and kings will come from your body. The land I gave to Abraham and Isaac, to you I will give it and to your seed after you I will give the land!" Elohim went away from him in the place where he had spoken to him. Jacob set up a stand in the place where he spoke to him: a standing stone. He poured a libation on it. He emptied oil on it. Jacob called the name of the place where Elohim had spoken with him Bethel. Jacob went to Isaac his father in Mamre/Kiriath-arba it is Hebron, where Abraham and Isaac sojourned. The days of Isaac were 180 years. Isaac expired. He died. He was added to his people, old and full of days. Esau and Jacob his sons buried him.

Genesis 36

This is Esau's genesis:

Esau took his wives, his sons and his daughters, all the souls of his house, his herds—all his livestock, all his fortune he made in the land of Canaan. He went to a land opposite his brother Jacob because their possessions were too great for settling together; the land of their sojourns could not sustain them due to their herds. Esau settled in the mountain of Seir. These are the names of the sheikhs of Esau, by name according to their clans and places: Sheikh Timna, Sheikh Alvah, Sheikh Jetheth, Sheikh Oholibamah, Sheikh Elah, Sheikh Pinon, Sheikh Kenaz, Sheikh Teman, Sheikh Mibzar, Sheikh Magdiel, and Sheikh Iram. They are the Sheikhs of Edom according to their settlements in the land of their tenure. This is Esau the father of Edom.

Genesis 37; 46–47; 49–50

Meanwhile, Jacob settled in the land of his father's sojourns, in the land of Canaan. This is Jacob's genesis:

Jacob and all his seed after him went to Egypt: his sons, the sons of his sons with him, his daughters and the daughters of his sons and all his seed he brought with him in Egypt. Israel resided in the land of Egypt in the land of Goshen. They held tenure in it. They fructified. They multiplied very much. Jacob lived in the land of Egypt 17 years. The days of Jacob, the years of his lifespan were 147. Jacob called for his sons. He commanded them. He ordered them "I am about to be added to my people, bury me next to my fathers, at the cave that is in the field of Ephron the Hittite, in the cave that is in the field of Machpelah, near Mamre in the land of Canaan where Abraham bought the field from Ephron the Hittite as burial tenure. There, they buried Abraham and Sarah his wife, there they buried Isaac and Rebekah his wife, and there I buried Leah: acquisition of the field and the cave in it from the sons of Heth!" Jacob finished instructing his sons; he added his feet onto the bed. He expired. He was added to his people. So his sons did according to what he had commanded them. His sons carried him to the land of Canaan. They buried him in the cave of the field of Machpelah, the field Abraham had bought as burial tenure from Ephron the Hittite near Mamre, but the sons of Israel fructified. They teemed. They multiplied. The land was filled with them.

Exodus 1–2; 6–7

Egypt enslaved them with brutality. They embittered their lives with a hard labour in mortar and bricks and every kind of toil in the fields; brutal was the forced labour by which they enslaved them. It lasted many days. The sons of Israel groaned because of the labour. They cried out. An outcry went up to the Elohim because of the labour. Elohim heard their groaning. Elohim remembered his treaty with Abraham, with Isaac and with Jacob. Elohim saw the sons of Israel. Elohim knew. Elohim spoke to Moses. He ordered him, "I am YHWH, I let myself be seen by Abraham, Isaac and Jacob as El Shaddai, but by my name YHWH I was not known to them. Nevertheless, I will validate my treaty with them to give them the land of Canaan, the land of their sojourns in which they sojourned. I have heard the groans of the sons of Israel whom Egypt is enslaving. I have remembered my treaty. Therefore, order the sons of Israel: 'I am YHWH, I will bring you out from under the burden of Egypt, I will deliver you from their slavery, I will redeem you with an outstretched arm and by great judgments. I will take you as my people. I will be your Elohim. You will know that I am YHWH your Elohim who is bringing you out from under the burden of Egypt. I will make you enter the land which I swore to give to Abraham, to Isaac and to Jacob. I will give it to you as inheritance—I am YHWH.'" Moses said so to the sons of Israel but they did not hear him because of the shortened breath and the hard slavery. YHWH said to Moses: "Enter, speak to Pharaoh King of Egypt so he will send the sons of Israel out of his land!" Moses said to YHWH: "If the sons of Israel did not listen to me, how will Pharaoh listen to me, since I am uncircumcised of lips!" YHWH ordered Moses: "See! I have set you as Elohim to Pharaoh, and Aaron your brother will be your prophet. You will speak everything I command you and Aaron your brother will speak to Pharaoh, he will send the sons of Israel from his land, but I will harden Pharaoh's heart. I will multiply my signs and my wonders in the land of Egypt, but Pharaoh will not listen to you. I will set my hand against Egypt. I will make my armies, my people the sons of Israel come out from the land of Egypt by great judgments. Egypt will know that I am YHWH when I stretch out my hand against Egypt and will make the sons of Israel come out from their midst!" Moses and Aaron did according to what YHWH commanded them; so they did. Moses was 80 years and Aaron 83 years old when they spoke to Pharaoh.

Exodus 7–8; 12; 14

YHWH ordered Moses and Aaron: "When Pharaoh tells to you: 'Give us a wonder!' you will order to Aaron: 'Take your staff and throw it before Pharaoh', it will be as a monster!" Moses and Aaron entered to Pharaoh. They did according to what YHWH commanded. Aaron threw his staff in front of Pharaoh and in front of his servants. It was as a monster. Pharaoh also called the wise-men and the wizards. The magicians of Egypt did the same by their mysteries. Each threw his staff. They were as monsters. Aaron's staff swallowed their staffs. Pharaoh's heart was strong and he did not listen to them, according to what YHWH had said.

YHWH ordered Moses: "Order to Aaron: 'Take your staff and stretch out your hand over the waters of Egypt, its streams, rivers, canals and over every gathering of water. They will be blood, blood everywhere in the land of Egypt even in the wooden and stone containers!" Moses and Aaron did so according to what YHWH had commanded. The blood was everywhere in the land of Egypt. The magicians of Egypt did the same by their mysteries. Pharaoh's heart was strong and he did not listen to them, according to what YHWH had said.

YHWH ordered Moses: "Order to Aaron: 'Stretch out your hand with your staff over the streams, over the rivers and over the canals, and make frogs come over the land of Egypt!'" Aaron stretched out his hand over the waters of Egypt. The frog came up and covered the land of Egypt. The magicians did the same by their mysteries. They made frogs come up on the land of Egypt, but he did not listen to them, according to what YHWH had said.

YHWH ordered Moses: "Order Aaron: 'Stretch out your staff and strike the dust of the land and it will be as gnats in all the land of Egypt!'" They did so. Aaron stretched out his hand with his staff. He struck the dust of the land. There was the gnat upon humankind and herd, all the dust of the land was gnats in all the land of Egypt. The magicians did the same by their mysteries in order to make gnats come out, but they could not. The gnat was on humankind and herd. The magicians declared to Pharaoh: "This is the finger of Elohim." Pharaoh's heart was strong so he did not listen to them, according to what YHWH had said.

YHWH ordered Moses and to Aaron in the land of Egypt: "This month is for you the first of months; it will be for you the first of the year's months. Speak to all Israel's congregation: 'on the tenth of this month, they will take a flock animal for a paternal house, a flock animal per house. If the household is too small let them share with the neighbouring household. It will be a male yearling without faults, from the sheep or from the goats. You will keep it with you until the fourteenth day of this month. All the community of Israel's congregation will slaughter it at twilight. They will take some of the blood and smear the doorposts and the lintel of the houses in which they will eat it. They will eat the flesh during that night, roasted. You will eat it with your loins belted, your sandals on your feet and your sticks in your hands; you will eat it in haste—it is a Passover for YHWH. I will pass in the land of Egypt in that night. I will strike every firstborn in the land of Egypt, from humankind to herd, even Egypt's gods. I will make judgements—I am YHWH—but the blood will be the sign on the houses you are in. I will see the blood and protect you. There will be no casualty among you as I strike the land of Egypt!" Moses called all the elders of Israel. He ordered them "select flock animals for your families and slaughter the Passover. Take a bunch of hyssop, dip it in the blood that is in the bowl and smear the lintel and the doorposts with the blood. But then, make sure no one goes out of the house until morning. YHWH will pass to injure Egypt. He will see the blood on the lintel and on the doorposts. YHWH will protect. On behalf of the Passover he will not let the destruction enter your house to injure. You and your sons will keep this observance as an everlasting decree! They went. The sons of Israel did according to what YHWH commanded to Moses and Aaron. So they did. In the middle of the night YHWH struck every first-born in the land of Egypt from Pharaoh's first-born who sat on his throne until the first-born of the prisoner who was in the dungeon, and every first-born of the herd. Pharaoh got up that night and all his servants and all Egypt. There was a great clamour in Egypt because there was not a single house without a dead in it. Pharaoh summoned Moses and Aaron at night. He ordered: "Get up, move out of my people, you and the sons of Israel. The sons of Israel moved out: about 600,000 infantry besides the toddlers. The dwelling of the sons of Israel in Egypt: 430 years. It happened at the end of 430 years, on that very day, all YHWH's armies went out from the land of Egypt. It is a night of observance for YHWH by those he caused to come out of the land of Egypt. That night is for YHWH, an observance by all the sons of Israel and their generations. The king of Egypt was informed that the people had run away. Pharaoh and his servants changed their minds. They said "What have we done? We sent Israel away from our slavery!" He harnessed his chariot and he took his people with him. He took 600 choice chariots and all the chariots of Egypt with three men on each. YHWH strengthened the heart of Pharaoh King of Egypt. He pursued the sons of Israel. YHWH ordered Moses: "Speak to the sons of Israel that they get a move on, and you, make high your staff and stretch out your hand over the sea and split it so the sons of Israel can enter inside the sea in the dry!" Moses stretched out his hand over the sea. YHWH made the sea go by a mighty east wind all that night. He turned the sea into a waste. The waters were split. The sons of Israel entered inside the sea in the dry, and the waters were for them a rampart on their right and on their left. Egypt pursued them. All Pharaoh's horses, his chariots and his riders entered behind them towards inside the sea. YHWH ordered Moses: "Stretch out your hand over the sea and the waters will return over Egypt, over his chariots and over his riders!" Moses stretched out his hand over the sea. The waters returned. They covered chariots and riders—all of Pharaoh's forces that had entered behind them in the sea. Not one was left, but the sons of Israel went in the dry inside the sea and the waters were for them a rampart on their right and on their left.

Exodus 16

The whole congregation of the sons of Israel lamented against Moses and Aaron in the wilderness. The sons of Israel said to them: "Will we now die in YHWH's hand while in the land of Egypt we used to stop by the cauldron of meat and eat bread to satiety? You made us come out to this wilderness to make this entire assembly die of famine." YHWH spoke to Moses: "I have heard the lament of the sons of Israel, tell them: 'In the morning you will be satiated with bread, then you will know that I am YHWH your Elohim!'" In the morning there was a layer of dew. The layer of dew evaporated; and look, on the face of the wilderness there was a thin flaking, thin like frost on the land. The sons of Israel saw. They said to one another, "What's that?" for they did not know what it was. Moses said to them: "It is the bread YHWH has given you for food. This is what YHWH has commanded: 'Pick a ration each, an omer per roll-call according to the number there is in his tent!'" The sons of Israel did so. Some picked much, some little. They measured it by omer and the much was not too much while the little was not too little, a ration for each one they picked. Morning by morning, they picked a ration for each. The house of Israel called its name "man." They ate manna till their arrival at the limits of the land of Canaan.

Exodus 25; 35–36; 40

YHWH spoke to Moses: "Speak to the sons of Israel. Receive a contribution from every man whose heart impels him to make a contribution for me, then make a sanctuary for me and I will reside among them." The men and the women as well came, everyone whose heart impelled brought brooches, ear-rings, signets, pendants, all sorts of golden objects and whatever gold one dedicated for YHWH. Whoever found himself with blue, purple and scarlet yarn or fine linen brought it. Skilled women spun by hand. They got blue, purple and scarlet yarn and fine linen. All the skilful ones made the Residence with ten curtains of finely twisted linen, blue, purple and scarlet yarn, with cherubim weaved into them by a skilled craftsman. The length of one curtain: 28 cubits, width 4 cubits per curtain; one measure for all the curtains. He joined five curtains one to one and five curtains he joined one to one. He made loops of blue purple on the edge of the first curtain from the end at the joining; so he did at the edge of the end curtain at the joining of the second. He made 50 loops in the first curtain and 50 loops he made at the end of the curtain that is at the second joining, the loops receiving one to one. He made 50 hooks of gold. He joined the curtains one to one by the hooks. The Residence was one. It was the first month in the second year in day one of the month; the Residence was set up and the glory of YHWH filled the Residence.

Leviticus 16

YHWH said to Moses "Speak to Aaron your brother. From the congregation of the sons of Israel he will take two he-goats for sin. He will take the two he-goats. Aaron will draw lots over the two he-goats, one for YHWH and one for the expelled guilt. Aaron will present the goat which the lot designated for YHWH and he will make it sinful. He will make the goat designated for the expelled guilt stand alive in front of YHWH as purgation through him by sending it for the expelled guilt to the wilderness. Aaron will lay his two hands on the head of the live goat and confess on it all the transgressions of the sons of Israel. All their wrongdoings and all their sins he will transfer them onto the head of the goat. Through a man of that time, he will send it to the wilderness. The goat will carry all their transgressions to an isolated land. He will send the goat in the wilderness and it will be for you an everlasting ordinance in month VII on the tenth of the month. You will humiliate your lives and you will do no work. It will be an everlasting ordinance for the purgation of the sons of Israel from all their sins once a year. It will be done as YHWH commanded to Moses.

Leviticus 23; 25

YHWH said to Moses: "Talk to the sons of Israel and explain to them the festivals of YHWH which you will call "holidays." These are my festivals:

Six days you will do work but the seventh day is Sabbath, a Sabbath minor, a holiday, all work you will not do; it is a Sabbath for YHWH in all your settlements.

These are the festivals of YHWH, holidays that you will have in their festivals: First month, in the fourteenth of the month at twilight: Passover for YHWH.

Fifteenth day of this month: pilgrimage of Unleavened Breads for YHWH, seven days you will eat unleavened breads.

YHWH said to Moses: "Tell the sons of Israel: 'The seventh month, day one of the month will be for you a minor Sabbath of remembrance, Blast holiday.'"

YHWH said to Moses: "Moreover, the tenth of the seventh month is the Day of Purgations. It will be a holiday for you; you will humiliate your lives. You will do no work on that very day since it is a day of purgations to purge you in front of YHWH your Elohim. Any being that will not be humiliated on that very day will be cut from its people, any being that will work on that very day. You will do no work—decree everlasting for your generations in all your settlements."

YHWH said to Moses: "Speak to the sons of Israel and you will order them 'When you enter the land that I am giving to you, the land will stop a Sabbath for YHWH. Six years you will sow your field, six years you will prune your vine and you will gather its produce, but the seven year will be a minor Sabbath for the land, a Sabbath for YHWH. Do not sow your field. Do not prune your vine. Do not harvest the after-growth. Do not pick the grapes of your uncut vine. It will be a Sabbath minor for the land. The Sabbath of the land will be your food, for you, for your slave, for your maid, for your hireling, for the resident migrating with you, for your cattle and for the wildlife that is in your land all its produce will be for food.

You will count seven Sabbaths of years, seven times seven years and it will be for you the days of the seven Sabbaths of years: 49 years. A horn will be blown in the seventh month, on the tenth of the month. On the day of purgations you will have a horn blown in all your lands. You will sanctify the year of the fiftieth year. You will proclaim a release in the land for all its residents. It will be a Jubilee for you. Everyone's tenure will be returned to its family on the Jubilee. It will take place for you on year 50. Do not sow, do not harvest the after-growth, and do not pick the vine because this Jubilee will be holy for you. From the steppe you will produce what you will eat in the year of this Jubilee, and each one will be returned to his tenure.

When you pledge something or someone to your fellow do not cheat each other. The number of years until the Jubilee will regulate the amount secured by the pledge. The amount will be proportional to the years until the Jubilee since what you are pledging is only the produce. The land must not be traded as freehold because the land is mine. You are only migrants and residents with me. For every plot of tenure land you will grant reclaim rights for the land. Whenever your brother borrows, he will pledge some of his tenure. Someone close to him may redeem his brother's pledge or the borrower himself may redeem it if he can. In that case, the number of years the lender used the pledge will be subtracted from the amount to be reimbursed to the lender. If he cannot afford it, the pledge remains in the hand of the lender until the year of the Jubilee. It is automatically released on the Jubilee. Tenure is then returned to its holder.

The sale of a residential house within a city can only be reclaimed within one whole year after its sale. After a whole year, a house within a walled settlement is validated as freehold to its buyer. It is not returned on the Jubilee. Village houses where there is no rampart are reckoned as the fields of the land around. Reclaim rights are granted for them and they are returned on the Jubilee.

Slaves and maids are to be bought from the neighbouring countries or from the sons of the residents born among you in your land. They will be for you as movables. You will transmit them to your sons after you as movables. For ever they are your slaves. But your brothers, the sons of Israel, you will not exploit them brutally.

When a migrant and resident with you prospers while your brother is short of cash, your brother can pledge himself to a migrant resident with you or to a branch of the migrant's family. He may, however, be redeemed by his redeemer, his uncle, the son of his uncle or a kinsman. Or he may redeem himself. In that case, the number of years he has worked for his lender will be subtracted to the amount he has to reimburse calculated on the basis of the number of years until the year of the Jubilee. The amount he has paid back by his work will be calculated at the current rate of wage workers. The more years to the Jubilee, the more he has to pay back. If only a few years remain until the Jubilee, he will have to pay back to his lender only the cost of a wage worker for these coming years. He will not exploit him brutally in your eyes. If he is not reclaimed, he will be released in the year of the Jubilee, him and his sons with him.'"

Numbers 1

YHWH spoke to Moses on day one of the second month of the second year since their coming out of the land of Egypt: "Levy the heads of all the congregation of the sons of Israel by clans, paternal dynasties, reckoning by name every male in their roll-call from twenty years old and over, every one going out with the army in Israel. You will muster them by their armies, you and Aaron. Take with you a man per tribe, each one a chief for his paternal house. These are the names of the men that stood with them:

> for Reuben: Elizur ben Shedeur
> for Simeon: Shelumiel ben Zurishaddai
> for Judah: Nahshon ben Amminadab
> for Issachar: Nethanel ben Zuar
> for Zebulun: Eliab ben Helon
> for Ephraim: Elishama ben Ammihud
> for Manasseh: Gamaliel ben Pedahzur
> for Benjamin: Abidan ben Gideoni
> for Dan: Ahiezer ben Ammishaddai
> for Asher: Pagiel ben Ochran
> for Gad: Eliasaph ben Deuel
> for Naphtali: Ahira ben Enan.

These were the ones called by the congregation, leaders of their paternal tribes. They were heads of thousands of Israel. Moses and Aaron took these men who were marked out by name, with the entire congregation assembled on day 1 of month II. They registered themselves according to their genealogy along their tribes by paternal dynasties by count of names from twenty years old and over in their roll-call. Total: 603,550.

Numbers 10; 13–14

On the twentieth of the second month of the second year, YHWH said to Moses:
"Send some men and they will tour the land of Canaan which I am giving to the sons
of Israel, one per paternal tribe, all of them leaders, heads of the sons of Israel. These
are their names:

> for the tribe of Reuben, Shammua ben Zaccur
> for the tribe of Simeon, Shaphat ben Hori
> for the tribe of Judah, Caleb ben Jephunneh
> for the tribe of Issachar, Igal ben Joseph
> for the tribe of Ephraim, Hoshea bin Nun
> for the tribe of Benjamin, Palti ben Raphu
> for the tribe of Zebulun, Gaddiel ben Sodi
> for the tribe of Manasseh, Gaddi ben Susi
> for the tribe of Dan, Ammiel ben Gemalli
> for the tribe of Asher, Sethur ben Michael
> for the tribe of Naphtali, Nahbi ben Vophsi
> for the tribe of Gad, Geuel ben Machi."

These are the names of the men that Moses sent to tour the land. Moses renamed
Hoshea bin Nun Joshua. Moses sent them to tour the land of Canaan. He ordered,
"Go up this way in the Negeb! Go up the mountain, check the land and the people
settled on it! Are they strong or weak, few or many? And the land in which they are
settled is it good or bad? What are the cities in which they are settled, are they in
camps or in fortresses? Is the land fat or lean, is there wood in it or none? You will
strengthen yourselves and take some of the fruit of the land." These were the days of
first grapes. They went up. They toured the land. They entered as far as a *wadi* of
grapes. They cut there a cane and a single bunch of grapes. It was carried with a
yoke for two. Also they took some pomegranates and figs. That place they called
Wadi Eshcol because of the bunch of grapes the sons of Israel cut there. They
returned from touring the land at the end of 40 days. They came back to Moses, to
Aaron and to the whole congregation of the sons of Israel. They reported to the
entire congregation. They showed them the fruit of the land. Then, they slandered
the land which they had toured for the sons of Israel: "The land we toured is a land
eating its inhabitants!" The entire congregation rose. They raised their voice. The
people cried that night. All the sons of Israel lamented against Moses and Aaron.
The whole congregation declared: "If only we had died in the land of Egypt or in
this wilderness! Is it not better for us to return to Egypt?" They said to each other:
"Let us choose a head; we had better return to Egypt." Moses and Aaron fell face
down in front of the general assembly of the congregation of the sons of Israel, but
Joshua bin Nun and Caleb ben Jephunneh, from those who had toured the land, tore
their cloaks. They said to the entire congregation of the sons of Israel: "The land we
toured is a very very good land." YHWH said to Moses and Aaron: "Until when will
this bad congregation lament against me? I have heard their lamentation against me.
Order to them: 'As surely as I live, announcement of YHWH, I will do to you just as I
heard you saying: in this wilderness your corpses will fall, all your musters, all your
numbers from twenty years old and over who lamented against me. I am YHWH, I
have spoken. I will do this to this entire bad congregation ganging against me. In this

wilderness they will be perfected. Here they will die except Joshua bin Nun and Caleb ben Jephunneh.'"

Numbers 20; 26–27

The sons of Israel—the whole congregation arrived at Mount the Mount. YHWH ordered Moses: "Call Aaron and Eleazar his son and go up Mount the Mount with them. Strip Aaron of his garments and put them on his son Eleazar. Aaron will be added and die there." Moses did as YHWH commanded. They went up Mount the Mount in the eyes of the whole congregation. Moses stripped Aaron of his garments. He put them on Eleazar his son. Aaron died there on top of the mountain. Moses came down with Eleazar from the mountain. The entire congregation saw that Aaron had perished. The entire house of Israel wept over Aaron for 30 days. YHWH ordered Moses and to Eleazar son of Aaron the priest: "Levy the heads of all the congregation of the sons of Israel from 20 years old and older by their paternal house, all those going out with the army in Israel. Moses and Eleazar the priest spoke with them in the steppes of Moab by the Jordan opposite Jericho. These were the muster of the sons of Israel: 601,730. YHWH ordered Moses: "Between these shall the land be divided, by lot, by count of names. You will increase the inheritance of a large group and diminish that of a small one. Each area will be proportional to the muster. By lot the land will be divided, by the names of their paternal tribes they will inherit, by drawing lots. You will share out inheritance between large and small groups." Those are the musters by which Moses and Eleazar the priest mustered the sons of Israel in the steppes of Moab by the Jordan opposite Jericho. Among these there was no one from the musters recorded by Moses and Aaron the priest in the wilderness because YHWH had ordered that they would die in the wilderness. So no one was left from them, except Caleb ben Jephunneh and Joshua bin Nun. YHWH ordered Moses, "Go up this Abarim Mountain, see the land I have given the sons of Israel." Moses said to YHWH: "May YHWH, the Elohim of the spirits of all flesh, appoint a man over the congregation, a man who will go out and will enter in front of them and who will cause them to go out and will cause them to enter, so that YHWH's congregation will not be like sheep without a shepherd." YHWH ordered Moses, "Take Joshua bin Nun, a man in whom is the spirit, and you will lay your hand on him. Then you will make him stand before Eleazar and before the entire congregation and you will commission him in their eyes. Then you will transfer some of your majesty onto him so that the whole congregation of the sons of Israel will listen to him. However, he will be subordinated to Eleazar the priest and will receive guidance from him by judgment of the Urim before YHWH. On his order they will go out, and at his command they will come in, him and all the sons of Israel with him, and the whole congregation!" Moses did according to what YHWH commanded him. He took Joshua. He made him stand before Eleazar the priest and the whole congregation. He laid his hands on him. He commissioned him, as YHWH said by Moses' hand.

Numbers 34; Deuteronomy 34

YHWH said to Moses: "Command to the sons of Israel, and you will order them, 'When you enter the land of Canaan, this is the land that will fall to you as share, the land of Canaan as to its boundaries. For you the southern boundary will be from the end of the Salt Sea at the East and its arrival at the Sea. The seaward boundary will be for you the Great Sea; this will be for you the western boundary. This will be for you the northern boundary: from the Great Sea for you it will turn towards Mount the Mount. From Mount the Mount it will turn towards the Sea of Kinnereth eastwards, the boundary will go down the Jordan and its arrivals will be at the Salt Sea; this will be for the land as to its boundaries around!'" Moses commanded the sons of Israel: "This is the land that you will endow by lot." Moses went up from the steppes of Moab to Mount Nebo, the head of Pisgah facing Jericho. YHWH caused him to see all the land, YHWH ordered him: "This is the land about which I swore to Abraham, to Isaac and to Jacob: 'To your seed I will give it,' I make you see it with your own eyes, but you will not enter there!" Moses died here. Moses was 120 years old when he died, his eyes were not dim and his jaw did not tremble. The sons of Israel wept over Moses in the steppes of Moab 30 days. The days of mourning for Moses were perfected,[8]

Joshua 4–5
so the people went up from the Jordan on the tenth of the first month. YHWH ordered Joshua: "Today I have rolled away the longing of Egypt from over you." The name of this place is Gilgal to this day. The sons of Israel camped in the Gilgal. They prepared the Passover on the fourteenth day of the month, in the evening in the steppes of Jericho. They ate from the yield of the land from the morrow of the Passover: unleavened bread and roasted grain on that very day. The manna stopped from the morrow of their eating from the yield of the land and there was no manna for the sons of Israel. They ate from the produce of the land of Canaan that year.

Joshua 14; 18
These are the ones who endowed the sons of Israel in the land of Canaan: Eleazar the priest, Joshua bin Nun and the heads of the fathers of the tribes of the sons of Israel. Their endowments were distributed by drawing lots according to what YHWH commanded by the hand of Moses. The whole congregation of the sons of Israel assembled at Shiloh, and the land was domesticated in front of them. They accomplished the division of the land.

---

8.   Here, as in Num 14:35, Pg uses √תמם rather than √כלה.

Part I

THE SABBATICAL CALENDAR AS BASIS
OF THE PRIESTLY DOCUMENT

Chapter 1

CREATION OF THE SABBATH (GENESIS 1:1–2:4)

Whatever is understood by the P siglum, Gen 1:1–2:4 constitute its introduction. While attempts have been made to trace earlier forms of the Creation narrative,[1] the tight structure of the heptameron is a token of its homogeneity.[2] It is a safe starting point to suggest that the introduction presents the main themes of the Pg narrative in a nutshell.

In the Beginning?

The classical rendering of the initial word as "In the beginning" is problematic since the notion of "beginning, start, onset" is expressed by חדל√ (Gen 8:4; Judg 13:5, 25; Hos 1:2), while the ordinal number ראשׁון denotes the first element of a series (Gen 8:13; Exod 12:2; 40:17; Lev 23:5; Num 10:13; 20:1). For the present purpose, the difference between "beginning" and "first" is significant. In common talk, first and beginning are similar enough to pass as synonyms. The confusion between "first" and "beginning" goes back to the LXX, which uses ἀρχὴ in Gen 1:1 and in Hos 1:2. Since they introduced other chronological changes (Gen 2:2; 5), it is not surprising that the translators downplayed the significance of בראשׁית, which in the Hebrew text marks the impossibility of a beginning at this point. The first narrative form (ויאמר) occurs in v. 3. Before v. 3, there is no proper beginning apart from the physical onset of writing. No action is being narrated. The first two verses only present the backdrop of what is about to happen. The full bearing of Gen 1:1 appears when it is compared with the first words of *Enuma eliš*.[3] The initial

---

1. P. Weimar, "Chaos und Kosmos," in *Mythos im Alten Testament und seiner Umwelt* (ed. A. Lange, H. Lichtenberger and D. Römheld; BZAW 278; Berlin: de Gruyter, 1999), 196–211.

2. O. H. Steck, *Der Schöpfungsbericht der Priesterschrift* (FRLANT 115; Göttingen: Vandenhoeck & Ruprecht, 1975).

3. J. M. Sasson, "Time…to Begin," in *"Shaʿarei Talmon": Studies in the Bible, Qumran, and the Ancient Near East* (ed. M. Fishbane; Winona Lake: Eisenbrauns,

words of the Mesopotamian creation myth translate as "When on high," introducing spatial categories immediately after the temporal "when": "When on high the skies were not yet named nor the earth below pronounced by name."[4] Pg delays the introduction of space (above and below) until day two, thus making the category of time the sole focus of day one, four and seven. As in Jer 26:1; 27:1; 28:1; 49:34, בראשית means "in the time of," normally referring to a particular reign.[5] Hence, instead of imagining a time and a space before creation like the incipit of *Enuma eliš*, or a time before the appearance of matter as does the concept of *creatio ex nihilo*,[6] Pg starts with initial time as some Egyptian texts do.[7] Yet, the initial time in בראשית is neither a beginning nor a cardinal number. Genesis 1:1 is the beginning of Pg and of the Bible, but not the beginning of creation nor the beginning of the week or even of the first day. Day one begins at the first dawn in v. 3 when light appears and ends

1992), 183–94 (188–89 n. 17), doubts that *Enuma eliš* influenced Gen 1 since Israel's theologians did not have access to Pritchard's *ANET* and because *Enuma eliš* was recited only in the inner recesses of Mesopotamian temples. According to Sasson, anything Genesis and *Enuma eliš* have in common is superficially connected and derives from a shared tradition. Gmirkin, *Berossus*, 135–39, traces the influence of *Enuma eliš* on Genesis through Berossus.

4. *CoS* 1:111, 391; S. Dalley, *Myths from Mesopotamia* (Oxford: Oxford University Press, 1992), 233.

5. J. M. Arambarri, "Gen. 1,1–2,4a. Ein Prolog und ein Programm für Israel," in *Gottes Wege suchend* (ed. F. Sedlmeier; Würzburg: Echter, 2003), 65–86 (67–68). Other meanings of בראשית are: "origin, fundament, premium quality" (Exod 23:19; 34:26; 1 Sam 15:21), "bloom" (Jer 2:3; 49:35; Ps 78:51), "firstling, ripe time" (Hos 9:10).

6. The skies and the land are actually created in vv. 7 and 9 respectively, but the hodgepodge (תהו ובהו), the darkness, the Deep (תהום), the wind or spirit and the waters are pre-existent. But *Creatio ex nihilo* postulates that matter was created. Wis 11:17; *Jub.* 2:1–2; *Ant.* 1.27 do not mention *creatio ex nihilo*. 2 Macc 7:28 is the first mention of it. Julian the Apostate (*C. Gal.* 49D–E) insists that Gen 1 does not mention it. It is through Christian exegesis that Rabbinic literature will accept it; see M. R. Niehoff, "*Creatio ex nihilo* Theology in *Genesis Rabbah* in Light of Christian Exegesis," *HTR* 99 (2006): 37–64; J. Barr, "Was Everything that God Created really Good?," in *God in the Fray* (ed. T. Linafelt and T. K. Beal; Minneapolis: Fortress, 1998), 55–65.

7. J. D. Currid, "An Examination of the Egyptian Background of the Genesis Cosmogony," *BZ* 35 (1991): 18–40 (30). See also M. Bauks, *Die Welt am Amfang* (Neukirchen–Vluyn: Neukirchener Verlag, 1997), 93–99, and W. Gross, "Syntaktische Erscheinungen am Anfang althebräischer Erzählungen: Hintergrund und Vordergrund," in *Congress Volume: Vienna, 1980* (ed. J. A. Emerton; Leiden: Brill, 1981), 131–45.

at twilight with the onset of the first night. At that point, the first cardinal number appears (אחד) as the first day is completed (v. 5). Day one, however, is merely the name of the first day of the week, but it does not constitute a beginning as such. The calendar begins on day four (see Table 1 below). To render this notion of indiscriminate time before the creation of days and calendar, the common formula "Once upon a time" seems to be the most fitting,[8] unless one wishes to stick closer to the *Enuma eliš* model with "In the initial period in which God…"[9] The fact that Pg does not hesitate to draw from the rich cosmological traditions of Egypt[10] and Mesopotamia[11] should not blind to the differences introduced in Gen 1. The hovering wind of v. 2 hints at the raging winds which bloated Tiamat's belly in the Babylonian myth and enabled Marduk to shoot the fatal arrow.[12] This is as far as Pg is willing to go with theogony. As for cosmogony, it is not the main focus of Gen 1 either. The burden of Gen 1 and of Pg is stated from the onset in v. 1, which starts with time (בראשית) and ends with land (ארץ), spanning the entire narrative which starts with time (Gen 1) and ends with land (Josh 18). To claim that Pg must close with the building of a temple because *Enuma eliš* does so fails to take into account the specificity of the biblical creation account.[13]

Cosmology

Besides *Enuma eliš*, Gen 1:1–2:4 integrates more recent influences. As Xenophanes (born about 570 B.C.E.) rejected theogony,[14] Pg presents a cosmogony with hardly a trace of theogony. The first creature is light.[15]

---

8.   See H. G. M. Williamson, "Once upon a time…?," in *Reflection and Refraction* (R. Rezetko, T. H. Lim and W. B. Aucker; Leiden: Brill, 2007), 517–28, for other places in the Hebrew Bible where this formula could be used profitably.

9.   R. Holmstedt, "The Restrictive Syntax of Genesis i 1," *VT* 58 (2008): 56–67.

10.   J. E. Atwell, "An Egyptian Source for Genesis 1," *JTS* 51 (2000): 441–77.

11.   However, D. Tsumura, *Creation and Destruction* (Winona Lake: Eisenbrauns, 2005), rejects the mythological aspects of *tohu wabohu* and *tehom*.

12.   *Enuma eliš* IV:100; *CoS* 1:111, 398; Dalley, *Myths*, 253.

13.   Against Nihan, *Priestly Torah*, 55.

14.   Diogenes Laertius 9.19; *de Melliso Xenophane Gorgia* (ed. Bekker and Brandis), 14.2, 8.

15.   Traces of a creation myth which presented the illumination of the sky and the earth as Anu's first creative act are found in Nabonidus's Harran stele; see P.-A. Beaulieu, "Nabonidus the Mad King," in *Representations of Political Power* (ed. M. Heinz and M. H. Feldman; Winona Lake: Eisenbrauns, 2007), 137–66 (153–54).

15.   D. Edelman, *The Origins of the "Second" Temple* (London: Equinox, 2005), 334–43.

Like Ezekiel, Gen 1:7 depicts a world where land and skies are enclosed beneath a two-dimensional vault.[16] Beyond the vault is water turning into clouds under the heat of the fire, the source of light, above the water. Similarly, Anaximander of Miletus imagined four wheels of eternal fire of different sizes, with cloud rims that let the light of the fire shine through spots, the stars. Another Milesian scholar, Anaximenes (died ca. 528) suggested that stars are pegged to the crystalline vault of heaven like nails (DK13A14).[17] Under the influence of the wind, the entire vault or the individual wheels rotate, carrying the stars with them. Celestial phenomena are entirely mechanical and recurring according to the size and the speed of the wheels. Relying on this understanding of a mechanistic cosmos, Thales was able to predict the occurrence of an eclipse in 585 B.C.E. which in turn precipitated profound theological turmoil.

Less elaborate, Gen 1 does not account for the movement of the heavenly bodies, but nevertheless presents striking parallels with conceptions developed at Miletus.[18] In Gen 1:18, Elohim sets the luminaries into the vault or dome inspired by the gabled top of Neo-Assyrian stelae[19] from which hang the divine emblems. The luminaries are translucent spots that let the light of the fire through, while birds fly across the surface of the same dome (Gen 1:20).[20] In v. 15, "great and small luminaries" reflect the relative sizes of the earth compared to the moon, a standard topic of ancient astronomy.[21] Stars pass below the horizon rather than into an

16. C. Uehlinger and S. Müller Trufaut, "Ezekiel 1, Babylonian Cosmological Scholarship and Iconography: Attempts at Further Refinement," *TZ* 57 (2001): 140–71.

17. H. Diels and W. Kranz, *Die Fragmente der Vorsokratiker* (Zurich: Weidmann, 1985).

18. B. Halpern, "Late Israelite Astronomies and the Early Greeks," in *Symbiosis, Symbolism, and the Power of the Past* (Winona Lake: Eisenbrauns, 2003), 323–52.

19. See J. Börker-Klähn, *Altvorderasiatische Bildstelen und vergleichbare Felsreliefs* (Mainz: P. von Zabern, 1982); M. Yon, "La stele de Sargon II à Chypre," in *Khorsabad, le plais de Sargon II, roi d'Assyrie* (ed. A. Caubet; Paris, 1995), 161–68. But see Uehlinger and Müller Trufaut, "Ezekiel," 153, for a flat firmament on a Neo-Assyrian seal impression. See M. Albani, *Astronomie und Schöpfungsglaube* (WMANT 68; Neukirchen–Vluyn: Neukirchener Verlag, 1992); M. Albani, *Der eine Gott und die himmlischen Heerscharen* (Leipzig: Evangelische Verlagsanstalt, 2000).

20. B. Halpern, "The Assyrian Astronomy of Genesis 1," *Eretz-Israel* 27 (2003): 74*–83* (76*).

21. A. C. Bowen and R. B. Todd, *Cleomedes' Lectures on Astronomy: A Translation of the Heavens* (Berkeley: University of California Press, 2004), 99–135. Cleomenes refutes the Epicurean view that the sun is as large as it appears to be. He demonstrates that the sun is larger than the earth and that the other heavenly bodies

underworld which this mechanical cosmology repudiates. In Gen 1:9–13, the land (not the planet) appears but it is not made. The land appears when the waters have been removed. The land is an unmade waterless surface that has neither substance nor thickness. The point is to undermine the underworld with its chthonic divinities which suggest the possibility of an afterlife and the power of ancestors.

Milesian cosmology was short-lived. Starting with Parmenides and the Saros Cycle (sixth–fifth century B.C.E.), the earth was conceived as a spherical planet. From the fifth century B.C.E. onwards, the earth had an underside. The assumption that stars are on a curved plane relative to the earth was discarded by Empedocles (ca. 492–432 B.C.E.) and Anaxagoras (ca. 500–428 B.C.E.).[22] Genesis 1 closely reflects a peculiar cosmology elaborated in Asia Minor which held sway for about one century between the careers of Xenophanes and Anaxagoras. Allowing a half-century lag for their ideas to percolate into Palestine, Gen 1 matches the state of scholarship in the first half of the fifth century B.C.E.

Sabbatical Calendar

Creative activity begins at v. 3 with the appearance of light, which marks the end of darkness (חשׁך, v. 2) and the beginning of day one. The refrain at the end of each day—"There was an evening. There was a morning"— indicates that, contrary to Babylonian days which started and ended at sunset, Pg's days start at sunrise and end at sunset.[23] The etymology of the word "morning" (בקר) supports this claim as it derives from a root which primary meaning is "to split." In Exod 7:15; Num 16:5; 1 Sam 9:19, בקר retains the original sense of the "morrow,"[24] when the appearance of light splits the day from the preceding night and separates calendar units. Once Judaism adopted a lunar calendar and the separation of days at sunset, בקר lost its original meaning and became a mere "morning," while the "morrow" was expressed through מחר, which

---

are not the size they appear to be. The wheel of the sun was deemed 27 or 28 times greater than the wheel of the earth, the wheel of the moon 19 times greater than that of the earth: DK 12 A 21= R21 Aetios 2 20:1; DK 12 A 11, R18.

22. D. Sider, *The Fragments of Anaxagoras: Introduction, Text, and Commentary* (2d ed.; Sankt Augustine: Academia, 2005).

23. Contra J. D. Levenson, *Creation and the Persistence of Evil* (San Francisco: Harper & Row, 1988), 123. See the bibliography in J. A. Wagenaar, *Origin and Transformation of the Ancient Israelite Festival Calendar* (BZABR 6; Wiesbaden: Harrassowitz, 2005), 140.

24. *HALOT*, 1:152.

originally had a wider meaning.[25] Although calendar days correspond to the nyctemeron, the distinction between day and night in Gen 1 signals that a day literally lasts only as long as daytime and that each day is separated by a night. The rejection of a 24-hour day (Gen 7:12) is crucial for determining the beginning of the festival of unleavened bread (Exod 12:18, discussed in Chapter 5 below).

The care with which Pg defines the duration of a day reflects the importance of time and the measure of time which constitute the theme of the first, fourth and seventh days. The centrality of day four, thematically and structurally, is underlined by the luminaries which are granted the most elaborate discussion of their purpose, more so than humanity's.[26] When humanity is considered the crown of creation or the main concern of Gen 1,[27] or when the focus is limited to the demythologization of the heavenly bodies on the fourth day,[28] the import of day four is missed, although it held a particular place in ancient cosmologies.[29] Verses 14–18 list seven functions, placing the rule of the day and of the night (v. 17) as the core of the structure of the fourth day, which itself forms the centre of the weekly structure of the whole creation account. This can be represented in the following way:

A   to separate between the day and the night (14a)
B   to (indicate) festivals, and days and years (14b)
C   to give light on the earth (15b)
D   to rule the day…to rule the night (16)
C'   to give light on the earth (17)
D'   to rule the day and the night (18a)
A'   to separate between the light and the darkness (18b)[30]

The calendrical purpose of the luminaries can hardly be more clearly stated.

The importance of the fourth day (Gen 1:14–19) goes beyond the mere imitation of the traditional cosmogonies since the sabbatical calendar must start every year with the fourth day of the week (Wednesday,

25. *HALOT*, 2:572: "in the future" (Exod 13:14; Deut 6:20).

26. W. Vogels, *Nos origines: Genèse 1–11* (L'horizon du croyant; Ottawa: Novalis, 1992), 44–47 (53); W. Vogels, "The Cultic and Civil Calendars of the Fourth Day of Creation (Gen. 1,14b)," *SJOT* 11 (1997): 163–80 (174).

27. D. Bergant, "Is the Biblical Worldview Anthropocentric?," *NTR* 4 (1991): 5–14.

28. A. S. Kapelrud, "The Mythological Features in Genesis Chapter I and the Author's Intentions," *VT* 24 (1974): 178–86.

29. Currid, "Examination," 36. B. Landsberger and J. V. K. Wilson, "The Fifth Tablet of Enuma Elish," *JNES* 20 (1961): 154–79.

30. Vogels, "Calendars," 172–73.

Mittwoch) in order to prevent the days of preparation of the Passover meal to fall on the Sabbath and to eliminate any coincidence of the Sabbath and the festivals. Although the day/night cycle starts on day one, day four of creation corresponds to the first day of the calendar (1 I) since there are no luminaries to rule the calendar before day four. Hence, day one is the beginning of the week, while day four is the beginning of the year. For this reason, rendering בראשית as "In the beginning" is misleading since Gen 1:1 is no beginning, neither the beginning of creation, nor the beginning of the week (both start in v. 3), nor the beginning of the calendar (which begins with day four).

While heavenly bodies traditionally determined days, months and years, Gen 1:14 ignores months from the list of calendrical elements regulated by the sun and the moon and mentions festivals instead. Whereas *Enuma eliš* stresses the importance of monthly cycles regulated by the moon,[31] Gen 1:14 reduces the moon to ruling the night; a meagre secondary role that fades into irrelevance since in Gen 1 it is actually the absence of sunlight that separates the day from the night.[32] Moreover, each month has several moonless nights while the moon is sometimes visible during the day. In spite of these drawbacks, Genesis retains the moon as a valid calendrical indicator, albeit not for monthly cycles. It is possible that the scholars who wrote Gen 1 had in mind a specific relation of the sun and the moon at the time of creation which is repeated after an approximate three-year cycle, a full or new moon at the vernal equinox.[33] Hence the moon remains useful for checking the synchronization of the calendar. As everything related to synchronization, this point is not explicit. It is merely hinted at since scribes made sure to retain their prerogatives by preventing sensitive information from falling into unauthorized hands (see Chapter 2). A bitter controversy over the function of the moon arose in the centuries around the turn of the era. The book of *Jubilees* excluded the moon by attributing the role of

31. *Enuma eliš* V:13–22; *CoS* 1:111, 399; Dalley, *Myths*, 255–26.

32. Pg underlines the "eclipse" of the moon in Gen 11:32 with the death of Terah in Haran, the location of a famous sanctuary dedicated to Sîn, the moon-god.

33. E. J. C. Tigchelaar, "Lights Serving as Signs for Festivals (Genesis 1:14b) in Enuma eliš and Early Judaism," in *The Creation of Heaven and Earth* (ed. G. H. van Kooten; Leiden: Brill, 2005), 31–48 (46–47). Cf 4Q319 (4QOtot) and Mishmarot (4Q320–330), both in DJD 21. Also possible is the moon's role in the "Lunar four" data, intervals between sunrise and moonset and moonset and sunrise: L. Brack-Bernsen, "Predictions of Lunar Phenomena in Babylonian Astronomy," in *Under One Sky* (ed. J. M. Steele and A. Imhausen; AOAT 297; Münster: Ugarit-Verlag, 2002), 5–19.

regulating the calendar to the sun alone (*Jub.* 2:9; 4Q216 VI.7),[34] while Ps 104:19 and Ben Sira denied the calendrical importance of the sun in regard to festivals.[35]

The seventh day completes the description of the calendar. The LXX, the Syriac tradition and most latter witnesses read at Gen 2:2 that Elohim completed his work on the sixth instead of the seventh day, aligning Gen 1 with Exod 20:11.[36] The Sabbath thus stands outside creation proper. The Sabbath becomes a period of rest after creation, which sets humankind rather than the Sabbath as the crown of creation. The shift of focus away from the Sabbath is reinforced today by the claim that the seventh-day Sabbath is older than Gen 1–2, although earlier biblical references to the Sabbath refer to the lunar cycle. Moreover, the primary meaning of √שבת has nothing to do with the notion of rest. Rest is designated by √נוח. On the seventh day, Elohim did not rest because he was not tired, in spite of a suggestion of the contrary in Exod 20:11. Such incongruous anthropomorphism is rejected by Isa. 40:28: "He does not faint or grow weary."[37] √שבת derives from Akkadian *šap/battum* ("to complete, bring to an end, fulfil"). As with Ugaritic *sappatum* ("intercalation")[38] and *šuptu* ("a station of the moon"),[39] ancient biblical evidence always refers to the Sabbath as the full moon: "new moon and Sabbath" (2 Kgs 4:23; Isa 1:13; Hos 2:13; Amos 8:5).[40] The pre-Pg legal

34. DJD 8: 16–17. Thanks to Helen Jacobus for this reference.

35. Tigchelaar, "Lights," 31–48. Compare Ps 104:19; Sira 33:7–9; 43:6–8; 50:6–7 and *Jub.* 2:8–10. Ezra and Nehemia use lunar and sabbatical calendars; see A. Sérandour, "A propos des calendriers des livres d'Esdras et de Néhémie," in *Etudes sémitiques et samaritaines offertes à Jean Margain* (ed. C.-B. Amphoux and U. Schattner-Rieser; Lausanne: Zèbre, 1998), 281–89.

36. See F. García Martínez, *Qumranica Minora*, vol. 2 (Leiden: Brill, 2007), 256–59.

37. G. Robinson, "The Idea of Rest in the Old Testament and the Search for the Basic Character of the Sabbath," *ZAW* 92 (1980): 32–42. The subsequent Hebrew, Syriac and Arabic meanings "to rest" all derive from the transformation carried out in Gen 1 and Exod 16 (the manna story), but have no etymological basis.

38. An intercalary period was added to the seven pentecontads (350 days) of the ancient Amorite year; see H. Lewy and J. Lewy, "The Origin of the Week and the Oldest West Asiatic Calendar," *HUCA* 17 (1942–43): 1–152.

39. D. E. Fleming, "A Break in the Line: Reconsidering the Bible's Diverse Festival Calendars," *RB* 106 (1999): 161–74 (174), doubts that biblical Sabbath derives from *shapattu* because at Ugarit the full moon is called *ym malʾat* (*KTU* 1.109.3, see 1.46.11) and at Emar ūmu Šaggari (Emar 373:44 [42], 171 [176], 187 [192]; 375:4).

40. See M. Albani, "Israels Feste im Herbst und das Problem des Kalenderwechsels in der Exilzeit," in *Festtraditionen in Israel und im Alten Orient* (ed.

corpora of the Bible do not display any connection of the seventh day with the Sabbath.[41] For the Babylonian lunar calendar, the new moon marked the beginning of the month and the full moon its middle. Each month was thus made of two "weeks" (new moon to full moon and full moon to new moon), the full moon bearing the Akkadian name *šapatum* from the root *šaba'* ("to be full") and not from *sebet* ("seven").[42] The Hebrew שׁמת cannot derive from Hebrew שׁמע ("seven") because Hebrew *ayin* never transforms into *taw*. The intermediary of Akkadian, which regularly drops guttural letters, in this case *ayin*, to obtain Hebrew שׁמת from *šabatum* renders the lunar aspect of the original biblical Sabbath inescapable. It is Gen 1 which shifts the meaning of the Sabbath from the full moon to the seventh day,[43] a move that may have been facilitated by the fact that the Babylonian Pleiades, the *sibitti*, derive their name from the word "seven" and are pictured as seven dots.[44]

In any case, the full import of the Genesis Creation narrative is missed when the Sabbath is considered as a mere appendix. While other Creation narratives circulated with no connection to the Sabbath,[45] Pg turned the creation story into the aetiology for the seventh-day Sabbath.[46] The Sabbath, rather than humanity, is the crown of creation. For this reason,

E. Blum and R. Lux; VWGT 28; Gütersloh: Gütersloher Verlaghaus, 2006), 111–56; W. W. Hallo, "New Moons and Sabbaths," *HUCA* 48 (1977): 1–18. The Yavne-Yam ostracon (ll. 5–6) does not support the seventh-day interpretation; see the discussion in Milgrom, III, 1960.

41.   Exod 16:22–26 is post-Pg; see Arambarri, "Prolog," 75. That the seventh-day Sabbath is a late invention is confirmed by the fact that it is not mentioned in Deuteronomy, except once in the Ten Words (Deut 5:12–15); see M. Weinfeld, "Sabbath, Temple and the Enthronement of the Lord," in *Mélanges bibliques et orientaux* (ed. A. Caquot and M. Delcor; AOAT 212; Kevelaer: Butzon & Bercker, 1981), 501–12. The earliest attestation of a seventh-day Sabbath is a record of brick delivery from Ptolemaic Egypt from around 280 B.C.E. at the earliest (*CPJ* 1:10).

42.   Robinson, "Rest," 32–42.

43.   N.-E. A. Andreasen, *The Old Testament Sabbath* (Missoula, Mont.: Scholars Press, 1972); G. Robinson, *The Origin and Development of the Old Testament Sabbath* (Frankfurt: Peter Lang, 1988).

44.   J. Black and A. Green, "Seven Dots," in *Gods, Demons and Symbols of Ancient Mesopotamia—An Illustrated Dictionary* (London: British Museum Press, 1992), 162.

45.   W. H. Schmidt, *Die Schöpfungsgeschichte der Priesterschrift* (WMANT 17; Neukirchen–Vluyn: Neukirchener Verlag, 1964), 70–73.

46.   M. Weinfeld, *The Place of the Law in the Religion of Ancient Israel* (VTSup 100; Leiden: Brill, 2004), 99.

Pg's creation is no anthropocentric text.[47] The aim of Pg's creation account is the setting up of a new rhythm serving as the basic unit of a different calendar.[48] The first, middle and last days of the heptameron deal specifically with the creation of time units. Hence, Gen 1 is a sabbatogony more than a cosmogony. *Jubilees* 6:28–32:38 and the Astronomical Book in *1 En* 72–82 fervently uphold the value of a non-Babylonian way of reckoning time commonly referred to as the Jubilee or Sabbatical calendar.[49] With 364 days per normal year, this perpetual calendar is made up of 52 whole weeks, which fixes the relationship of the days of the month with the days of the week (Table 1). Every year, the Sabbath falls on the same day of the month. The travels of the Patriarchs are planned to respect the seventh-day rest and during the Exodus the children of Israel do not start off or arrive on a Sabbath day. In fact, most dated events in the Hebrew Scriptures are calculated according to the 364-day calendar to preserve the sanctity of the Sabbath.[50] There are only two exceptions. Esther 9:15 dates the massacre of 300 inhabitants of Susa on the fourteenth day of Adar.[51] This day, though, is not necessarily a Sabbath since Adar indicates that Esther does not use the sabbatical calendar, which uses numbered months only. With a lunar calendar, it is necessary to know the exact year to determine the date of the Sabbath. As for Solomon's building his temple, 2 Chr 3:2 dates it clearly on a Sabbath, perhaps to underline that the whole project was doomed from the beginning.

47. U. Neumann-Gorsolke, *Herrschen in den Grenzen der Schöpfung* (WMANT 101; Neukirchen–Vluyn: Neukirchener Verlag, 2004), 300.

48. C. H. Gordon, "The Seventh Day," *UF* 11 (1979): 299–302; K. A. D. Smelik, "The Creation of the Sabbath (Gen. 1:1–2:3)," in *Unless Some One Guide Me...* (ed. J. W. Dyk et al.; Maastricht: Shaker, 2001), 9–11 (10).

49. See the following works by A. Jaubert: *La date de la cène* (Paris: Gabalda, 1957), 32–38; *The Date of the Last Supper* (trans. I. Rafferty; New York: Alba House, 1965); "The Calendar of Qumran and the Passion Narrative in John," in *John and Qumran* (ed. J. A. Charlesworth; London: Geoffrey Chapman, 1972), 62–75. See also J. S. Croatto, "Reading the Pentateuch as a Counter-text," in *Congress Volume: Leiden, 2004* (ed. A. Lemaire; VTSup 109; Leiden: Brill, 2006), 383–400. The term "solar calendar" is inappropriate and should be avoided; see U. Glessmer, "Calendars in the Qumran Scrolls," in *The Dead Sea Scrolls After Fifty Years* (ed. P. Flint and J. VanderKam; Leiden: Brill, 1999), 213–78 (231).

50. R. T. Beckwith, "The Significance of the 364-day Calendar for the Old Testament Canon," in *Calendar, Chronology and Worship* (ed. R. T. Beckwith; Leiden: Brill, 2005), 54–66.

51. B. Z. and S. Wacholder, "Patterns of Biblical Dates and Qumran's Calendar: The Fallacy of Jaubert's Hypothesis," *HUCA* 66 (1995): 1–40.

Table 1. *The Sabbatical or 364-day Calendar*

Day	Weekday	Months I, IV, VII, X					Months II, V, VIII, XI					Months III, VI, IX, XII				
4	Wednesday	1	8	15	22	29		6	13	20	27		4	11	18	25
5	Thursday	2	9	16	23	30		7	14	21	28		5	12	19	26
6	Friday	3	10	17	24		1	8	15	22	29		6	13	20	27
7	Sabbath	4	11	18	25		2	9	16	23	30		7	14	21	28
1	Sunday	5	12	19	26		3	10	17	24		1	8	15	22	29
2	Monday	6	13	20	27		4	11	18	25		2	9	16	23	30
3	Tuesday	7	14	21	28		5	12	19	26		3	10	17	24	31

Many scholars consider that the sabbatical calendar originated in the mid-third century B.C.E. on the basis of the oldest manuscripts of the Astronomical Book contained in the book of *Enoch*.[52] Since several texts found in the caves near Qumran also use this calendar, one fragment even refers to it explicitly,[53] the sabbatical calendar is often viewed as an impractical invention of a peripheral sectarian group opposed to a hypothetical "normative Judaism," if such a norm ever existed.[54] This requires understanding that all the biblical dates that avoid activity of the Sabbath day were added or modified during the third century B.C.E., implying that peripheral groups re-dated events in the entire Pentateuch to fit their calendar and that the "official" Judaism which they opposed duly transmitted their dating system! It is preferable to understand the dates of the Pentateuch as original. All the dates in the Pentateuch that fit the sabbatical calendar represent Pg's chronological system. This system

52. Beckwith, "Significance," 56.

53. 4Q252 II 3 is the only non-reconstructed reference to a 364-day year; see G. J. Brooke, "4QCommentaries on Genesis A and Genesis D," in *Qumran Cave 4, XVII, Parabiblical Texts, Part 3* (ed. G. J. Brooke et al.; DJD 22; Oxford: Clarendon, 2003), 198–99.

54. J. C. VanderKam, "The Origin, Character, and Early History of the 364-Day Calendar: A Reassessment of Jaubert's Hypotheses," *CBQ* 41 (1979): 390–411, reprinted in VanderKam, *From Revelation to Canon* (SJSJ 62; Leiden: Brill, 2000), 81–104 (97 n. 55); M. G. Abegg, "The Calendar at Qumran," in *Judaism in Late Antiquity*. Part Five, *The Judaism of Qumran: A Systemic Reading of the Dead Sea Scrolls*. Vol. 1, *Theory of Israel* (ed. J. Neusner and A. J. Avery-Peck; HdO I/56; Leiden: Brill, 2001), 145–71 (150). Reflecting the 364-day calendar, see 1Q32; 1Q34; 4QMMT; 4QShirShabb; 4Q252 frag. 1ii.3; 4Q317–30; 4Q319–336; 4Q365; 4Q559; 6Q17; 11QTemple; 11QPs³ Dav Comp 27.6; cf. S. Talmon, "Calendars and Mishmarot," in *Encyclopedia of the Dead Sea Scrolls* (ed. L. H. Schiffman and J. C. VanderKam; Oxford: Oxford University Press, 2000), 1:108–17; T. H. Lim, "The Chronology of the Flood Story in a Qumran Text (4Q252)," *JJS* 43 (1992): 288–98.

was modified when the dominant group imposed a calendar reform which replaced the sabbatical calendar with a Babylonian calendar, either during the Seleucid era, or already during the reign of Artaxerxes II (404–358 B.C.E.). Artaxerxes introduced a calendar reform celebrating the return of a sun-like Mitra and of Sîn, two divinities which the Zoroastrianism of previous Persian rulers had suppressed.

The book of *Jubilees* holds a particular place among the supporters of the sabbatical calendar. In spite of its vibrant defence of the sabbatical calendar, Jubilees contains three Sabbath violations.[55] I interpret this paradox as demonstrating that *Jubilees* is defending the traditional scriptural calendar rather than an innovative one. The large amount of secondary material inserted into the original narrative, which was based upon the sabbatical calendar (Pg), made it impossible for the writers of the book of *Jubilees* to maintain the original system. This means that the sabbatical calendar is older than the mid-third century B.C.E.

In fact, a schematic 364-day year is already attested by the Assyrian treatise MUL.APIN composed around the beginning of the first millennium.[56] The earliest copy of this text dates to the seventh century B.C.E. Since the MUL.APIN schematic year is the most likely source for the 364-day calendar of the Bible,[57] there is no need to wait until the third century B.C.E. for its appearance in biblical texts. It could have reached Palestine as early as the Western Assyrian campaigns of the Sargonid kings. Therefore, Shemaryahu Talmon claims that the 364-day calendar is rooted in the biblical era[58] and James VanderKam narrows the biblical era to the early centuries of the second temple.[59] At one point, the

---

55. *Jub.* 5:3 (the animals enter the ark); 18:1–15 (Abraham's return to Beersheva); 44:1 (Jacob's sacrifice at the Well of Oath); see R. T. Beckwith, "The Qumran Temple Scroll and Its Calendar: Their Character and Purpose," in Beckwith, ed., *Calendar, Chronology and Worship*, 67–66 (18).

56. H. Hunger and D. Pingree, *MUL.APIN, an Astronomical Compendium in Cuneiform* (AfOB 24; Horn: F. Bergern & Söhne, 1989).

57. See W. Horowitz, "The 364 Day Year in Mesopotamia, Again," *NABU* (1998) 49: online at http://www.achemenet.com/recherche/textes/babyloniens/nabu /nabu.htm. See also W. Horowitz, "The 360 and 364 Day Year in Ancient Mesopotamia," *JANES* 24 (1996): 35–41; J. P. Britton, "Treatments of Annual Phenomena in Cuneiform Sources," in Steele and Imhausen, eds., *Under One Sky*, 21–78 (24). I am indebted to Helen Jacobus for these references and her clarifications.

58. S. Talmon, "Qumran Studies: Past, Present and Future," *JQR* 85 (1994): 1–31 (28).

59. VanderKam, "Origin," 103. This hypothesis is at least a century old; see B. W. Bacon, "Calendar of Enoch and Jubilees" *Hebraica* 8 (1891–92): 79–88 (124–31). See also the bibliographical citations in VanderKam, "Origin," nn. 9–10.

Babylonian lunar calendar was reintroduced at Jerusalem, replacing the sabbatical calendar, which provoked the controversy reflected in the book of *Jubilees* and some Dead Sea Scrolls.[60] Rabbinic Judaism uses the Babylonian calendar to this day, while the sabbatical calendar can be as old as the writing of Gen 1 and Pg. The date of Pg is further discussed in the Conclusion.

Like humankind, the Sabbath is blessed. Unlike humankind, or all other creatures, the Sabbath is also sanctified (Gen 2:3). As the only creature to be blessed and sanctified,[61] the Sabbath is the foundation of time and the measure thereof. Setting humanity as the crown of creation misses out the primacy of time in the first, fourth and seventh days. However, Gen 1:1–2:4 present only the first elements of the calendar, the day and the week. The full range of calendrical indications is presented further on in the Pg narrative. For this reason, Gen 2:3 explicitly notes that "Elohim created in order to continue to make" (ברא לעשות), insisting that creation is accomplished, but that divine activity is not completed, not until every aspect of the sabbatical calendar is delineated and not until every human group is settled permanently on a viable territory, which takes place in Josh 18.[62]

Fundamental Goodness

A last element in Pg's introduction needs to be underlined in order to show the coherence of the entire narrative. The formulae "it was good" (Gen 1:4, 10, 12, 18, 21, 25, 31) and "it was so," or, better, "it was firmly established" (√כון) constitute a refrain within the Creation narrative. Firmness is ascribed to the dome (v. 7), the separation of the waters from the dry (v. 9), vegetation (v. 11), luminaries (v. 15), animal life (v. 20 [in the LXX] and 24), and food (v. 30). Humanity is not listed since it is capable of violence which undermines the stability of its existence.

60. See J. C. VanderKam, "2 Maccabees 6,7a and Calendrical Change in Jerusalem," *JSJ* 12 (1981): 52–74, reprinted in *From Revelation to Canon*, 105–27. Detailed analysis of various non-biblical texts based on heptadic cycles is provided by C. Berner, *Jahre, Jahrwochen und Jubiläen* (BZAW 363; Berlin: de Gruyter, 2006).

61. A unique phenomenon in the whole of the Old Testament (Exod 20:11 quoting Gen. 2:3); see Arambarri, "Prolog," 77.

62. B. Barc, "Du temple à la synagogue," in *KATA TOYΣ O' «selon les Septantes» Mélanges offerts en hommage à Marguerite Harl* (ed. G. Dorival and O. Munnich; Paris: Cerf, 1995), 11–26 (17); E. A. Knauf, "Seine Arbeit, die Gott geschaffen hat, um sie auszuführen," *BN* 111 (2002): 24–27.

Instead, humankind is blessed. The day and night cycle (day 1) is not declared firm either since it will be interrupted once by the Flood when primeval waters return as agents of purgation. For this reason, day two (Gen 1:6–8) is the only day without a confirmation of goodness. By contrast, the separation water/dry land is deemed firm and good (Gen 1:9–10) since the ark prevented the Flood from drowning all breathing creatures.

On the whole, creation is very good (Gen 1:31), which produces a sharp contrast with the following story of the Garden of Eden. Genesis 2–4 undermines the fundamental goodness of creation and seeks an alternative myth for the origin of evil.[63] Genesis 2–4 are still widely considered as an earlier Creation narrative attributed to J, but an increasing number of studies now understand Gen 2–4 as a disputation text dealing more with wisdom than with creation.[64] The demise of the Solomonic J reverses the order of dependence, freeing the Eden narrative and other non-Pg elements in Gen 1–11 to be considered as post-Pg.[65]

63. Such myth prevails in Enochic literature, with which Pg entertains close links (see Gen 5:23–24). For further discussion see P. R. Davies, "Sons of Cain," in *A Word in Season* (ed. J. D. Martin et al.; JSOTSup 42; Sheffield: JSOT Press, 1986), 35–56.

64. J. M. Sasson, "The mother of all… 'Etiologies'," in *"A Wise and Discerning Mind": Essays in Honour of Burke O. Long* (ed. S. M. Olyan and R. C. Culley; BJS 325; Providence, RI: Brown University Press, 2000), 205–20. Gen 2–4 are read as a polemical rejection of human ability to choose between good and evil; see D. Carr, "The Politics of Textual Subversion: A Diachronic Perspective on the Garden of Eden Story," *JBL* 112 (1993): 577–95. On the assimilation of late wisdom themes into Torah theology, see E. Otto, "Die Paradieserzählung. Eine nachpriesterschriftliche Lehrerzaehlung in ihrem religions-historischen Kontext," in *"Jedes Ding hat seine Zeit…" Studien zur israelitischen Weisheit* (ed. A. A. Diesel et al.; BZAW 241; Berlin: de Gruyter, 1996), 167–92. See J. M. Husser, "Entre mythe et philosophie. La relecture sapientielle de Genèse 2–3," *RB* 107 (2000): 232–59; K. Schmid, "Die Unteilbarkeit der Weisheit," *ZAW* 114 (2002): 21–39.

65. See Otto, "Paradieserzählung," 167–92; T. Krüger, "Das menschliche Herz und die Weisung Gottes," in *Rezeption und Auslegung im Alten Testament und in seinem Umfeld* (ed. R. G. Kratz and T. Krüger; OBO 153; Fribourg: Universitätsverlag; Göttingen: Vandenhoeck & Ruprecht, 1997), 65–92; J. Blenkinsopp, "A Post-exilic Lay Source in Genesis 1–11," in *Abschied vom Jahwisten* (ed. J. C. Gertz, K. Schmid and M. Witte; BZAW 315; Berlin: de Gruyter, 2002), 49–62; E. Bosshard-Nepustil, *Vor uns die Sinflut* (BWANT 165; Stuttgart: Kohlhammer, 2005).

The Sabbath as Sacred Rhythm

One caveat must be entered concerning the notion of time, a notoriously difficult philosophical concept. Protestant ideology tried to prove that the genius of Israel expressed itself through the action of YHWH in history in opposition to the mere repetition of myths in the cult.[66] Ancient Egypt had in fact conceptualized linear and cyclical notions of time well before Israel.[67] The Sabbath and the perpetual calendar based upon it set up a rhythm that pertains to a cyclical aspect of time. Whether time itself is a legitimate concept is also questionable. Jack Sasson claims that Elohim created time in the first day and space on the second day.[68] Singling out time as a dimension or reality distinct from space reflects a Newtonian concept of reified time.[69] Rather than the disputable notion of time as an autonomously flowing entity, the Sabbath and Gen 1 are the creation of a sacred rhythm. Since none of the Hebrew words referring to time appear in Gen 1, it is more accurate to refer to the creation of a sacred calendar. Calendars coordinate human activities and natural processes with one another[70] rather than measure an abstract time flow.

The Exclusivity of Sabbath Sacredness

Conventional exegesis of Gen 1 focuses primarily on anthropological matters and overlooks the fact that the first, fourth and seventh days are devoted exclusively to the creation of rhythms. Yet, the importance of the Sabbath is underlined by the exclusive attribution of sanctity to the Sabbath. Elohim not only blesses the Sabbath as he blesses other creatures, he also sanctifies it. The Creation narrative culminates with the Sabbath as a unique repository of holiness. This produces a tension with other categories of sanctity—holy mountain, holy land, holy city, holy temple and holy priesthood—none of which, however, appear in Pg.

Etymologically, the notion of sanctity or holiness conveys aspects of segregation of persons or things from common use. To sanctify is to

66. G. von Rad, *Theology of the Old Testament*, vol. 2 (Louisville: Westminster John Knox, 2001); J. Muilenburg, "The Biblical View of Time," *HTR* 54 (1961): 225–53; J. Barr, *Biblical Words for Time* (London: SCM, 1962).

67. J. Assmann, "Zeit und Geschichte in frühen Kulturen," in *Time and History* (ed. F. Stadler and M. Stöltzner; Frankfurt: Ontos, 2006), 489–508.

68. Sasson, "Time," 191–93.

69. S. Stern, *Time and Process in Ancient Judaism* (Oxford: Littman Library of Jewish Civilization, 2003), 21; P. C. W. Davies, *Space and Time in the Modern Universe* (Cambridge: Cambridge University Press, 1977), 32–55.

70. Stern, *Time*, 57.

grant a particular status, to clean, purify, dedicate or consecrate. Holiness bears upon economic matters since consecrated objects may become free from taxation or seizure, their use being reserved to certain people (Korban in Mark 7:11, Islamic *waqf*). Holiness is applied to soldiers and their weapons as they sanctify themselves before battle, specifically by abstaining from intercourse with women (1 Sam 21:4–6). Ordinary Israelites are also urged to consecrate themselves before festivals (2 Kgs 10:20; 2 Chr 35:6). The notion underlying such calls to sanctification is that daily life defiles and renders one unfit for religious activities. Israelites are called to sanctify themselves either because YHWH is holy or they will be sanctified because YHWH is holy (Lev 11:44; 19:2; 20:7). The difference between these two concepts, human self-sanctification or divine sanctification of humans, is huge. Yet, they agree on one point. Both are conditioned by the observance of rites and commands (Num 15:40). By contrast, the sanctification of the Sabbath by Elohim in Gen 2:3 is independent of any human activity. A possibility thus opens for the isolation of two distinct concepts of holiness within Priestly traditions.[71]

That a hierarchy of notions of holiness exists within the broad category of priestly literature is suggested by a scholar who cannot be suspected of hostility to things holy. Jacob Milgrom makes the astonishing claim that "Never in Scripture do we find that God sanctifies space."[72] This means that the many holy places in the Hebrew Bible and across the Levant are cases of self-proclaimed sanctity lacking direct divine approval. Sacred space belongs to tradition, a tradition not endorsed by any biblical text. One would think that the sanctity of Jerusalem and its temple is undisputed. Yet, a quick survey of the relevant texts confirms Milgrom's claim that Jerusalem is no exception. The holiness of Jerusalem and of Zion has no direct divine sanction.

The Tabernacle Moses built in the wilderness is divided between the Holy and the Holy of Holies.[73] These structures are said to be holy but they are not places as such since, despite their common English translation, they lack any spatial indicators. These holy places are no places at all since they were mobile structures constructed and erected in the wilderness. The wilderness is nowhere in particular. Sanctity renders holy structures extra-territorial. Claims that the Land of Israel is holy

---

71. J. G. Gammie, *Holiness in Israel* (Minneapolis: Fortress, 1989), 9–70 subsumes the Priestly Code, the Holiness Code, Ezekiel and the Chronistic History under the single category of "Priestly" understanding of holiness.

72. Milgrom, III, 1962.

73. קדש הקדשים appears in Exod 26:33–34; 28:29, 35, 43; 29:30–31; 38:24; 39:1, 41; Lev 6:16, 30; 7:6.

because the Tent of Meeting was eventually set up in it are highly suspect.[74] If the holiness of Zion becomes a major theme after 70 CE, when the land becomes inaccessible and remote,[75] in the Hebrew Bible the link of Zion with the place where YHWH will choose to rest his name (Deut 12; 14; 16; 26) is severed since the Torah never names this resting place. In fact, the Torah never mentions Jerusalem or Zion. The holiness of Zion and Jerusalem are cases of self-proclaimed holiness (Ps 93:2).[76]

The impossibility of establishing a link between the wilderness tent and the Jerusalem temple is illustrated by 1 Chr 16:39 and 2 Chr 1:3, which attempt to fill the gap by claiming that the Tabernacle made by Moses in the wilderness was later set up in Gibeon. The Chronicler could not have the Tabernacle erected in Jerusalem because the Tent of Meeting set up in the temple by Solomon (1 Kgs 8:4 MT) is not mentioned in the episode of David's bringing the ark into the city of David (2 Sam 6:1–19). Hence, the Chronicler concluded that the Tent had been stored at the greatest possible high place mentioned in his source, Gibeon (1 Kgs 3:4), before Solomon brought it into the temple,[77] in clear contradiction to the explicit claim that the Tent of Meeting was erected in Shiloh (Josh 18:1). To overcome the difficulty, 2 Chr 22:19 has David ordering the building of a house for the ark and the holy vessels and thus forges the missing link between the wilderness sanctuary and the Jerusalem temple. The Chronicler was well aware of the deficit of legitimacy suffered by the edifice he was meant to extol. A holy of holies is mentioned three times in connection with the temple at Jerusalem (1 Kgs 6:16; 7:50; 8:6), but again, this holiness is self-attributed and YHWH is never displayed as sanctifying the temple.

74. Against J. Joosten, *People and Land in the Holiness Code* (VTSup 67; Leiden: Brill, 1996). Judah is once referred to as a holy ground (אדמת הקדש, Zech 2:16). Doubts are expressed by the very builder of the temple over its suitability as a divine abode when Solomon asks whether Elohim will dwell on the land at all (1 Kgs 8:27). Jeremiah's desecrating sermon at the gate of the house of YHWH is a clear refusal to attribute much significance to the temple of Jerusalem (Jer 7:2, 4). Zechariah's vision of contaminating holiness which will sanctify every pot in Jerusalem and Judah (Zech 14:21) appears as the opposite of Jeremiah's strategy. Yet, hyperbolic sacralization has the same effect as radical desacralization. If everything is holy, the concept of holiness is emptied of its substance.

75. D. J. Harrington, "The 'Holy Land' in Pseudo-Philo, 4 Ezra, and 2 Baruch," *Emanuel* (2003): 661–72.

76. D. J. A. Clines, "Sacred Space, Holy Places and Suchlike," in his *On the Way to the Postmodern* (JSOTSup 293; Sheffield: Sheffield Academic Press, 1998), 542–54.

77. G. N. Knoppers, *1 Chronicles 10–29* (AB 12A; Garden City: Doubleday, 2004), 653.

Isaiah speaks much of holiness, but he ascribes it mostly to God. The few designations of Jerusalem or Zion as a holy mountain in divine oracles (Isa 11:9; 27:13; 52:1; 56:7; 57:13; 65:25) always refer to the eschatological Zion, the Jerusalem of the end of times or outside time. Ezekiel 20:40; 42:13; 43:12; 44:19; 45:1–7 are equally eschatological. The non-existent holy space is replaced by a coming era. When Zeph 3:11 refers to Zion as the "mountain of my holiness," the holiness in question refers to God rather than to the mountain. Hence, Milgrom is right, YHWH is never said to grant holiness to any particular place, not even to Jerusalem or to its "sanctuary."

The location of the burning bush may be considered an exception to Milgrom's claim since YHWH tells Moses that "the place upon which you are standing is a holy ground" (Exod 3:5). This is the second mention of holiness in the Torah, after that of the Sabbath in Gen 2:3. The order to remove shoes underlines the sanctity of the place, treated as if it were a sanctuary.[78] Yet, the holy ground upon which Moses stands is devoid of architectural features and devoid of any precise geographic indicator. The ground in question is beyond the wilderness. The only point of reference is Midian which encompasses the modern Hejaz in northern Saudi Arabia. The other geographical marker in Exod 3:5 is Horeb, qualified as the mountain of Elohim. Moses' encounter with the burning bush "beyond the wilderness from Midian" indicates that the holy ground is not a land, nor a country, not even a place, and no sanctuary was ever built upon it. It stands outside geography. It cannot be located. Sanctified time takes precedence over sanctified space.[79]

78. E. Tigchelaar, "Bare Feet and Holy Ground," in van Kooten, ed., *The Revelation of the Name YHWH to Moses*, 17–36; R. Bartelmus, "Begegnung in der Fremde. Anmerkungen zur theologischen Relevanz der topographischen Verortung der Berufungsvisionen des Mose und des Ezechiel (Ex 3,1–4,17 bzw. Ez 1,1–3,15)," *BN* 78 (1995): 21–38; L. Beard, "From Barefootedness to Sure-footedness: Contrasts Involving Sacred Space and Movement in the Bible," *JS* 14 (2005): 235–60.

79. R. Hayward, "The Sanctification of Time in the Second Temple Period: Case Studies in the Septuagint and Jubilees," in *Holiness Past and Present* (ed. S. C. Barton; London: T&T Clark International, 2003), 141–67 (141). According to Y. Z. Eliav (*God's Mountain: The Temple Mount in Time, Place, and Memory* [Baltimore: The Johns Hopkins University Press, 2005]), the "sacredness" of the Temple Mount in Jerusalem arose from an absence. Eliav notes (p. 240): "From a temple enclosure serving the sanctuary at its center and devoid of any independent value, this space evolved into the Temple Mount, an autonomous entity with the stature of a holy mountain in every sense of the word. Ironically, then, the space became the Temple Mount only when it no longer had a temple—the Temple Mount is a Mount without a Temple."

The holy ground passage is repeated almost verbatim when Joshua stands for the first time in Canaan (Josh 5:15).[80] The commander of the army of the Lord alludes directly to Moses in front of the burning bush. The scene is set by Jericho, or even in Jericho (ביריחו, Josh 5:13). The only difference with the formulation in Exodus is that the word אדמה ("soil, ground") is dropped, which further prevents the transfer of this holiness to a particular location.

In agreement with Milgrom's claim that God never sanctifies space in the Bible, the holiness of priests and cultic objects is another case of self-attributed sanctity. In spite of the importance of priests and temple in Exodus, Leviticus, Numbers, Ezekiel and Zechariah, YHWH is never presented as consecrating priests or sanctuaries. It is Israel who grants holiness to priests because they offer food for their god (Lev 21:7–8). Therefore, it is far from obvious that the building of a sanctuary is the natural outcome of Elohim's sanctification of the Sabbath.[81] In fact, Elohim's sanctification of the Sabbath may well be the factor which prevented the sanctification of any earthly sanctuary and priests in the Bible, in spite of the heavy stress on the importance of Jerusalem in latter parts of the Hebrew Scriptures. Therefore, assuming that the notion of holy time is naturally transferable to the cultic apparatus misses a crucial distinction maintained throughout the Hebrew Scriptures. Although the scribes who penned the long description of the Tabernacle derived their income more or less directly from the Jerusalem temple, they felt compelled to respect Pg's strict limitation of divinely conferred holiness to sabbatical rhythms. All attempts to connect the Jerusalem temple to Gen 1 are cases of special pleading which are blind to this remarkable phenomenon.

The exclusive holiness of the Sabbath is a characteristic of Pg, a criterion for the identification of Pg in the rest of the Pentateuch. That the holiness of the Sabbath is not tied in any way to its observation by the first humans is a hallmark of Pg's theology, which coheres with Pg's notion of unconditional grace displayed by the sign of circumcision (Gen 17). As soon as YHWH's presence is understood as conferring holiness to space, Pg's central tenet of holiness reserved to time is lost, and the door is opened to Deuteronomistic notions of conditional grace such as this:

80. C. G. den Hertog, "Jos 5,4–6 in der griechischen Übersetzung," *ZAW* 110 (1998): 601–6.

81. *Pace* M. Bauks, "La signification de l'espace et du temps dans 'l'historiographie sacerdotale'," in *The Future of the Deuteronomistic History* (ed. T. Römer; BETL 147; Leuven: Leuven University Press, 2000), 29–45 (44).

...it is righteousness and perfection that will save Israel, just as it saved Noah... Should Israel refuse to recognize the categories of holiness engrained in P's worldview, YHWH will destroy the nation like a sacrifice...[82]

The categories of holiness this quote refers to are obviously not those of Pg, which always insists on unconditional grace and never places human obedience as a prerequisite to divine blessing. The trail of holy rhythms (rather than time) can be followed right through the Pentateuch thanks to the sabbatical calendar. This is the task of the next chapters.

82. D. Janzen, *The Social Meanings of Sacrifice in the Hebrew Bible* (BZAW 344; Berlin: de Gruyter, 2004), 101.

Chapter 2

INTERCALATION OF THE SABBATICAL CALENDAR

After establishing the week as the basic unit of the sabbatical calendar, Pg presents a numerical list in the form of ages of ancestors. Genesis 5 is the first inventory transmitting mostly names and numbers, which sets Pg apart from standard narratives. Such lists facilitate the identification of Pg because they are so peculiar, yet they also render its understanding difficult because the interpretation of such lists is far from obvious. The difficulty is complicated here and in Gen 11 by the fact that three textual traditions are preserved. It has long been suspected that the major differences between MT, LXX and SP are not accidental but result from carefully construed systems. Once the principles governing each system are identified, it should be possible to determine which of them is more likely to represent Pg's chronology.[1] The enterprise has, however, proved daunting.[2] A number of textual variants within each system complicate

1. J. Skinner, *A Critical and Exegetical Commentary on Genesis* (Edinburgh: T. & T. Clark, 1910), 135.

2. M. Barnouin, "Recherches numériques sur la généalogie de Genèse V," *RB* 77 (1970): 347–65; M. Wojciechowski, "Certains aspects algébriques de quelques nombres symboliques de la Bible," *BN* 23 (1984): 29–31; C. J. Labuschagne, "The Life Span of the Patriarchs," in *New Avenues in the Study of the Old Testament* (ed. A. S. van der Woude; OTS 25; Leiden: Brill, 1989), 121–27; D. W. Young, "The Influence of Babylonian Algebra on Longevity Among the Antediluvians," *ZAW* 102 (1990): 321–35; D. V. Etz, "The Numbers of Genesis V 3–31," *VT* 43 (1993): 171–89; L. R. Bailey, "Biblical Math as Heilsgeschichte?," in *A Gift of God in Due Season* (ed. R. D. Weis and D. M. Carr; JSOTSup 225; Sheffield: JSOT Press, 1996), 84–102; G. Borgonovo, "Significato numerico delle cronologie bibliche e rilevanza delle varianti testuali (TM-LXX-SAM)," *RSB* 9 (1997): 139–67. R. Heinzerling, "'Einweihung' durch Henoch? Die Bedeutung der Altersangaben in Genesis 5," *ZAW* 110 (1998): 581–89; B. Barc, "La chronologie biblique d'Adam à la mort de Moïse," *LTP* 55 (1999): 215–26; B. Gardner, *The Genesis Calendar: The Synchronistic Tradition in Genesis 1–11* (Lanham: University Press of America, 2001); G. Larsson, "Septuagint versus Massoretic Chronology," *ZAW* 114 (2002): 511–21; D. W. Young, "The Step-down to Two Hundred in Genesis 11,10–25,"

the task, though progress has been made on biblical calendars thanks to data from the Dead Sea Scrolls. Hence, the facile claim that "it is possible to discover in the text whatever we wish, for the figures are flexible and can be made to fit all sorts of numerical combinations..."[3] is unconvincing since numbers are a lot less flexible than the sources and redactors manipulated by critical exegesis with little external control. For this reason the numerological lists resists explanation. Without claiming to "break the code," the aim here is to recover some clues to demonstrate the coherence of these lists with Gen 1.

The first name of the list in Gen 5 is Adam, who is presented as a male ancestor, in contradiction to Gen 1 where Adam designates humankind. The tension has been used to negate the existence of a Priestly narrative.[4] Whereas Gen 1:27–28 and 5:2 depicts "the adam" as humankind, both male and female, in Gen 5:1, 3 "Adam" is an individual male who corresponds to Adamu the second of the legendary Assyrian kings. The decidedly egalitarian concept of the sexes in Gen 1 is thus carefully meshed with the list of male ancestors which consciously imitates the Assyrian kings lists.[5] Yet the presence of two kinds of Adam is not enough to prove that Gen 5 cannot belong to the same narrative than Gen 1. Pg's hand is clearly visible in the replacement of the reign lengths of the Assyrian King Lists by the age at fatherhood which reflects Pg's constant anxiety over human multiplication.[6] Enoch further points to the coherence of Gen 1 and 5.

Everything in Gen 5 points to Enoch's special significance. Enoch represents the seventh generation, he walks with the Elohim before his rapture at age 365 (Gen 5:23). Not only does Enoch not die, but in all three traditions (MT, LXX, SP) his lifespan is about half of the lifespan of the other antediluvian ancestors. The name Enoch "Initiated" stands out as particularly positive compared to the names of the ancestors from the fourth generation onwards, names which anticipate the violence that

ZAW 116 (2004): 323–33. D. W. Young, "The Sexagesimal Basis for the Total Years of the Antediluvian and Postdiluvian Epochs," *ZAW* 116 (2004): 502–27; B. Barc, "Bible et mathématiques à la période hellénistique," in Amphoux, Frey and Schattner-Rieser, eds., *Études sémitiques et samaritaines*, 269–79.

3. U. Cassuto, *A Commentary on the Book of Genesis* (Jerusalem: Magnes, 1964), 258.

4. Campbell and O'Brien, *Rethinking*, 111–12.

5. *CoS* 1:135, 463; A. K. Grayson, "Königslisten und Chroniken," in *Reallexikon der Assyriologie* (ed. E. Ebeling and B. Meissner; Berlin: de Gruyter, 1980), 6:89–101.

6. Gen 1:28; 9:1; 10–11; 21:2–5; 25:13–26; 35:11; 36:6–43; 46:7; 47:27; Exod 1:7; 12:37; Num 1:46.

caused the Flood (see Gen 6:11).[7] Had Enoch lived 364 years rather than 365, the presence of the sabbatical calendar in the Bible would be obvious. However, virulent objections have been published against such presence because Enoch's 365 years are reflected in the duration of the Flood, which in turn is supposed to prove that the 364-day calendar is not used by the Flood narrative.[8] To counter this claim it is necessary to demonstrate that number 365 is congruent with the sabbatical calendar and indicates that the basic 364-day year needs intercalation.

Abraham's Lifespan

In spite of variations in the relative length of daylight and darkness, weeks, months, and years are accounted in whole numbers of days since no other cycle impresses itself as inescapably on our senses.[9] However, the number of days between sightings of the new moon varies between 29 and 30 days,[10] so that twelve lunar cycles approximate 354 days, about 11 days short of the solar year. Calendars are doomed to be out of synch with awkward consequences with regard to seasons.[11] While the Moslem calendar functions without intercalation, most calendars synchronize the lunar cycle to the solar one in order to keep the months in step with the seasons. Mesopotamian scholars devoted much effort to observing and recording moon risings and settings to determine in advance whether the new month marked by the appearance of the new crescent would be hollow (29 days) or full (30 days).[12]

Like its Assyrian ancestor MUL.APIN, the Jubilee calendar offers the notable advantage of being independent of the moon, with the length of

---

7. Little-Smith (Kenan) Rendered-El-Mad (Mahalalel), Went-Down (Jared), Throwing-A-Spear (Methuselah) and Sword (Lamech).

8. Wacholder and Wacholder, "Patterns," 26. A weaker argument is based on the fact that *Jubilees* rejects all notion of intercalation. This does not prove that it is also the case in the Bible: *pace* Wacholder and Wacholder, "Patterns," 29; R. T. Beckwith, "The Essene Calendar and the Moon," *RQ* 59 (1992): 457–66.

9. L. Depuydt, "History of the heleq," in Steele and Imhausen, eds., *Under One Sky*, 79–107 (80).

10. Synodic months (the time in which the moon returns to conjunction) vary between 29.27 and 29.83 days, a difference of about 13.5 hours, with the shortest months in summer. See ibid., 82–83.

11. D. E. Fleming, *Time at Emar: The Cultic Calendar and the Rituals from the Diviner's Archive* (Winona Lake: Eisenbrauns, 2000), 211.

12. Brack-Bernsen, "Predictions," 5–19; J. Ben-Dov and W. Horowitz, "The Babylonian Lunar Three in Calendrical Scrolls from Qumran," *ZA* 95 (2005): 104–20.

months determined in advance (see Table 1).[13] MUL.APIN has an approximate lunar/solar synchronization with an extra month intercalated every third year: ([354 days × 3] + 30 days): 3 = 364 days. This is too approximate to be used as a working calendar since over a day and a half is missing every year, which makes it impossible to keep pace with the synodic year. The problem could be solved in two ways. Adding one whole week every 6-year cycle, plus an extra week every 84 years (14 six-year cycles) produces a 365.2068-day year, 51 minutes short of the exact tropical year (365.2422 days).[14] Over the full term of 84 years the cycle coincides exactly with 1039 lunations.[15] Another intercalation method is attested in 4Q319 and 4Q503, which use a seven-year cycle with a whole week added every seventh year, plus an additional week every twenty-eighth year: (365 × 28) + 7 = 365.25 × 28.[16] Both methods are suitable for intercalation of the 364-day calendar presented in Gen 1 since intercalating a whole week at a time preserves the sacred rhythm of the seventh-day Sabbath and does not interfere with the requirement to start every year on a Wednesday. Both methods use a two-step intercalation, either a 6/84-year or a 7/28-year scheme. In both cases, the first stage functions with a mean year of 365 days although normal years have only 364 days. Hence Enoch's age refers directly to this first stage of intercalation. Elohim cut Enoch's life down to the correct length to legitimate the first stage of intercalation. What about the second intercalation scheme?

Shem's genesis (Gen 11:10–26) supplies a list of ten generations from Shem to Terah (LXX), or from Shem to Abram since Kainan is missing from MT and SP. Listed are the ages of first begetting and the years of remaining life. Only the postdiluvian begetting ages are relevant for

13. Albani, *Astronomie*, 173–72.

14. U. Glessmer, "Der 364-Tage Kalendar und die Sabbatstruktur seiner Schaltungen in ihrer Bedeutung für den Kult," in *Ernten was man sät* (ed. D. R. Daniels, U. Glessmer and M. Rösel; Neukirchen–Vluyn: Neukirchener Verlag, 1991), 379–98; and "Horizontal Measuring in the Babylonian Astronomical Compendium MUL.APIN and in the Astronomical Book of 1En," *Henoch* 18 (1996): 259–82.

15. Gardner, *Calendar*, 179.

16. M. Testuz, *Les idées religieuses du livre des Jubilés* (Geneva: Droz, 1960), 127–28; A. R. C. Leaney, *The Rule of Qumran and Its Meaning* (London: SCM, 1966), 85; U. Glessmer, "Calendars in the Qumran Scrolls," in Flint and Vander-Kam, eds., *The Dead Sea Scrolls After Fifty Years*, 213–78. Alternatively, the extra days could be intercalated in one block of 49 days every Jubilee year; for more on this, see S. B. Hoenig, "Sabbatical Years and the Year of Jubilee," *JQR* 59 (1969): 222–36.

calculating the duration of the post-diluvian era. Since Shem fathered Arpachshad two years after the Flood (Gen 11:10), these two years should theoretically be included in the count. However, Shem was 100 years when the Flood started (Gen 5:32; 7:6) and he still was 100 years old two years after the Flood (Gen 11:10). By this device, Pg indicates that the Flood corresponds to a suspension of time. The implications of the suspension are discussed below with the Flood chronology. For the time being, the discrepancy is enough to justify the exclusion of these two years from the count (Table 2).

Table 2. *The Post-Diluvian Era*

	MT	*LXX*	*SP*	*Pg*
Shem				
Arpachshad	35	135	135	135
Kainan	—	130	—	130
Shelah	30	130	130	130
Eber	34	134	134	134
Peleg	30	130	130	130
Reu	32	132	132	132
Serug	30	130	130	130
Nahor	29	79	79	29
Terah	70		70	70
Abram leaves Haran	75		75	75
Total	*365 = Enoch*	*1000*	*1015*	*1095 = 3 × 365*

The postdiluvian period is marked by a sharp reduction of life-span, ending with dislocation and reproductive disorders. In sharp contrast to the one people/one land principle featured by the Table of Nations (Gen 9), Terah moves out of Ur of the Chaldeans after the death of his son and goes to Haran with his childless son Abram and his orphaned grandson Lot. Sarai is the first attested barren woman and Lot is the first orphan (Gen 11:28). Then Abram and Lot leave for Canaan without Terah. According to the MT and the LXX, Terah dies at age 205, remaining 60 years on his own in Haran, famous for its cult of the lunar god.[17] Adding the begetting ages of the postdiluvian ancestors from Arpachshad (Gen 11:10) to Terah (Gen 12:4) gives the length of the postdiluvian period. The textual traditions present several models. The MT adds Abram's 75 years when he left Haran to the begetting ages of the post-diluvian

17. The SP eliminates the extra 60 years, a *lectio facilior* having Abram wait until Terah dies before leaving for Canaan but missing the symbolic value of these 60 years alone in lunar Haran. Why Acts 7:4 follows SP rather than the LXX remains to be explained. Was Stephen a Samaritan?

ancestors to reach a total of 365 years between Arpachshad's birth and Abram's departure from Haran. These 365 years reproduce Enoch's lifespan and block any further intercalation by indicating that mean-years are the same before and after the Flood. This runs contrary to what Pg envisaged since it infers that the violence against the solar cycle produced by a faulty calendar continues. Over the same period, the SP produces a sum of 1015 year, not a significant number. The LXX tallies a total of 1000 years between Arpachshad's begetting of Kainan and Nahor's begetting of Terah.[18] One thousand years bears no particular significance within the sabbatical system but belongs to a decimal system which places the Cyrus edict in *anno mundi* 4999 and the return from Exile in year 5000.[19] Before deciding which Pg's original calculation was, the problem posed by the omission of Kainan in the MT and the SP requires some explanation.

The primacy of Kainan is supported by the parallelism Noah//Terah established by their fathering of three sons in the same year (Gen 5:32; 11:26).[20] Whether Shem–Ham–Japheth and Abram–Nahor–Haran were triplets or were born from different mothers is irrelevant since the list ignores women.[21] Those "triplets" provide the clue that solves the riddle of Kainan in the postdiluvian list in Gen 11, and the number of Toldot in Pg's narrative. The fact that Abram has no Toldot,[22] contrarily to Terah (Gen 11:27) shores up Kainan's presence in Pg. Kainan's cancellation places Abraham in the tenth postdiluvian generation in parallel to Noah who stands in the tenth antediluvian generation and who, like Abram, received a *berît*. Kainan's cancellation makes Abraham's first year one of the key dates in a chronology which has to be much later than Pg since it presupposes the formation of the Torah, the Historical books and

18.   135 + 130 + 130 + 134 + 130 + 132 + 130 + 79 = 1000 years.

19.   P. Sacchi, "Measuring Time Among the Jews," in *The Early Enoch Literature* (ed. G. Boccaccini and J. J. Collins; Leiden: Brill, 2007), 95–118 (111).

20.   Gardner, *Calendar*, 245, against Hughes, *Secrets*, 9.

21.   T. Hieke, *Die Genealogien der Genesis* (HbS 39; Freiburg: Herder, 2003), 119 n. 351, rejects and considers absurd the notion of triplets fathered by Noah and Terah, a position defended by H. Gunkel, *Genesis* (Göttingen: Vandenhoeck & Ruprecht, 1910), 157.

22.   E. A. Knauf, "Der Exodus zwischen Mythos und Geschichte," in *Schriftauslegung in der Schrift* (ed. R. G. Kratz, T. Krüger and K. Schmid; BZAW 300; Berlin: de Gruyter, 2000), 73–84 n. 18. For an attempt to create a Toldot for Abraham, see F. M. Cross, *Canaanite Myth and Hebrew Epic* (Cambridge, Mass.: Harvard University Press, 1973), 303: "Gen. 25:19b, 'Abraham begot Isaac', gives the appearance of being a gloss by a scribe who missed a heading, 'these are the generations of Abraham.'" Abraham is not one of the links on the Toldot chain but a bifurcation, the point from which start two parallel lines; see Ziemer, *Abram*, 367–69.

Maccabees.[23] Gerhard Larsson, however, considers Kainan a secondary addition belonging to the LXX's fitting the biblical chronology into Manetho's Pharaonic dynasties. According to Larsson, the Alexandrian scholars increased the duration of the postdiluvian era to make sure that Manetho's earliest dynasties did not find themselves dated before the biblical Flood. The problem is that the LXX's limitation of Terah's 205 years to his stay in Haran rather than to his whole lifespan does not lengthen the postdiluvian era (see Gen 11:32). When the LXX integrates within the 430 years of Exod 12:40 not only the dwelling of the sons of Israel in Egypt (MT) but also their time in the land of Canaan, it even reduces the postdiluvian era. Hence, Larsson's argumentation does not account for every LXX difference. On the contrary, the requirement to fit Manetho's chronology can be understood as the only reason why the LXX did not remove Kainan as MT and SP did, and thus disproves Larsson's contention that Kainan is secondary. I consider Kainan as part of Pg's original system, although this does not imply that all the LXX's begetting ages are also original.

The original count devised by Pg requires combining the LXX's begetting ages of the first seven generations (with Kainan) with the MT's ages for the last three positions in the list to obtain 1095 years (Table 2 above). A sum of 1095 years represents three cycles of 365 years, indicating that the mean 365-day year obtained with the intercalation of a week every seventh year is only valid for three consecutive cycles. This is a first clue. The next clue relative to the second stage of intercalation is provided by Abraham's death notice: "And these are the days of the years of the lifespan of Abraham which he lived: a hundred and seventy-five years. He expired. Abraham died in a good senescence, elderly and sated of days. He was added to his people" (Gen 25:7–8). This is the most elaborate and complete lifespan notice in Genesis (compare Gen 23:1; 25:7, 17; 47:28), if not in the entire Pentateuch (compare Num 20:28; Deut 34:7). Not only "days of years of lifespan" are mentioned (ימי שני־חיי), but Abraham is graced with a very laudatory obituary: "a good senescence, elderly and sated of *days*"[24] (בשיבה טובה זקן ושבע ימי)—a hint that Abraham's 175 years are a significant total not only of

---

23. Anno mundi 1600 + 1200 to the first year of Solomon's temple AM 2800 (1 Kgs 6:1) + 1200 to Hanuka AM 4000; see Hughes, *Secrets*, 46. H. Jacobus ("The Curse of Cain [Jub. 8.1–5]: Genealogies in Genesis 5 and Genesis 11 and a Mathematical Pattern," *JSP* 18 [2009]: 207–32), Kainan's removal corresponds to a process at work on other ancestors holding the thirteenth position on a generational line.

24. Following the *BHS*'s suggested addition of ימי supported by six Hebrew manuscripts, SP, LXX and the Syriac.

years but also of days. 175 years represent 25 cycles of 7 years, which explains his call to be whole (חמים) in Gen 17:1.[25] It is ironic to ask a man about to be circumcised to be whole, unless wholeness refers to his lifespan. Abraham's perfect lifespan of 175 years provides the exact length of the second cycle of intercalation. An intercalated period of 175 years yields the following results:

Intercalated sabbatical calendar (365-day year):
$$([364 \times 7] + 7) \times 25 = 63,875 \text{ days}$$

Julian calendar (365.25-day year):
$$365.25 \times 175 = 63,918.75 \text{ days}$$

Present reckoning of tropical year:
$$365.2422 \times 175 = 63,917.385 \text{ days}$$

With the intercalation of one whole week every seventh year, after 175 years the sabbatical calendar is out of synch by 42.385 days, which requires intercalating six extra weeks: $([364 \times 7] + 7) \times 25 = 63,875 + (6 \times 7) = 63,917$ days. Abraham's lifespan thus suggest the length of a second intercalatory scheme which is only about 0.4 days short of the present reckoning of the tropical year. In comparison, over the same 175 years period the Julian calendar is about 1.3 days longer than the true solar year. Hence, the sabbatical calendar is not as impractical as is often claimed.[26] Utopia prevails in Zech 14:6–9, which imagines the suppression of daily and seasonal cycles, but the sabbatical calendar achieves an impressive level of accuracy and regularity.[27]

With the requirement to intercalate only whole weeks on seven-year cycles, 175 years is the logical number for a complete cycle of intercalation. At this point of the narrative, there is no indication of how to insert these six additional weeks. In theory, they could be introduced at any given point, as long as whole weeks are introduced. Yet, regularity requires spreading them evenly across the 175-year cycle. The text provides the solution a little further on.

The Size of the Curtains of the Residence (Exodus 36)

The last clue for the intercalation of the sabbatical calendar is found in the second part of the book of Exodus, some of the most daunting chapters of the Bible. The Tabernacle to be built in the wilderness is

---

25. The same word is used in 4Q252 to indicate a *complete* year; see DJD 22: 193–99 (198–99).

26. Wacholder and Wacholder, "Patterns," 1–40.

27. Against Sérandour, "Calendriers," 288.

described in great detail, first as divine instruction, and then again as accomplishment (Exod 25–40). The passage in question is found both in the instructions (Exod 26:2–6) and as their accomplishment:

> All the wise of heart among the doers of the work made the Residence with ten curtains of finely twisted linen of blue, purple and scarlet yarn, with cherubim made into them by a skilled craftsman. The length of one curtain: 28 cubits, width 4 cubits per curtain; one measure for all the curtains. He joined five curtains one to one and five curtains he had joined one to one. He made loops of blue purple on the edge of the first curtain from the end at the joining; so he did at the edge of the end curtain at the joining of the second, 50 loops he made in the first curtain and 50 loops he made at the end of the curtain that is at the second joining, the loops receiving one to one. He made 50 hooks of gold. He joined the curtains one to one by the hooks. The Residence was one (Exod 36:8–13).

The significance of the size of the curtains extends beyond the mere description of the Residence to supply the last clue for the intercalation of the sabbatical calendar. Enoch's 365 years (Gen 5:23) indicate a first cycle of intercalation of one week every seventh year, a yearly sequence of 52–52–52–52–52–52–53 weeks. Since 365-day mean years are about a quarter of a day too short, Abraham's lifespan of 175 years establishes the length of the overall cycle into which the remaining weeks have to be intercalated to keep track with the solar year. The rhythm of insertion of the missing weeks is provided by the size of the curtains (28×4 cubits). Every twenty-eighth year a second week is added. Between year one and year 168, 30 weeks are inserted at regular intervals of 7 and 28 years. A last week is added at the end of year 175, which completes the cycle. Upon the completion of the cycle, the intercalation scheme reverts back to the beginning. Each cycle thus consists of 175×52 weeks + 31 intercalatory weeks = 9131 weeks (Table 3).

Table 3. *Intercalation Scheme*
(Year Number / Number of Weeks in that Year)

1/52	29/52	57/52	85/52	113/52	141/52	169/52
2/52	30/52	58/52	86/52	114/52	142/52	170/52
3/52	31/52	59/52	87/52	115/52	143/52	171/52
4/52	32/52	60/52	88/52	116/52	144/52	172/52
5/52	33/52	61/52	89/52	117/52	145/52	173/52
6/52	34/52	62/52	90/52	118/52	146/52	174/52
7/53	35/53	63/53	91/53	119/53	147/53	175/53
8/52	36/52	64/52	92/52	120/52	148/52	
9/52	37/52	65/52	93/52	121/52	149/52	
10/52	38/52	66/52	94/52	122/52	150/52	
11/52	39/52	67/52	95/52	123/52	151/52	

12/52	40/52	68/52	96/52	124/52	152/52
13/52	41/52	69/52	97/52	125/52	153/52
14/<u>53</u>	42/<u>53</u>	70/<u>53</u>	98/<u>53</u>	126/<u>53</u>	154/<u>53</u>
15/52	43/52	71/52	99/52	127/52	155/52
16/52	44/52	72/52	100/52	128/52	156/52
17/52	45/52	73/52	101/52	129/52	157/52
18/52	46/52	74/52	102/52	130/52	158/52
19/52	47/52	75/52	103/52	131/52	159/52
20/52	48/52	76/52	104/52	132/52	160/52
21/<u>53</u>	49/<u>53</u>	77/<u>53</u>	105/<u>53</u>	133/<u>53</u>	161/<u>53</u>
22/52	50/52	78/52	106/52	134/52	162/52
23/52	51/52	79/52	107/52	135/52	163/52
24/52	52/52	80/52	108/52	136/52	164/52
25/52	53/52	81/52	109/52	137/52	165/52
26/52	54/52	82/52	110/52	138/52	166/52
27/52	55/52	83/52	111/52	139/52	167/52
28/<u>54</u>	56/<u>54</u>	84/<u>54</u>	112/<u>54</u>	140/<u>54</u>	168/<u>54</u>

Hiding the last key for the intercalation of the sabbatical calendar in the curtains of the Residence may smack of charlatanism. However, ancient literary works did not address the general public; rather, they served as points of departure for discussions with pupils. For instance, according to Diogenes's report (9.6), Heraclitus deliberately wrote an obscure book that he hid in the temple of Artemis so that it would not be despised by the populace.[28] Pg likewise hides intercalation data in unexpected places, dropping clues for the initiated but leaving the non-initiated clueless. The Dead Sea Scrolls have revealed the existence of a bitter controversy over calendrical matters, a controversy which the protagonists considered highly significant. The intercalation of the sabbatical calendar links Creation, Enoch, Abraham and the wilderness Residence into a coherent whole. That the Residence supplies the last element of the description of the fully intercalated sabbatical calendar confirms Pola's claim (see the Introduction) that the Residence belongs to Pg and leads to an examination of how the Residence relates to the Tabernacle.

Residence versus Sanctuary

Exodus 25–40 are crammed with descriptions of a number of structures that do not fit into a coherent whole. The Residence (משכן) is the most basic structure over which stands the Tent of Meetings (אהל מועד). The

---

28. Quoted by Ø. Andersen, "The Significance of Writing in Early Greece—A Critical Appraisal," in *Literacy and Society* (ed. K. Schousboe and M. T. Larsen; Copenhagen: Akademisk Forlag, 1989), 73–90 (82–83).

"Tabernacle" of modern translations is based on the LXX's translation of two distinct realities in the Hebrew (משכן and אהל) by the same Greek word (σκηνή). Besides the Tent of Meetings at the centre of the camp, which only the Aaronid priesthood enters, there is another tent pitched outside the camp entered by anyone seeking an oracle from YHWH.[29]

The impossibility of arranging these various constructions into a coherent whole is demonstrated by the LXX, which transmits major differences in the second part of Exodus. The changes in the LXX are not due to a translator's carelessness[30] but to a deliberate process of harmonization.[31] The LXX translators tried to fit the Residence into the Tabernacle while the MT merely juxtaposes them. The differences between the MT and the LXX in Exod 36:8–39:32 reveal that the literary growth of the second half of Exodus was extensive and took place later than Pg, during or after the first Greek translations of the text. Because it took place so much later, the integration of the Residence into the Tent has left traces in the versions.

The Old Latin *Monacensis* manuscript shows that the LXX, before its harmonization with the MT, contained hardly any structural elements of acacia wood and fewer curtains than are described in the Tabernacle tradition.[32] Hence, *Monacensis* indicates that the earlier structure erected in the wilderness was much simpler than the Tabernacle. This view is coherent with the description of the ten-curtain Residence in Exod 36:8–13 (see above), which mentions no beams. The Residence is made of two sets of five curtains sown together. Each set has 50 loops and the two sets are held together with 50 hooks that connect the 100 loops. The Masoretic vocalization of מחברת ("joint") and שפת ("edge") suggests that the 50 loops are put at one end of each set and that the end product

---

29. Fragments of this tradition were preserved in Exod 33:6–11; Num 11:16–17; 12:4–10; Deut 31:14–15; I. Knohl, "Two Aspects of the Tent of Meeting," in *Tehillah le-Moshe* (ed. M. Cogan, B. K. Eichler and J. H. Tigay; Winona Lake: Eisenbrauns, 1997), 73–79; C. Dohmen, "Das Zelt ausserhalb des Lagers," in *Textarbeit* (ed. K. Kiesow and T. Meurer; Münster: Ugarit Verlag, 2003), 157–69.

30. As claimed by D. W. Gooding, *The Account of the Tabernacle* (Cambridge: Cambridge University Press, 1959).

31. A. Aejmelaeus, "Septuagintal Translation Techniques," in *On the Trail of Septuagint Translators* (Kampen: Kok Pharos, 1993), 116–30.

32. P.-M. Bogaert, "L'importance de la Septante et du 'Monacensis' de la Vetus Latina pour l'exégèse du livre de l'Exode (chap. 35–40)," in Vervenne, eds., *Studies in the Book of Exodus*, 399–428 (414–15); P.-M. Bogaert, "La construction de la tente (Ex 36–40) dans le *Monacensis* de la plus ancienne version latine," in *L'enfance de la Bible hébraïque* (ed. A. Schenker and P.-M. Bogaert; Geneva: Labor et Fides, 2005), 62–76.

has the shape of a long rectangular fabric made of two rectangular carpet hooked together in the middle (Figure 1).[33]

Figure 1. *Single Joint*

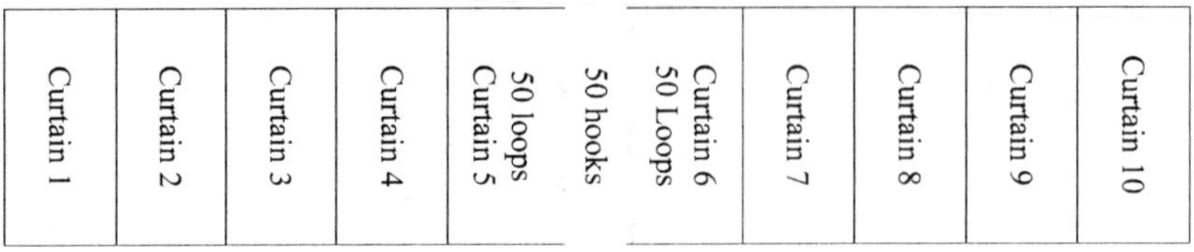

Curtain 1	Curtain 2	Curtain 3	Curtain 4	50 loops Curtain 5	50 hooks	Curtain 6 50 Loops	Curtain 7	Curtain 8	Curtain 9	Curtain 10

However, without vocalization מחברת and שפת can be read as a plural ("joints, edges") in *scriptio defectiva*, as are the other feminine plurals in this passage (מקבילת ללאת יריעת). In this case, there are 25 loops at both ends of each set and two joins with 25 hooks each. Instead of forming a rectangle, the ten curtains are hooked on both sides and stand as walls delimiting a space without any opening (Fig. 2). The absence of opening and the closing remark on the oneness of the Residence (ויהי המשכן אחד, Exod 36:13) fit the description of the Residence in Exod 36:

Figure 2. *Double Joint*

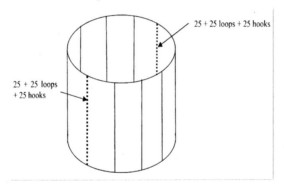

25 + 25 loops + 25 hooks

25 + 25 loops + 25 hooks

Once the structure was turned into a foreshadowing of the temple of Jerusalem, which the priests had to enter to perform rituals, Exod 37:1–13 LXX transformed the MT's doorless Residence into a tent by inserting the description of a veil functioning as a door (37:4–6 LXX), which was taken from the MT's description of the Tent in Exod 36:35–38. Logically, the description of the way the ten curtains are sown in two sets joined with golden hooks (Exod 36:10–13 MT) is deleted from the LXX, as is the MT's description of the eleven-curtain Tent (Exod 36:14–34 MT), which

33. See M. Chyutin, *Architecture and Utopia in the Temple Area* (LSTS 58; New York: T&T Clark International, 2006), 19 Fig. 1:6a.

is merely juxtaposed to the ten-curtain Residence. The subsequent elaboration of the "Tent over the Tabernacle" is composed of two unequal sets, one of five curtains of 4 × 30 cubits each and the other with six curtains. This roof of goat hair doubled with leather (Exod 36:19) is followed with a long description of roofing, frames, beams, screens, ark, table, lamps, altars, poles, basins, court, hangings, pillars and vestments. In spite of the details, the paraphernalia fails to explain how the ten curtains of Exod 36:8–13 stand because the Tent is literally superposed onto the original Residence. On the basis of these observations, Pg's account of the fabrication and setting up of the Residence can be recovered from the bulk of Exod 25–40:

> [25:1] YHWH spoke to Moses: [2]"Speak to the sons of Israel. Receive a contribution from every man whose heart impels him to make a contribution for me. [8]Then make a sanctuary for me and I will reside among them." [35:22]The men and the women as well came, everyone whose heart impelled brought brooches, ear-rings, signets, pendants, all sorts of golden objects and whatever gold one dedicated for YHWH. [23*]Whoever found himself with blue, purple and scarlet yarn or fine linen brought it. [25]Skilled women spun by hand. They got blue, purple and scarlet yarn and fine linen. [36:8*]All the skilful ones made the Residence with ten curtains of finely twisted linen and blue, purple and scarlet yarn, with cherubim weaved into them by a skilled craftsman. [9]The length of one curtain 28 cubits, width 4 cubits per curtain; one measure for all the curtains. [10]Someone joined five curtains one to one and five curtains he joined one to one. [11]He made loops of blue purple on the edge of the first curtain from the end at the joining; so he did at the edge of the end curtain at the joining of the second. [12]He made 50 loops in the first curtain and 50 loops he made at the end of the curtain that is at the second joining, the loops receiving one to one. [13]He made 50 hooks of gold. He joined the curtains one to one by the hooks. The Residence was one. 40[17] It happened in the first month in the second year in [day] one of the month; the Residence was set up [34b]and the glory of YHWH filled the Residence.

Exodus 35:22 continues directly from the instructions in Exod 25:1–2, 8. As in Gen 1:27, women are mentioned besides men since they usually own jewels as heirloom and dowry. The gold ornaments in v. 22b are turned into hooks (Exod 36:13). Although the offering (תנופה) for YHWH in the last part of the verse corresponds to a particular type of consecration in Ps texts (Exod 29:24, 26; Lev 7–14), there is no reason to exclude it from Pg.

The textiles in Exod 35:23 correspond to the material of the curtains (Exod 36:8), except the goat hair used for the eleven curtains of the Tent (Exod 36:14). The leather for the roof is also secondary (Exod 36:19) since the Residence is roofless. The Residence has no need of the silver, bronze, acacia, gems, spices, oil, and incense collected in Exod 35:24, 27–28. The women and wise men make the curtains of the Residence, rendering Bezalel and Oholiab redundant (Exod 35:30–36:7). The Cherubim embroidered into the ten curtains are guardians of the Residence.[34] They stand up vertically, as they did in Assyrian palaces, while the Ps redaction places the ten curtains of the Residence horizontally with the consequence that the cherubim fly on the ceiling of the Tent as angels do in baroque churches.[35]

Once, in Exod 25:8, YHWH refers to the Residence as a sanctuary (מקדש). Although this seems to contradict the exclusive sanctity of the Sabbath in Gen 2:3 (see above), in fact it confirms it since the size of the curtains of the Residence have a calendrical function. The Residence is a sanctuary in the sense that it supplies the last clue of intercalation of the sabbatical calendar. Its oneness and its circular shape signify the complete intercalation cycle.

The curtains are joined together by an anonymous person (ויחבר, Exod 36:10).[36] It is probable that the anonymity indicates that the identity of the assembler is irrelevant because the Residence requires no priests, no Levitical specialists or clergy of any kind. As is the case for the slaughter of the Passover lamb, anyone is entitled to assemble the Residence, contrary to Num 3–5 (Ps), which reserve the handling of the Tabernacle to the Levites. However, in Pg's much shorter text, the "he" who assembles the curtains of the Residence for the first time can be read as Moses since YHWH's order to Moses to make the Residence stands only seven verses earlier (Exod 25:2). Therefore, Pg agrees with 1 Chr 21:29, which credits Moses with the work. The Residence is set up on the first day of the second year after the Exodus, on a Wednesday, corresponding to the day of the creation of the calendar (Gen 1:14).

Having no door, the Residence contains no altar or cultic gear whatsoever. The Residence simply enables YHWH to reside among his people. This is at loggerheads with all texts that revolve around temples and priests. Economic motives required the subsuming of Pg's Residence into the Tent of Meetings, which has a clear sacrificial purpose controlled by a priestly caste. Hence, when Peter Weimar claimed that Pg

34. D. Launderville, "Ezekiel's Cherub: A Promising Symbol or Dangerous Idol?," *CBQ* 65 (2003): 165–83. J. L. Craig, "Text and Textile in Exodus," *JANES* 29 (2002): 17–30.

35. Chyutin, *Architecture*, 36: "the cloth embroided with a design of cherubim symbolize 'the host of the skies,' whose place is in the firmament."

36. H. Utzschneider, *Das Heiligtum und das Gesetz* (Fribourg: Universitätsverlag; Göttingen: Vandenhoeck & Ruprecht, 1988), 201, insists that Moses took little part in the fabrication process.

only describes an empty tent, he was not radical enough.[37] Pg's wilderness structure is indeed empty, but it is not even a tent!

Considering Exod 25–40 as a uniform "priestly" textual block is misleading since it erases the particularity of Pg's Residence, which has no cultic function and is not attended by any priest. If those chapters cover up the Residence with the Tent without erasing it, the cultic paraphernalia of the Tent of Meeting should not be attributed to Pg, in spite of the fact that parallels in ancient creation narratives culminate with the construction of a temple establishing the cult of the creator.[38] The Tent of Meetings and the wilderness cult certainly follow the ancient pattern that connects creation and cult, but these elements are secondary to Pg's non-cultic enclosure.[39] Parallels from Deuteronomy and Kings are sometimes adduced to claim that the wilderness cult must prefigure the temple at Jerusalem. These parallels merely prove the undisputed point that the final redactions understood the Tent of Meeting as a prefiguration of the Jerusalem temple.[40] The same can be said about parallels established between the Tabernacle and Creation. The six-fold graded holiness in and around the Tabernacle supposedly reflects Gen 1.[41] Alternatively, the seven speeches in Exod 25–31 are said to correspond to the seven days of creation, though the equation is forced.[42] The original sin

37. P. Weimar, "Sinai und Schöpfung," *RB* 95 (1988): 337–85 (383).

38. E. Blum, *Die Komposition der Vätergeschichte* (Neukirchen–Vluyn: Neukirchener Verlag, 1984), 310 n. 83–85.

39. N. Lohfink, "Die Abänderung der Theologie des priesterlichen Geschichtswerks im Segen des Heiligkeitsgesetzes," in *Wort und Geschichte* (ed. H. Gese and H. P. Rüger; Kevelaer: Butzon & Berker, 1973), 129–36 (132–33 n. 5); V. Fritz, *Tempel und Zelt* (WMANT 47; Neukirchen–Vluyn: Neukirchener Verlag, 1977); Weimar, "Sinai," 337–85. T. E. Fretheim, "The Priestly Document: Anti-Temple?," *VT* 18 (1969): 312–29, even suspected Pg was opposed to rebuild a temple at Jerusalem.

40. E. Cortese, "The Priestly Tent," *Liber Annuus* XLVIII (1998): 9–30.

41. A. Ruwe, *"Heiligkeitsgesetz" und "Priesterschrift"* (FAT 26; Tübingen: Mohr Siebeck, 1999), 103–20.

42. P. J. Kearney, "Creation and Liturgy," *ZAW* 89 (1977), 375–87. The light of Gen 1:3 corresponds to the lamps (Exod 27:20–21; 30:7–8) and the Sabbath refers to Gen 2:1–3. The other parallels are far-fetched: the opposition between "over and below" (day 2) supposedly reflects Exod 30:14 "twenty years and over"; Kearney finds the sea of Gen 1:10 in 1 Kgs 7:23 and the sun and the moon as far as Ps 89:21. In spite of such loose connections, C. H. T. Fletcher-Louis, "The Cosmology of P and Theological Anthropology in the Wisdom of Jesus ben Sira," in *Of Scribes and Sages*, vol. 1 (ed. C. A. Evans; LSTS 50; London: T&T Clark International, 2004), 69–113, considers that the intertextuality between Sir 24 and 50 proves Kearney's claim that Gen 1 and Exod 25–40 belong together. As far as I can see,

of the Creation–Tabernacle connection is best illustrated by an excursus on temple and creation in the Priestly order of Gen 1, which claims that this chapter "points to a vision of a holy universe…presents the cosmos as the divine holy place…to be understood not simply as holy, but as a holy place such as a sanctuary."[43] The author of these lines insists that holy time *and space* are adumbrated in Gen 1 in order to support the claim that Gen 1 foreshadows the covenant on Mt Sinai.[44] This claim has no support in the text. Genesis ascribes holiness to the Sabbath and to the Sabbath only. The connection with Sinai is pure fabrication facilitated by the attribution of an indiscriminate P sign to both Gen 1 and the Tabernacle material in Exodus. In spite of the large amount of added material, Pg's laconic description of the Residence stands out as a doorless, priestless structure, a square peg that never fits the round hole of the Tent of Meetings and the wilderness cult.

If it is devoid of cultic activity, the Residence is nevertheless presented as a sanctuary (מקדש, Exod 25:8). Yet, the sanctity of the residence does transfer to space since the Residence is a portable structure set up in the wilderness. On the contrary, this second mention of sanctity underlines the calendrical function of the Residence described above. Within a network of tight mathematical correspondences between Gen 5; 25 and Exod 36, the Residence coheres with Pg's theology of unconditional divine favour presented through the signs of the rainbow and circumcision (Gen 9; 17). The Residence's sole function is to enable YHWH's presence among his people throughout the wilderness era, a presence that, like the rainbow and circumcision, is effective without the agency of a priest. The existence of a continuous Pg narrative extending from Gen 1 until at least the end of Exodus gains strength. Before finding out how far it continues, the sabbatical calendar hypothesis should be submitted to the test of the classical piece of biblical chronology, the Flood narrative.

Fletcher-Louis's article reveals that Ben Sira was well aware of the contradictions between Pg's understanding of the Sabbath and Ps's Sabbath sacrifices and that Sira was at pains to show that those who work during the Sabbath do not sin (Sir 24:22).

43. M. S. Smith, *The Pilgrimage Pattern in Exodus* (JSOTSup 239; Sheffield: Sheffield Academic Press, 1997), 112–14.

44. Ibid., 16.

Chapter 3

THE SABBATICAL CALENDAR IN THE FLOOD NARRATIVE

The traditional source division between J and P is largely responsible for the failure to understand the different chronologies superposed in the Flood narrative. As mentioned in the Introduction, the demise of the Graf–Wellhausen system of sources has freed some elements in the first chapters of Genesis traditionally attributed to J, which can now be absorbed into Pg when they fit Pg's calendrical and theological parameters. The aim here is to recover the chronology based on the sabbatical calendar in the Flood narrative.

For Pg, violence (חמס, Gen 6:11) is the sole cause of the Flood since violence "decayed the land".[1] The decay is not moral corruption, as it is in Gen 6:1–9 ("J"), but as a natural process of over-ripening, one of the meanings of √שחת, due to the very long lifespans of Gen 5. Rather than presenting the antediluvian ancestors as models of eternal youth, they are equated with fruits that waited too long, suggesting a problem of timing rather than of immorality. All flesh is responsible for the violence (Gen 6:12), including the animals, and it is justice when they die in the Flood. The fish and the sea monsters are spared since they are not responsible for bloodshed (see Gen 9:5).[2] The same root (שחת) is also used to describe Elohim's intervention (Gen 6:13). Instead of presenting the Flood as a punishment of immoral behaviour, Pg presents it as a homeopathic treatment of the decaying violence by the same decaying process that runs its full course.[3] Rather than enforcing a punishment to

---

1. N. Lohfink, "Original Sins in the Priestly Historical Narrative," in his *Theology of the Pentateuch* (Minneapolis: Fortress, 1994), 106–10. On the same characterization of the sin of Nineveh in Jon 3:8, see L. Schrader, "Kommentierende Redaktion im Noah–Sintflut–Komplex der Genesis," *ZAW* 110 (1998): 489–502.

2. H.-J. Stipp, "Alles Fleisch hatte seinen Wandel auf der Erde verdorben," *ZAW* 111 (1999): 167–86.

3. This meaning of the Flood (מבול) is retained in Syrian Arabic, which uses √bwl, "to qualify decay due to aging, overuse or humidity"; see A. Barthélemy, *Dictionnaire Arabe–Français* (Paris: Geuthner, 1935), 70.

end illicit actions, as suggested by the "J" passage, Elohim drives events to their logical conclusion (see also Num 14:2, 28–29).

The Beginning of the Flood and Its Date

The study of the chronology of the Flood narrative faces the problem that textual variants produce different years for the date of the Flood and different days for its beginning. The year of the Flood is calculated by adding the ages of first begetting of the ten antediluvian generations provided in Gen 5 (Table 4):[4]

Table 4. *The Year of the Flood*

	MT	*LXX*	*SP*
Adam	130	230	130
Seth	105	205	105
Enosh	90	190	90
Kenan	70	170	70
Mahalalel	65	165	65
Jared	162	162	62
Enoch	65	165	65
Methuselah	187	167	67
Lamech	182	188	53
Noah's age at the Flood	600	600	600
Total	*1656*	*2262*	*1307*

The Flood began when the rain started (Gen 7:11) on 17 II 1307 (SP), 1656 (MT) or 2262 (LXX). The lack of clear criteria hinders the search for the original chronological system or the identification of the system closest to the original.[5] The sabbatical calendar supplies the missing criterion.

4. See the tables in Hughes, *Secrets*, 7 and 12, but note the misprint (p. 7) where the central column reproduces SP's dates instead of the LXX's, while the right column lists LXX's not SP's data!

5. Borgonovo, "Significato," 143, is in favour of the MT as transmitting the original version. G. Larsson, "The Chronology of the Pentateuch," *JBL* (1983): 401–9, considers that the SP and the LXX are rationalizations of the MT chronology while alterations in the other direction make no sense. According to him, the Alexandrian translators harmonized the text they received from Jerusalem with Alexandrian chronographical science to fit Manetho's Pharaonic dynastic list into the biblical postdiluvian era. Since Manetho's list covered almost 3000 years of uninterrupted Pharaonic dynasties, adding 100 years to the postdiluvian ages at primogeniture shifted the Flood back before the first Pharaohs. F. Bork, "Zur Chronologie der

Symbolically, the MT and LXX's dates seem to make more sense than the SP's since their hexadic basis reverses the heptadic scheme of creation. The destructive connotation of the number 6 is signalled by the 600 years of Noah's age when the Flood occurred and the sixfold occurrence of the word מבול ("flood") in Pg's Flood narrative.[6] The ark's measurements ($300 \times 50 \times 30$ cubits, Gen 6:15) are also base six figures. According to the hexadic criterion, the MT's Flood date makes the most sense since, from creation to the 17th day of the second month of year 1656, there is a total of 602,467 days: $(1655 \times 364) + 30$ (month I of year 1656) + 17 (in month II). 602,467 days are one day short of 600,000 days + 6 years + 6 months + 6 weeks + 60 days: $600,000 + 2184 (6 \times 364) + 182 (30 + 30 + 31 + 30 + 30 + 31) + 42 (6 \times 7) + 60 = 602,468$ days. Symbolically, the Flood resulted in the complete destruction of all but one family (Gen 6:19). One can argue that the week of creation should be subtracted from year 1 since it is already counted as a separate period. According to the Sabbatical calendar, New Year's Day is always on Wednesday (day 4) because God created the calendar on the fourth day of creation when he created the heavenly luminaries. Three days can be removed from year 1, yielding a total of 602,464 days. In this case, the missing four days symbolize Noah and his three sons, who did not perish in the Flood, and the four days that are added at the end of months III, VI, IX and XII (Table 1).

This symbolically significant sum of days can only be reached on the basis of the MT's figure with a non-intercalated sabbatical calendar. I take this as indicating that the MT's Flood date reflects a chronology more in line with the Creation story than is the case with the ages of primogeniture in the LXX and the SP.[7] *Jubilees* 6:32–38 claim that the violence prevailing during the antediluvian era (Gen 6:11) was in part violence against the sacred rhythm of time. This is not explicit in the text of Genesis but it is possible to read the huge lifespan of the antediluvian ancestors in Gen 5 as a hint to the lack of intercalation. Since non-intercalated years are too short, they inevitably result in a longer lifespan for

---

biblischen Urgeschichte," *ZAW* 47 (1929): 206–22, and R. W. Klein, "Archaic Chronologies and the Textual History of the Old Testament," *HTR* 67 (1974): 255–63, favour the LXX. Hughes, *Secrets*, 11–13, prefers SP.

6. Gen 6:17; 7:17; 9:11 (×2), 15, 28.

7. Cassuto, *Genesis*, 261, uses 365-day years and finds 600,000 days from Creation to Flood. J. Oppert, "Chronology," in *Jewish Encyclopedia* (New York: Funk & Wagnells, 1901–1916), 4:64–68, finds 86,407 weeks in the MT's 1656 years at the Flood, which he considers close to $86,400 = 72 \times 1200$, which corresponds to Berossos's total of 72×1200 Roman lustra (= 6,000 years).

everyone, including the animals, although a day and a quarter per year hardly account for Methuselah's 969 years!

The choice of the MT's date of the Flood leads to the favouring of the MT's date for the beginning of the Flood, which differs from the LXX's. It is often claimed that the Flood lasts a whole year. In fact, it begins on 17 II (MT/SP) or 27 II (LXX) and ends according to all three textual traditions on 27 II (Gen 7:11; 8:14). The ten-day difference at the beginning of the Flood is explained as resulting from the use of different calendars comprising 354 or 364 days, although this does not help decide which system is original. Hendel claims that 17 II in the MT and SP is original since it is supported by *Jubilees* and by 4Q252.[8] Table 5 shows the dates of the Flood narrative in the main textual traditions:

Table 5. *Synopsis of Flood Chronologies*

Gen.	MT/SP	LXX	Jubilees	4Q252	1 Enoch	Vulgate	Pg*
7.11	17 II	27 II	17 II (5.23)	17 II (1.4)	One year	17 II	17 II
8.4	17 VII	27 VII	—	17 VII (1.10)	(106.15)	27 VII	27 VII
8.5	1 X	1 XI	1 X (5.30)	+ 40 days (1.12)		1 X	1 XI[9]
8.13	1 I	1 I	1 I (5.30)	1 I (1.22)		1 I	1 I
8.14	27 II	27 II	17 II (5.31)	17 II (2.1)		27 II	27 II
			27 II (5.32)				
			1 III (6.1)				

From the LXX onwards there is a tendency to simplify by having the Flood last one whole year, as 4Q252 twice states,[10] by modifying either the date of the Flood's beginning (LXX) or the date of its end (4Q252). Hendel's proposal that *Jubilees* and 4Q252 reflect the original text is difficult to sustain since the number of days is as significant as having a

---

8.   R. S. Hendel, "4Q252 and the Flood Chronology of Genesis 7—8," *DSD* 2 (1995): 72–79, explains the LXX's variations by a series of errors, first in word division and then haplography which first took place in Gen 8:14 MT, carried over into Gen 8:14 LXX and on which basis Gen 7:11 LXX was corrected: בשבעה עשר יום > בשבעה עשרים יום > בשבעה עשרים. I wish to that Helen Jacobus for drawing my attention to this reference.

9.   The date of the appearance of the mountain top, 1 X (MT) or 1 XI (LXX), plays no role in the overall chronology, but since the beginning of the verse signals a gradual decrease until the tenth month, 1 XI is more logical than 1 X.

10.   DJD 22: 193–99 (198–99): "[2.2] the earth dried up on the first day of the week, on that day Noah went forth from the ark at the end of a [2.3] complete year of 364 days, on the first day of the week, in the seventh [2.4] (vacat) one and six (vacat) Noah from the ark at the appointed time, a [2.5] complete year (vacat) and Noah awoke from his wine…"

complete year, and having the Flood begin on the 17th or on the 27th makes all the difference in the count of days. The book of *Jubilees*, a staunch defender of the 364-day calendar, manages to transmit both the exact-year simplification and MT's system. Working from the final text of the Torah with the numerous post-Pg additions, which effectively clouded the original system, *Jubilees* split the end of the Flood into three different dates. The viewing of the dry land (17 II), the opening of the ark and the freeing of the animals (27 II) and Noah's coming out (1 III) are spread over two weeks whereas they occur on the same day in the biblical text. The land is thus dry on the 17th instead of the 27th day, while the 27th is connected to the exit of the animals.[11] The problem now is to identify the system of dates which is likely to correspond to Pg's.

Duration of the Flood in Weeks and Months

In Pg's framework (rather than a vague P), it can be expected that the number of weeks of the Flood should also be symbolically significant. To obtain a significant number of weeks for the duration of the Flood, I use the sabbatical calendar's unique system of 30-day months plus an extra day for months III, VI, IX and XII (see Table 1). Then, the period of actual destruction when the ark is afloat has to be considered as a time gap rather than being integrated into the calculation. The actual Flood duration is a chronological void. The calendar is abrogated because by its lack of intercalation it contributed to the over-ripening of the ante-diluvian world. Lastly, it is necessary to choose the MT date for the Flood's onset (17 II, Gen 7:11) and the LXX date for its end (27 VII, Gen 8:4). The apparent weakness entailed by such mixture of textual traditions is compensated by two features that can hardly be accidental. It provides a seven-month period between the resting of the ark and its opening, seven months to turn the devastated land into a dry land capable of producing life (Gen 1:9–10). These seven months underline the positive value of the creation heptad. Furthermore, by placing these seven months between months VII and II, Pg signals that the years of the sabbatical calendar always have twelve months, and that they are not intercalated with a thirteenth month, as was common for lunar calendars. Calculating the duration of the Flood with the sabbatical calendar and such time gap provides the following result (Table 6):

11.   J. C. VanderKam, *The Book of Jubilees* (Sheffield: Sheffield Academic Press, 2001), 35–36; J. T. A. G. M. van Ruiten, *Primaeval History Interpreted* (Leiden: Brill, 2000), 206–24.

Table 6. *Pg's Flood Chronology Reckoned with the Sabbatical Calendar*

Gen 7.11	Rain starts on 17 II	
Gen 7.12	40 days of rain	40
Gen 7.17	Ark afloat, time gap	
Gen 8.4	Ark rests on 27 VII (LXX)	
Gen 8.13	Ark uncovered on 1 I	156 (3 + 30 + 31 + 60 + 31 + 1)
Gen 8.14	Ark opened on 27 II	56 (29 + 27)
	Total	*252 days (6 × 6 × 7)*

The hexadic number (6×6) of full weeks is significant. The entire Flood lasts 36 weeks, a symbolic multiplication of the number 6 as the cipher for destruction, while the number 7 (the number of days in the week) indicates the persistence of creation within the duration of the Flood itself. The use of a time gap is attested in ancient literature[12] and reproduced in the presentation of Sinai (Ps) as a time during which there was neither birth nor death (compare Exod 38:26 and Num 1:46). The time gap within the Flood narrative is also confirmed by the ages of Noah and Shem. According to Gen 5:32, Noah fathered Shem, Ham and Japheth when he was 500 years old. One hundred years later, the Flood wiped out the earth when Noah was 600 years old (Gen 7:6) and his sons 100 years old. According to Gen 11:10, Shem engendered Arpachshad two years after the Flood, at the age of 100 years, although two years after the Flood he should have been 102 years old.[13] Hence, Shem did not age during his stay in the ark. He was 100 years old at the onset and at the conclusion of the Flood. The same principle applies to Noah, who was 600 during the Flood, lived 350 years after the Flood and died at age 950 (Gen 9:28–29). The two-year discrepancy signals the time-gap and solves the *crux interpretum* of Shem's age when he fathers Arpachshad two years after the Flood.[14] Fully coherent with Gen 1, this sabbatical

12. F. Bovon, "The Suspension of Time in Chapter 18 of Protoevangelium Jacobi," in F. Bovon, *Studies in Early Christianity* (Tübingen: Mohr Siebeck, 2003), 226–37.

13. The LXX solves the problem by considering Japhet as the elder in Gen 10:21: Larsson, "Chronology," 405.

14. F. H. Cryer, "The Interrelationships of Gen. 5,32; 11,10–11 and the Chronology of the Flood (Gen. 6–9)," *Biblica* 66 (1985): 241–61 (248), considers that Shem was born at some point after Noah's 500th year. For K. Stenring, *The Enclosed Garden* (Stockholm: Almqvist & Wiksell, 1966), 89, the genealogies indicate the time of conception (hence the Hiphil), not the time of birth. Therefore one year must be added to every fathering year to get the actual birthdate. According to Borgonovo, "Significato," 161, the two-year difference reveals that the value of the Jubilee is 50 years instead of 49 (49×2) +2 = 100, although the genealogies are

chronology of the Flood narrative confirms that Creation and Flood belong to Pg. All versions with a whole year (17th–17th or 27th–27th, see Table 5 above) are simplifications or outright rejections of the sabbatical calendar.

The De-sabbatization of the Flood Narrative

The sabbatical calendar renders the identification of a significant numerological system in the Flood narrative possible. The simplicity of the system, based on hexads and heptads, is a token of the existence of the sabbatical calendar in an earlier version of the Flood narrative. On the basis of its coherence with Gen 1, this earlier version can be ascribed to Pg. However, the criterion of the sabbatical calendar requires slight modifications of the traditional distribution of sources within the Flood narrative. My delimitation of Pg's Flood narrative is supplied in the Appendix. Only the main differences are presented here.

The forty days of rain (Gen 7:12, 17b) are traditionally excluded from the P narrative, but they should be attributed to Pg since they are an essential component of Flood chronology identified in Table 6. The ark is not afloat on the first day of rain but after 40 days of continuous downpour. The moment the ark is afloat marks not the beginning of the Flood but the suspension of time until the ark rests on Ararat. By contrast, the two periods of 150 days while the ark is afloat (Gen 7:24; 8:3) belong to a secondary addition which introduce into the narrative a calendar composed exclusively of 30-day months (6 months × 30 days = 150 days) in order to avert the use of the 364-day calendar with its cycle of 30/30/31-day months.

The forty days and the two extra weeks of waiting for the dove's return with signs of fresh vegetation do not belong to Pg's Flood narrative. The fact that they play upon motifs already present in Mesopotamian Flood stories does not prove that they must belong to a pre-Pg narrative, traditionally attributed to J. In fact, the non-Pg elements within the Flood narrative as identified here do not constitute an independent narrative since some of the J elements are attributed to Pg. They all introduce calendrical and theological elements intended to align the narrative with later theological and calendrical developments.

based on the sabbatical calendar which supports a 49-year Jubilee. Hughes, *Secrets*, 18, considers the two years after the Flood to be a secondary addition. Other suggestions are found in C. Westermann, *Genesis* (Minneapolis: Fortress, 1984), 1:42–47, and Gardner, *Calendar*, 243.

For instance, the insertion of sexual deviation as another reason for the Flood (Gen 6:1–8) diverts the attention away from Pg's critique of violence and bloodshed. The addition of seven pairs of clean animals follows a similar aim as it justifies their sacrifice (Gen 7:1–10; 8:20–21). Because the passage mentions YHWH rather than Elohim, it was traditionally attributed to J, since in Pg YHWH only appears under that name in Exod 6:2. There is, however, no need to postulate a pre-Pg Flood narrative, in spite of the fact that Noah's sacrifice imitates Utnapishtim's.[15] Pg's omission of extra pairs of clean animals is consistent with its rejection of sacrifices.[16] Their introduction into Pg's narrative is consistent with the transformation of Pg's Residence into the Tent of Meeting in Exod 26–40 (see Chapter 2) and the introduction of the purity laws of Leviticus into Pg's notion of bloodless atonement (see Chapter 5). The extra pairs of clean animals in the ark belong, with Noah's holocausts, to a broad redaction inserting sacrificial theology because Pg rejected holocausts by claiming that shedding animal blood is acceptable to Elohim only if the victims are used to feed humans (Gen 9:3).

For Pg, the situation after the Flood is not fundamentally different from the antediluvian world. Creation stasis is recovered through the purge of the Flood. The goodness of creation is recovered, but at a price. Antediluvian vegetarianism is gone. Domestication is replaced by terror since humans can now eat any animal that has life in it (Gen 9:3). The ideal of vegetarianism is given up. The only restriction is that the animals eaten must have had life in them, forbidding the consumption of carrion. The authorization of meat consumption is therefore a licence to kill. Animals of every kind may be eaten, at least land animals. This excludes the distinction of pure and impure among land animals which is also at loggerheads with the fundamental goodness of creation. It has been argued that creational goodness was lost after the Flood since the domination of humans over the animals in Gen 1:28 is replaced by the harsher terms of fear and dread in Gen 9:2. This is a definite change from creational order, but does it imply that the "very good" is lost?[17] An

---

15. J. H. Tigay, *The Evolution of the Gilgamesh Epic* (Philadelphia: University of Pennsylvania Press, 1982), 296.

16. B. Halpern, "Biblical versus Greek Historiography," in *Das Alte Testament—ein Geschichtsbuch?* (ed. E. Blum, W. Johnstone and C. Markschies; Münster: LIT, 2005), 101–27 (107).

17. So M. Köckert, "Das Land in der priesterlichen Komposition des Pentateuch," in *Von Gott reden* (ed. D. Vieweger and E.-J. Waschke; Neukirchen–Vluyn: Neukirchener Verlag, 1995), 147–62 (150–51). G. Hepner, "Israelites Should Conquer Israel," *RB* 113 (2006): 161–80, interprets the non-mention of בכשׂ, which he

affirmative answer requires ignoring that √כבש is restated in Josh 18:1 and that Caleb and Joshua declare the land of Canaan "very good" in Num 14:7. This introduces the issue of the delimitation of Pg and where it ends. These crucial issues for the understanding of Pg's coherence are dealt with in the second part of this study through the land theme. It is enough here to note that the Flood did not destroy the land and the heavens. The Flood is not a de-creation[18] but a purgation. The status *ante quo* is indeed not recovered since meat consumption is introduced. Yet, the sacrificial and purity system of Leviticus are not implied by the fact that animals may be killed because every animal is good for eating. This precludes rather than prefigures the sacrificial system established on degrees of purity and sanctity. Moreover, the limitation of bloodshed to food purposes contradicts the principle of sacrifice since sacrifice diverts part or the whole of the victim away from human consumption. Deriving the notion of sacrifice from the authorization to kill animals for food is even less likely in the light of the recommendations in Gen 9:5–6, which act as safety rails against the inherent danger of the licence to kill animals which is likely to breed again the violence that caused the Flood.[19] Killing animals for food is a concession to the violence prevailing before the Flood. Does the bloodshed entailed by the necessity to feed oneself support the notion of atonement through the blood of an animal? The analysis of the Day of Atonement in Chapter 5 provides a negative answer.

Creation—Flood Coherence

Campbell and O'Brien claim that the Creation narrative and the Flood narrative do not have the same origin because the windows of the heavens, the fountains of the great deep and the mountains (Gen 7:11, 20; 8:2), which play a significant role in the P Flood narrative, are not mentioned in Gen 1. Campbell and O'Brien add that the dome created in the second day does not appear in the Flood, the provision of food differs between 1:29–30 and 9:3, and terms for animals in the Flood narrative

---

translates "conquest," as the indication that the land (prefiguration of Canaan) does not belong to all the sons of Noah. If the land indeed prefigures Canaan in Gen 1, the Table of Nations in the next chapter proves that the promise of Canaan to Abraham's seed does not deprive others from their own land.

18. *Pace* J. D. Currid, *Ancient Egypt and the Old Testament* (Grand Rapids: Baker, 1997), 113–17.

19. O. H. Steck, "Der Mensch und die Todesstrafe," *TZ* 53 (1997): 323–34; E. A. Knauf, "Grenzen der Toleranz in der Priesterschaft," *BK* 58 (2003): 224–27.

lack the logic of Gen 1.[20] To counter the claim of distinct origins, I adduce a number of thematic correspondences.

The animals entering the ark are described as in Gen 1:25 "according to their kind," with no clean/unclean distinction (Gen 6:20; 7:14–16). The mention of 40 nights besides the 40 days corresponds to Creation days, which do not include the night (Gen 1:5, 14 and 7:12, 17 LXX). The mountain tops become visible, as did the dry ground in Gen 1:9. The post-diluvian blessing reiterates the injunction to multiply (Gen 1:28; 9:1, 7). Elohim caused *a wind* to pass over the land (Gen 1:2; 8:1). Blowing over the flooded land as it did on day three of creation, this wind displays the same concept of a pre-existent land that remains ever present. The Flood merely covers the land—only terrestrial life is destroyed. The coherence is thus greater than the details adduced to silence it. Yet it is the sabbatical calendar which supplies by far the clearest evidence of the coherence of Creation with the Flood narrative.

The application of the sabbatical calendar to the chronological problems of the Flood narrative produces remarkable results. Lasting exactly 36 weeks, the hexads mark the Flood's destructive power while the heptad underlines that creation remains present and that the Flood is neither a de-creation nor a return to pre-creational chaos. Noah's family and a couple of land animal of every kind, without pure/impure distinction, are safely tucked in the ark, which experiences a suspension of time while the ark is afloat. For this reason, Noah and his sons do not age during their stay in the ark. The antediluvian violence which caused the Flood has a chronological aspect, as much as do the creation of the Sabbath, Enoch's and Abraham's lifespan and the curtains of the Residence. The Flood underlines the need for intercalation, while it also states major theological themes to be developed in the rest of Pg: violence, food and blood.

The Flood narrative confirms the validity of the sabbatical calendar hypothesis, its presence in the Torah and its link with the Pg narrative which gains an impressive chronological and theological coherence. Confirming that Pg uses an intercalated 364-day calendar goes a long way towards clarifying the extent of the influence of the Enochic tradition upon the editors of the Pentateuch, a problem that is felt acutely in the study of calendar material of the Dead Sea Scrolls.[21] The editors of the Pentateuch did not align the text under the influence of *1 Enoch* and *Jubilees*. To the contrary, *1 Enoch* and *Jubilees* are upholders of Pg's

---

20. Campbell and O'Brien, *Rethinking*, 113–15.
21. See Glessmer, "Calendars," 235.

calendar, which they considered as the repository of the legitimate scriptural tradition. The Pg tradition was intentionally muddled, albeit not erased, by Pentateuch editions which set off the calendar controversy displayed in the Dead Sea Scrolls. In this controversy, the upholders of the 364-day calendar were traditionalists reacting against reformers who introduced some kind of lunar calendar. The outcome was a messy compromise, with the survival of the seventh-day Sabbath, which became a hallmark of Judaism,[22] within the overall framework of a lunar year. The Otot and Mishmarot texts attempt an impossible synchronization of two mutually exclusive systems.[23]

22. For the Roman era, see M. Stern, ed., *Greek and Latin Authors on Jews and Judaism*, vol. 1 (Jerusalem: Israel Academy of Science and Humanities, 1976), 319, 325, 349.

23. M. Albani, "Die lunaren Zyklen im 364-Tage-Festkalender von 4QMischmerot/4Qse," *Mitteilungen und Beiträge* 4 (1992): 3–47 (40).

Chapter 4

The Final Eras of the Priestly Document

Once the sabbatical chronology of the Flood narrative and the intercalation scheme of the calendar have been recovered, the overall chronology of the Priestly Document can be pieced together. As can be expected, Pg is organized in seven eras. Creation, the first era, has been discussed in Chapter 1. Chapter 2 examined the implications of the antediluvian era, while the Flood and the postdiluvian periods were discussed in Chapter 3. Abram's departure from Haran marks the end of the postdiluvian era and the onset of the next period.

Period of Wanderings

The division of the Pg narrative varies slightly from traditional approaches, which distinguish a patriarchal era from the Exodus. For Pg, the departure from Egypt is the occasion to present the first festival of the year (Passover, see below), though it does not mark the end of a period. The Exodus constitutes the last leg of a period of wanderings initiated by Abram's departure from Haran and closing with the setting up of the Residence on 1 I 02 after crossing the sea:

Abraham begets Isaac (Gen 21:5) 25 years after leaving Haran (Gen 12:4)	25
Isaac begets Esau and Jacob at 60 (Gen 25:26)	60
Jacob in Egypt at 130 (died at 147 after 17 years in Egypt, Gen 47:28)	130
The Israelites stayed 430 years in Egypt (Exod 12:40)[1]	430
Residence set up on 1 I of year 2 after crossing the sea (Exod 40:17)	1
Total	*646*

There are 646 years between Haran and the completion of the Residence. 646 years is 40 years short of 14 jubilees ($2 \times 7 \times 49 = 686$). The jubilee

---

1. Again, I follow the MT. The SP and LXX include within these 430 years the sojourn of the patriarchs in Canaan: LXXB = 435.

is an obvious sabbatical unit. The 40 years missing to complete 14 jubilees are the time the sons of Israel spent in the wilderness before settling in the land of Canaan.

Wilderness Era

Once YHWH resides among his people, the narrative is coming close to resolution. The sons of Israel constitute the last landless human group. All of Noah's offspring received a land of their own (Gen 10), but disruptions in Terah's Toldot led to his displacement to Haran and then to Canaan. The land of Canaan being settled with Hittites, Esau settles in Transjordan with his uncle Ishmael while Jacob settles in Egypt until his seed is violently enslaved. The Exodus enables the sons of Israel to escape Pharaoh's brutality. YHWH provides daily manna to sustain his people on their way to the land. After a census of the adult males in Num 1, Moses is instructed to send surveyors, the "spies" of traditional translations, in order to prepare the allotment of the land of Canaan and make sure that resources are equated to needs. In the final text, the sending of the land surveyors is not dated. The closest date is 20 II of the second year after the crossing of the sea, which now corresponds to the moment when the cloud rose for the first time from over the tabernacle to lead the way (Num 10:11). In my delimitation, however, the cloud and the tabernacle do not belong to Pg. Hence, once this secondary material is removed, the date in Num 10:11a relates directly to YHWH's order to send some men to inspect the land in Num 13:1:

> [10:11] On the twentieth of the second month of the second year, [13:1] YHWH said to Moses: [2]"Send some men and they will tour the land of Canaan…

In this case, the land surveyors are sent on day 20 of month II in the second year, that is, 400 days after the crossing of the sea: $364 + 30 + 6 = 400$.

Then, the surveyors return with fruits of the land as tokens of its fertility. The question is how to interpret such fertility: How could such a good land remain empty of inhabitants unless it eats them?[2] Misinterpreting

---

2. The land filled with giants (Num 13:28–33) does not fit Pg's picture, is secondary and reaches back as far as Gen 6:1–8 (Ps). The failure to recognize the giants as a later addition warps the understanding of the rest of Pg. Lohfink, "Original Sins," 111, considers the giants as "an expanded motif from the old sources that is not precisely covered by the naming of the sin as 'slander of the land.'" In most cases, the contradiction between an anthropophagous land which is thus empty and a land peopled with giants is not noted (R. Achenbach, "Die Erzählung von der

the emptiness of fertile Canaan (Num 13:23, 26) as meaning that it is anthropophagous (Num 13:32 // Ezek 36:12–14), the surveyors present a slanderous report (דבה, Num 13:32), a last complication that enables the plot to rebound. Instead of setting off to take possession of their holding, the people deduce that it is preferable to go back to Egypt or die in the wilderness. YHWH hears the complaint of the sons of Israel and acts upon it according to a strict concept of proportional retribution already applied in Exod 16:12. The sons of Israel wait until the generation that left Egypt dies in the wilderness. While the sending of the land surveyors should have marked the end of the wilderness period, the slander of the good land and the refusal to enter it transform days into years. According to the "one day is one year" principle (Num 14:34 Ps?), the initial 400 days in the wilderness become forty years, obtained by the difference between Moses' eighty years when he spoke to Pharaoh (Exod 7:7) and his death on the eastern shore of the Jordan River at age 120 (Deut 34:7). To point out the chronological significance of the forty years in the wilderness, Num 14:35 (Pg) states that the Exodus generation was perfected (יתמו ושם ימתו). Like the occurrence of √תמם in Abraham's lifespan (Gen 17:1; 25:8), the perfection has more to do with the calendar than with moral character. The significance of these forty years and of the fourteen jubilees which the eras of wanderings and of wilderness produce remains to be found.

The Torah ends with Moses' death and the entry of the sons of Israel is presented in the book of Joshua. This canonical division, however, is artificial. Pg continues into Joshua and narrates the peaceful settlement of the sons of Israel in the land of Canaan (see Chapter 10 below).[3] In this long version of Pg, the completion of the days of mourning for Moses is followed immediately by a laconic mention of the crossing of the Jordan on the tenth day of month I (Josh 4:19). Compared to the elaborate crossing described in Josh 3, this is a matter-of-fact note reflecting Pg's notion of an empty Canaan, which requires no army, no priests and no spies sent in advance. The sons of Israel arrive just in time to put into practice the festival calendar of Lev 23 by finding a wild lamb in the land

gescheiterten Landnahme von Kadesch Barnea," *ZABR* 9 [2003]: 56–123 [98–99]), or the presence of giants leads to the conclusion that Pg presupposes a military conquest under the leadership of Joshua (Schmidt, *Studien*, 223; N. Rabe, *Vom Gerücht zum Gericht* [Tübingen: Francke, 1994], 410–13). C. Levin, *Der Jahwist* (FRLANT 157; Tübingen: Vandenhoeck & Ruprecht, 1993), 376, however, removes the giants at the end of v. 32.

3. E. A. Knauf, "Die Priesterschrift und die Geschichten der Deuteronomisten," in Römer, ed., *The Future of the Deuteronomistic History*, 101–18 (113–15).

of Canaan that they will eat during their first Passover in the land. The seven periods of the overall chronology are as follows:

Creation:	1 week
Antediluvian:	600,000 days + 6 years + 6 months + 6 weeks + 59 days
Flood:	36 weeks
Drying out:	7 months
Postdiluvian:	3 cycles of seven 365-day mean years
Wanderings:	14 jubilees—40 years
Wilderness:	from 400 days to 40 years

Since calendars regulate daily life by setting the date of festivals, it is time to consider the festivals of the sabbatical year.

Chapter 5

YEARLY FESTIVALS (LEVITICUS 23*)

The concern displayed by Pg over the calendar and its intercalation continues with a section dealing with festivals. Calendars regulate the celebration of festivals by setting apart holy days which the entire community celebrates simultaneously. Festivals are mentioned in Gen 1:14 and the complete yearly festival cycle is delineated in Lev 23. However, studies have never attributed much material from Leviticus to Pg mainly because Martin Noth considered that Pg, being is a narrative document, excluded *de facto* the presence of "legal" material from Pg.[1] Only the consecration of Aaron and the first sacrifice on the wilderness altar in Lev 8 and 9 were traditionally attributed to Pg.[2] Recent studies by Frevel and Pola have been even more stringent by excluding Leviticus from Pg altogether (see appendix). Yet, the requirement of genre purity is dubious and several authors are now challenging the Nothian dogma postulating that narratives do not include "legislative" material.[3] In the wake of this new trend, I suggest that the calendar material in Lev 23 and 25 is likely to belong to Pg since parts of these chapters obviously cohere with the sabbatical calendar.

Attributing parts of Lev 23 and 25 to Pg runs, however, into another problem since these chapters belong to the Holiness code (HC) commonly

1. Noth, *Überlieferungsgeschichte*, 48. Noth had considerable difficulties in defining P. See R. Rendtorff, *Das überlieferungsgeschichtliche Problem des Pentateuch* (BZAW 147; Berlin: de Gruyter, 1977), 112, or p. 126 in the English translation, *The Problem of the Process* (trans. J. Scullion; JSOTSup 89; Sheffield: JSOT Press, 1990).

2. See the useful chart in P. P. Jenson, *Graded Holiness* (JSOTSup 106; Sheffield: JSOT Press, 1992), Appendix 1, which lists the delimitation of Pg by Holzinger, Noth, Elliger, Weimar and Lohfink.

3. A. Ruwe, "The Structure of the Book of Leviticus in the Narrative Outline of the Priestly Sinai Story (Exod 19:1–Num. 10:10*)," in *The Book of Leviticus* (ed. R. Rendtorff and R. A. Kugler; VTSup 93; Leiden: Brill, 2003), 55–78 (57); J. Schaper, *Priester und Leviten im achämenidischen Juda* (FAT 31; Tübingen: Mohr Siebeck, 2000), 44–47; Nihan, *Priestly Torah*.

viewed as a separate document. Most studies of Leviticus identify two major schools and documents, designated as H (holiness school) and P (priestly school). How P relates to H is far from clear.[4] Even more problematic for the present concern is the relationship between Pg and the P of Leviticus studies. These documents are incompatible in terms of theology,[5] and Jacob Milgrom has never clarified how P and Pg stand in relation to each other,[6] although he has a paragraph on H's polemics against P, D, and even JE.[7] In fact, the isolation of HC from the bulk of Leviticus is considered artificial by some scholars.[8] It partly results from anachronistic notions which view ancient law collections as modern codes. Ancient law codes did not reflect actual judicial practice which was based on precedents, administrative measures[9] and on customary law. Hence legal collections were not codes in the modern sense.[10]

4. Discussion by J. Stackert, *Rewriting the Torah* (FAT 2/52; Tübingen: Mohr Siebeck, 2007), 12–29.

5. D. Janzen, *The Social Meanings of Sacrifice in the Hebrew Bible* (BZAW 344; Berlin: de Gruyter, 2004), makes a description of P in Genesis and Exodus which corresponds to Pg, but goes on with P in Leviticus, which turns into a quasi-Dtr theological position: "...obedience is the key... [I]t is righteousness and perfection that will save Israel, just as it saved Noah... Should Israel refuse to recognize the categories of holiness engrained in P's worldview, YHWH will destroy the nation like a sacrifice..." (p. 101). What is left of Pg's unconditional *berît*?

6. J. Milgrom, "A Response to Rolf Rendtorff," *JSOT* 60 (1993): 82–85.

7. Milgrom, II, 1352–61.

8. V. Wagner, "Zur Existenz des sogennanten 'Heiligkeitsgesetzes'," *ZAW* 86 (1974): 307–16; J. Blenkinsopp, *The Pentateuch: An Introduction to the First Five Books of the Bible* (New York: Doubleday, 1992), 224; R. Rendtorff, "Is it Possible to Read Leviticus as a Separate Book?," in *Reading Leviticus* (ed. J. F. A. Sawyer; JSOTSup 227; Sheffield: Sheffield Academic Press, 1996), 22–35 (27–29). B. Britt and P. Creehan, "Chiasmus in Leviticus 16,29–17,11," *ZAW* 112 (2000): 398–400, find a literary unit spanning from Lev 16 to 17, but see D. P. Wright, "The Fallacies of Chiasmus," *ZABR* 10 (2004): 143–68.

9. R. Westbrook, "Cuneiform Law Codes and the Origin of Legislation," *ZA* 79 (1989): 201–22.

10. These "codes" do not constitute an authoritative body of laws enforced by courts. Before the codification of the Anglo-Egyptian laws and the *Code algérien*, oriental judicial systems did not function with codes; see J. Schacht, *An Introduction to Islamic Law* (Oxford: Clarendon, 1964), 100–101. Even the Shariaᶜ is not a law code, but an unwritten jurisprudence loosely based on the narratives of the Quran through the interpretation of four different schools. The canonization of the Torah did not render oral legal tradition obsolete as indicated by the importance of the oral Torah for the Pharisees. On the opposite side, it is noteworthy that the books of Ezra and Nehemiah hardly display the application of laws written in the Torah; see H. Maccoby, "Holiness and Purity," in Sawyer, ed., *Reading Leviticus*, 153–70 (167 and 169 n. 22). Possible exceptions are the celebration of the Feast of Booths (Neh

Collections of laws belonged to royal propaganda[11] and to the scribal school but played little or no role in the practice of judges.[12] The many thousand court dockets recovered from southern Mesopotamia never cite Hammurabi's code in actual judicial proceedings, despite its being recopied as part of the scribal curriculum for over a millennium.[13] The goring ox and the injured pregnant woman, not to speak of the castratrix (Deut 25:11), are as common in legal collections as they are rare in actual life because they are paradigmatic school exercises.[14] Since the HC and the other ancient legal collections belong more to the realm of narratives than to judicial practice, parts of HC can be attributed to the Pg narrative when they agree with the criteria delineated so far.

In Lev 23, YHWH's festivals are holy convocations and holidays. This is only the third occurrence of קדשׁ√ in Pg, after Elohim's sanctification of the Sabbath (Gen 2:3) and the mention of the Residence as a sanctuary (Exod 25:8). Leviticus 23:4 repeats v. 2 and frames the Sabbath in v. 3 to organize the festivals upon the succession of Sabbaths. The originality of Pg's festival calendar lies in the weekly sabbatical rhythm since the festival cycle attested in the library found at Emar (Tell Meskene, Syria) already clusters festivals around the equinoxes with spring and autumn seven-day festivals.[15] Leviticus 23 merely inserts the Sabbath into a

8:14–17//Lev 23:40–42; see L. L. Grabbe, "The Priests in Leviticus," in Rendtorff and Kugler, eds., *The Book of Leviticus*, 207–24 [222]); and the midrash of Lev 18:24–30 in Ezra 9:11–12 to establish a prohibition against mixed marriages (see A. Schenker, "What Connects the Incest Prohibitions with the Other Prohibitions Listed in Leviticus 18 and 20?," in Rendtorff and Kugler, eds., *The Book of Leviticus*, 162–85 [178–79]).

11. R. Westbrook, "What is the Covenant Code?," in *Theory and Method in Biblical and Cuneiform Law* (ed. B. M. Levinson; JSOTSup 181; Sheffield: Sheffield Academic Press, 1994), 15–36 (32), which explains why Isa 10:1 equates the writing of laws with injustice.

12. R. Harris, *Ancient Sippar* (Leiden: Nederlands Historisch-Archaeologisch Instituut, 1975), 116–17.

13. B. M. Levinson, "The Right Chorale," in *Not in Heaven* (ed. J. P. Rosenberg and J. C. Sitterson Jr.; Bloomington: Indiana University Press, 1991), 129–53 (147).

14. J. J. Finkelstein, *The Ox that Gored* (Philadelphia: American Philosophical Society, 1981), 14–20; H. Liss, "The Imaginary Sanctuary: The Priestly Code as an Example of Fictionality in the Hebrew Bible," in *Judah and the Judeans in the Persian Period* (ed. O. Lipschits and M. Oeming; Winona Lake: Eisenbrauns, 2006), 663–90.

15. D. Arnaud, *Emar*, vol. 4 (Paris: Recherche sur les civilisations, 1986–87); D. E. Fleming, "The Israelite Festival Calendar and Emar's Ritual Archive," *RB* 106 (1999): 8–34. The closest parallel to Lev 23 and 25 is Emar's zukru; see ARM XXVI 5:7; I 131:10–16; XXVI 405:3; XXVI 216:11; Fleming, *Time*; D. Charpin,

Bronze Age festival tradition. Since the sabbatical calendar prevents festivals falling on the Sabbath, the Sabbath governs the festival calendar but is never merged with the festivals. Months I and VII have exactly the same number of days and their Sabbaths are in the same position. Both months start with a Wednesday (see Table 1). Therefore, the sabbatical calendar provides a criterion to identify non-sabbatical additions in Lev 23. Only festivals fixed in relation to the Sabbath belong to Pg. Tenufah and Shabuot (Lev 23:9–21) are excluded since they are determined by the maturity of the grain and their date cannot be fixed in advance. This leaves two pairs of festivals determined by the Sabbath: Passover and Massot (Unleavened breads) on 14 and 15–21 I, Teruah (Blast) and Kippurim (Purifications) on 1 and 10 VII:

> [23:1]YHWH said to Moses: [2]"Talk to the sons of Israel and explain to them the festivals of YHWH which you will call 'holidays.' These are my festivals: [3]Six days you will do work but the seventh day is Sabbath, a Sabbath minor, a holiday, all work you will not do; it is a Sabbath for YHWH in all your settlements. [4]These are the festivals of YHWH, holidays which you will have during their festivals:
> [5]First month, in the 14th of the month at twilight: Passover for YHWH. [6]Fifteenth day of this month: pilgrimage of Massot for YHWH, seven days you will eat unleavened breads."
> [23]YHWH said to Moses: [24]"Tell the sons of Israel: 'In the seventh month, day 1 of the month will be for you a minor Sabbath of remembrance, Blast holiday.'" [26]YHWH said to Moses: [27a]"Moreover, the 10th of the 7th month is the day of purgations. It will be a holiday for you; you will humiliate your lives. [28]You will do no work on that very day since it is a day of purgations to purge you in front of YHWH your Elohim. [29]Any being that will not be humiliated on that very day will be cut from its people, [30a]any being that will work on that very day. [31]You will do no work—decree everlasting for your generations in all your settlements."

Even in its final form, Lev 23 displays limited interest in sacrificial matters.[16] This is corrected in the longer version of this calendar in Num

---

"Les mois Uwarum et Sebûtum," *NABU* (1989) 93: 66; D. E. Fleming, "Seven-Day Siege of Jericho in Holy War," in *Ki Baruch Hu* (ed. R. Chazan, W. W. Hallo and L. H. Schiffman; Winona Lake: Eisenbrauns, 1999), 211–28; Hallo, "Moons," 1–13; W. Sallaberger, *Der kultische Kalender der Ur III-Zeit* (Berlin: de Gruyter, 1993), 37–96; B. Groneberg, "Die Tage des šigû," *NABU* (1989) 9: 7–10; G. Wilhem, *Grundzüge der Geschichte und Kultur der Hurriter* (Darmstadt: Wissenschaftliche, 1982), 96; G. Pettinato, *The Archives of Ebla* (Garden City: Doubleday, 1981), 72; A. Archi, "The Archives of Ebla," in *Cuneiform Archives and Libraries* (ed. K. R. Veenhof; Leiden: Nederlands historisch-archaeologisch Instituut, 1986), 74.

16. K. Grünwaldt, *Das Heiligkeitsgesetz Leviticus 17–26* (BZAW 271; Berlin: de Gruyter, 1999), 299.

28–29, which adds sacrifices for normal days, for the Sabbath, new moon and Massot.[17] Offering sacrifices on the Sabbath (Num 28:9) subverts the requirement of human idleness decreed for the first time in Pg in v. 3.[18] This means that the offerings mentioned in Lev 23:8, 13, 18, 25, 27, 36 are secondary. As the whole of Num 21–25, they have to be attributed to Ps, which, besides introducing sacrificial theology into Pg, erases the sabbatical calendar by downplaying the importance of the Sabbath once months became lunar again, as they had been before Pg.[19]

Leviticus 23:3, 24 refer to the Sabbath and to Teruah as Sabbath *shabbaton* (שבתון), a feature often regarded as part of a secondary revision of the Priestly calendar.[20] It is translated as a superlative, "complete rest," based on the dubious premise that the *-on* ending transforms a noun into an adjective with a superlative shade.[21] Superlatives, however, are often built with the plural (as in Song of Songs), while the ending *–on* is diminutive rather than superlative.[22] Rather than a "solemn day of rest," a Sabbath *shabbaton* is a small or ordinary Sabbath compared to special Sabbaths.[23] Nowhere do we find mentions of great Sabbaths, though the mentions of *shabbaton* suggest that Sabbaths *shabbaton* are comparatively less solemn than other festive days, simply because they are more frequent. The ordinary seventh day and the Day of Blasts are thus minor Sabbaths rather than superlative Sabbaths. The difference is not the amount of activity permitted but their relative solemnity compared to the Day of Atonement and the Jubilee. When the sabbatical calendar was replaced by a lunar calendar, various *shabbaton*s[24] were added, obliterating Pg's distinction. The focus shifted away from the festive character

17. Ibid., 297; Milgrom, III, 1979.

18. Milgrom, II, 1406.

19. Against K. W. Weyde, *The Appointed Festivals of YHWH* (FAT 2/4; Tübingen: Mohr Siebeck, 2004), 18, who claims the opposite because "it is difficult to imagine that the author of Num 28:9–10, provided that the legislation in Lev 23:3 was available to him, would reduce the significance of the seventh day."

20. Wagenaar, *Origin*, 85, suggests that in Lev 23:23–24 (the single occurrence of *shabbaton* in his reconstruction of the Priestly calendar) it coincides with the pre-exilic New Year on 1 VII and thus, according to the etymology of Shabbat, has the connotation of end, stop of the year.

21. *HALOT*, 4:1411.

22. J. Barth, *Die Nominalbildung in den semitischen Sprachen* (Hildesheim: Olms, 1967), §196.

23. As distinguished by the Samaritan calendar; see S. Powels, "The Samaritan Calendar," in *The Samaritans* (ed. A. D. Crown; Tübingen: J. C. B. Mohr, 1989), 681–742 (734–37).

24. Non-Pg *sabbaton* in Exod 16:23; 31:15; 35:2; Lev 16:31; 23:24, 32, 39.

towards the prohibition of work, the infringement of which divine directive became liable to the death penalty (Exod 31:12–17 Ps). Pg only requires the death penalty for breaches of the solemnity of Kippurim (vv. 29–30) in order to underline the importance of this festival for Pg's unique atonement system.

The theoretical presentation of the calendar in Lev 23 is completed with passages describing the circumstances of the first celebration of each yearly festival except Teruah. These passages are scattered across Pg and inserted at the relevant moment of the narrative of Israel's past. They are presented below in the order of their presentation in Lev 23, which corresponds to their chronological order within the yearly cycle.

Passover (Exodus 12)

Passover is the first festival of the sabbatical year (Lev 23:5) and the first one celebrated by the sons of Israel (Exod 12). There is no consensus on what belongs to Pg in Exod 12.[25] If Pg does include ritual regulations and calendrical material, Exod 12 is a key element. The Passover as apotropaic slaughter used to be attributed to JE. While Pg most likely took over an older ritual connected to the Exodus, there is no need here to attempt to recover literary strata older than Pg.[26] Any element fitting the requirements of the sabbatical calendar may be attributed to Pg. The application of this principle leads to the attribution of most of Exod 12 to Pg, except the unleavened bread (Exod 12:8, 15–20, 39, see below on Massot) and a few other details (see the translation of the Priestly document at the outset of the present study).[27]

25. Lohfink (see Appendix) and L. Schmidt, *Studien zur Priesterschrift* (BZAW 214; Berlin: de Gruyter, 1993), 29–32, remove everything until v. 37. Elliger, Weimar, Pola and Gertz keep v. 1 and vv. 3–14, while Noth goes as far as v. 20 (Noth).

26. The criteria used to recover the old Passover are unreliable at best: cult centralization, historicizing, non-ritual meal, nomadic rite; see U. Dahm, *Opferkult und Priestertum in Alt-Israel* (Berlin: de Gruyter, 2003), 114–72.

27. The burning of the leftovers in v. 10 is secondary since v. 4 insists that households should join to make sure that there are no leftovers. It may prepare the insertion of burnt offerings into Pg at Gen 8:20 and Lev 16 and 23. The prescription not to boil the lamb (v. 9) is redundant after v. 8. It is a reaction against Deut 16:7; Exod 29:31; Lev 6:28; Num 6:19. The mixed crowd and livestock (v. 38) are required for the sacrifices in the wilderness (Exod 40:29; Lev 8–10) and the thirsty flocks in Num 20:4–11. Pg has no sacrifice (see below on *yom kippur*) and the Israelites are not accompanied by flocks. Hence the catechism section (Exod 12:25–27) is also likely to be secondary since עבדה "service" or "slavery" has negative

Exodus 12:2 supplies a crucial calendrical component missing from Gen 1:14, namely, that month I is the month when Passover is celebrated.[28] This information is crucial since the sabbatical calendar rejects named months and designates months exclusively by numerals. Exodus 12:3–5 omit the word "day" after "the tenth" to underline the fact that Passover is celebrated at night. This is congruent with "the fourteenth of the month" in Lev 23:5. The lamb is kept until the fourteenth *day* (v. 6) and slaughtered at sunset.[29] It is then eaten during the night that separates the fourteenth and the fifteenth days. For this reason, Exod 12:42 insists on the character of Passover as taking place at night. The preparation of the Passover lamb never happens during a Sabbath but always on a Tuesday (Table 1), thus preserving the requirement of Sabbath idleness (Lev 23:3).

Exodus 12 displays other features that conform to the Pg narrative. The stress on having enough mouths to eat all the meat is in line with the authorization to kill animals for food only (לאכלה, Gen 9:2–3). Avoiding waste of meat underlines that eating animals is a concession which involves a dangerous amount of violence.[30] Bloodshed is never trivial. For this reason, the lamb in Exod 12:27 is slaughtered (שחט) rather than sacrificed (זבח), stressing that no sacrifice is involved,[31] contrary to what

connotations in Pg (Exod 1:14; 2:23), and since זבח ("sacrifice") is never used by Pg because killing animals is only permitted for the feeding of humans (Gen 9:3). The mention of Passover as pilgrimage (חג, v. 14) contradicts the home celebration by suggesting that Passover is to take place at sanctuaries under the supervision of priests (Deut 16:3–6; 2 Chr 35:16; Ezek 35:21–25). Verse 31b belongs to the strand in which Moses asks Pharaoh to let the people go and worship YHWH in the wilderness (Exod 3:18; 4:23; 7:16) while Pg's v. 31a presents the Exodus as Pharaoh's manumission of his Hebrew slaves. The plundering of the Egyptians (vv. 35–36) explains the origin of the gold for the cherubim, lamp stand and altar built in the wilderness (Exod 25; 30). Pg's Residence has no need of this (see above on the intercalation of the calendar).

28. D. J. A. Clines, "The Evidence for an Autumnal New Year in Pre-Exilic Israel Reconsidered," in his *On the Way to the Postmodern*, 371–94.

29. Wagenaar, *Origin*, 174. Literally, "between the evenings" (בין ערבים).

30. By contrast, Ps elevates the holocaust, waste *par excellence*, as the paradigm of selfless devotion to sustain their economic interests; see J. W. Watts, *Ritual and Rhetoric in Leviticus: From Sacrifice to Scripture* (Cambridge: Cambridge University Press, 2007), 72–73.

31. P. Laaf, *Die Pascha-Feier Israels* (BBB 36; Bonn: Hanstein, 1970), 113; W. H. Schmidt, *Exodus, Sinai und Mose* (Darmstadt: Wissenschaftliche Buchgesellschaft, 1990), 57; A. Marx, *Les systèmes sacrificiels de l'Ancien Testament* (VTSup 105; Leiden: Brill, 2005), 212.

is the case in Ezek 45:22 and Deut 16:1–8.[32] Sacrifice involving the offering of at least a portion of the meat to a divinity contravenes the strict limitation of bloodshed to food purposes. This unique Pg feature is often missed due to the large amount of sacrificial material added into Pg, which aligns the Torah with the traditional use of sacrifices as one taxation method among others. The fact that anyone may slaughter the Passover lamb in Exod 12:6 confirms Pg's opposition to sacrifices. For Pg, Passover founds the congregation (עדה, Exod 12:3, 6) but it does not foreshadow the cult.[33] Pg's ברית (Gen 9; 17) requires no cult to propitiate an angry deity since all covenantal requirements are independent from human obedience. Hence the blood is only a sign (Exod 12:13). We now turn to Pg's second yearly festival.

Manna and Massot
(Exodus 16; Leviticus 23:6; Joshua 5:10–12)

Contrary to Passover celebrated in Exod 12 before its mention in the calendar in Lev 23, the festival of Massot (Unleavened Bread)[34] is prescribed in Lev 23, while its first celebration is delayed until the arrival in the land in Josh 5. It is, however, anticipated by the gift of manna in Exod 16. Manna is eaten in the wilderness until it is replaced by wild grain when the sons of Israel celebrate their first ever Massot festival following their first Passover in Canaan. Hence, in Pg, Massot recalls the first "proper" meal eaten in the land after the manna ceased. The following Pg material can thus be identified, as it coheres with the elements of the sabbatical calendar in Lev 23:6:

> Exod 16:2 The whole congregation of the sons of Israel lamented against Moses and Aaron in the wilderness. ³The sons of Israel said to them: "Will we now die in YHWH's hand while in the land of Egypt we used to stop by the cauldron of meat and eat bread to satiety? You made us come out to this wilderness to make this entire assembly die of famine." ¹¹YHWH spoke to Moses: ¹²*"I have heard the lament of the sons of Israel, tell them: 'In the morning you will be satiated with bread, then you will know that I am YHWH your Elohim!'" ¹³*In the morning there was a layer of dew. ¹⁴*The layer of dew evaporated; and look, on the face of the wilderness, there was

---

32. Wagenaar, *Origin*, 130, citing Wellhausen, *Prolegomena*, 98; K. Grünwaldt, *Exil und Identität* (BBB 85; Frankfurt: Hain, 1992), 82–83.

33. *Pace* J.-L. Ska, "De la relative indépendance de l'écrit sacerdotal," *Biblica* 76 (1995): 396–415 (406).

34. Etymology unknown, although there is a possible link with Persian-period seals found in Yehud with *m-s-h* inscription; see J. R. Zorn, J. Yellin and J. Hayes, "The *m-(w)-s-h* Stamp Impressions," *IEJ* 44 (1994): 161–83.

a thin flaking, thin like frost on the land. [15]The sons of Israel saw. They said to one another, "What is that?" for they did not know what it was. Moses said to them, "it is the bread YHWH has given you for food. [16*]This is what YHWH has commanded: 'Pick a ration each, an omer per roll-call according to the number there is in his tent!'" [17]The sons of Israel did so. Some picked much and some little. [18]They measured by omer and the much was not too much while the little was not too little, a ration for each one they picked. [21a]Morning by morning, they picked a ration for each. [31a]The house of Israel called its name "man" and [35b]the manna they ate until their arrival to the limits of the land of Canaan.

[Josh 4:19*] So the people went up from the Jordan on the tenth of the first month. [5:9] YHWH told Joshua: "Today I have rolled away the longing of Egypt from you. The name of this place is Gilgal to this day." [10]The sons of Israel camped in the Gilgal. They prepared the Passover on the 14th day of the month, in the evening in the steppes of Jericho. [11]They ate from the yield of the land from the morrow of the Passover: unleavened bread and roasted [grain] on that very day. [12]The manna stopped from the morrow of their eating from the yield of the land and there was no manna for the sons of Israel. They ate from the produce of the land of Canaan on that year.

In Pg's manna episode, the murmurs of complaint are a legitimate expression of grief by the sons of Israel who find themselves destitute in the wilderness and are legitimately anxious about their survival. For Pg, it is not a sin to be hungry and Elohim refers to food several times (Gen 1:29; 9:3). Manna is provided immediately after the Exodus since the Israelites would have experienced hunger right after crossing the Reed Sea rather than a month and a half later. Manna is YHWH's response to a legitimate lament (ויליני, Exod 16:2–3) rather than the first episode of guilty murmurs.[35] As Israel's Elohim, YHWH is responsible to attend to his people's need. YHWH supplies bread from the skies (v. 4), a bloodless provision reflecting antediluvian vegetarianism. Hence, the quails are secondary.[36] YHWH promises bread for the morning and for the first time addresses the formula "you will know that I am YHWH" to Israel, whereas before it was only addressed to Egypt (Exod 7:5). The moment Israel eats manna; the people know that YHWH is Israel's Elohim.[37] Therefore, the sons of Israel cannot be accused of revolt against YHWH since it is through the gift of manna that YHWH is first revealed to them.[38]

---

35. Frankel, *Murmuring*, 14–26.

36. Ibid., 111–13.

37. D. E. Gowan, *Theology in Exodus* (Louisville: Westminster John Knox, 1994), 174.

38. YHWH was revealed to Moses in Exod 6:2.

It is also possible that the double ration of manna on Fridays is secondary. On the one hand, it underlines Sabbath sanctity and thus seems to fit Pg's parameters. Yet, Pg only states the prohibition of work on the Sabbath in Lev 23:3 and the sons of Israel, as do all sons of Adam, get hungry even on the Sabbath. It is therefore likely, although not certain, that Pg conceived that the manna was provided on a daily basis even on the Sabbath. It is only when the land is reached that the daily provision of manna ends (Josh 5:12). Until that point in the narrative, no particular prescription is attached to the Sabbath as the festival calendar is to be enforced in the settlements of the sons of Israel (Lev 23:3) and not before. This wilderness is a non-land, a place of death rather than the idealized location.[39] Seen as a suspension of space, the wilderness era corresponds to the suspension of time during the Flood (see Chapter 3). While time is reckoned during the wilderness era, the wilderness is marked by nameless mountains (see Chapter 9). The importance of the River Jordan as limit of the wilderness is underlined by a string of word-plays using the same root (עבר) relating to space ("the *steppe* [ערבות] of Jericho"), to time ("the two *evenings* [ערבים]"), and to food ("the *produce* [מעבור] of the land," Josh 5:10–11).[40] The Jordan crossing thus marks the return to ordinary life, to agriculture and to a meat diet. The manumitted Hebrew slaves had no flocks with them in the wilderness and survived solely on manna. They arrive in the land of Canaan on 10 I, just in time to select a Passover lamb (Exod 12:3) out of the wild animals waiting for them in the empty land of Canaan (Num 13:32 below). This is hardly more miraculous than the provision of manna.

Jan Wagenaar suggests that the mention of Massot in Lev 23:6 is a secondary insertion to compensate the addition of Succoth in the seventh month.[41] Since unleavened bread is on the menu of the Israelites' first meal in Canaan after the cessation of manna (Josh 5:11), I see no reason to consider Massot as secondary. The delay in presenting the feast of Massot is simply due to Pg's narrative sequence. Another reason to retain Massot within Pg is that Lev 23:6 sets the beginning of Massot on the fifteenth day, as does Josh 5:11 on the morrow of Passover.[42] This

---

39. S. Talmon, "The Desert Motive," in *Biblical Motifs* (ed. A. Altmann; Cambridge, Mass.: Harvard University Press, 1966), 31–63.

40. A. G. Auld, *Joshua* (Leiden: Brill, 2005), 129.

41. J. A. Wagenaar, "The Priestly Festival Calendar and the Babylonian New Year Festivals," in *The Old Testament in Its World* (ed. R. P. Gordon and J. C. de Moor; OTS 52; Leiden: Brill, 2005), 218–52.

42. See also 11QT 11:6–12 and 4Q326.

agreement in the timing of Massot *after* Passover supports the presence of Pg elements in Exod 12, Lev 23 and Josh 5 that are coherent with Gen 1. While another tradition sets it on the fourteenth day,[43] Exod 16:1 dates the gift of Manna on 15 II, thus retaining the original day, but adding one month in order to make room for the insertion of an earlier mention of Massot in Exod 13:3–10. That this is a secondary insertion can be argued from the fact that it is linked with the borrowing of Egyptian gold in Exod 12:34–36 and that it is dated in the month of Abib while Pg's months are numbered and not named. Also, Exod 12:29–31a, 42 (Pg) set Passover, the killing of the Egyptian first-borns and the Exodus at night, which coheres with the strict day/night distinction in Gen 1. In Josh 5:11 and Lev 23:6, unleavened bread is eaten on the morrow of the Passover (15 I) while the thrust of Exod 12:15–20 (non-Pg) is that *massot* are eaten already on 14 I. The difference results from another counting method. The Passover lamb is always killed at sunset on 14 I. With Pg's days starting at sunrise and ending at sunset, the lamb is killed at the end of day 14 and eaten during the night which separates days 14 and 15.[44] Massot then starts on day 15 at sunrise. "On the morrow of their eating from the produce of the land" (Josh 5:12), that is, on 16 I, the manna ceased (שבת). But with days starting and ending at sunset, Passover is eaten at the beginning of day 15, at night, when Massot has already started and thus unleavened bread is eaten together with the Passover.[45] The recourse to Gen 1 solves the crux of the date of Massot and demonstrates the calendrical coherence of Pg. For Pg, Massot does not celebrate the last meal in Egypt, as it does in Exod 13:3–6, but the first meal prepared with Canaanite produce. Calendar and land themes are thus spliced together. Manna is miraculous bread provided in the wilderness the day *after* the first Passover in Egypt and it stops upon arrival in the land *after* the celebration of the first Passover in the land.

43. Exod 12:14; 13:6; 16:3; Num 9:11; Ezek 45:21; 2 Chr 30:21; 35:17; Ezra 6:22. G. Hepner, "The Morrow of the Sabbath is the First Day of the Festival of Unleavened Bread (Lev. 23,15–17)," *ZAW* 118 (2006): 389–404.

44. The LXX of Josh 5 also fuses Passover with the beginning of Massot and harmonizes Josh 5 with non-Pg texts (Exod 12:19–20). Auld, *Joshua*, 15, notes: "And the sons of Israel made the Pasha on the fourteenth day of the month at evening…; and they ate of the grain of the land unleavened and new [loaves]. In this day the manna left off, after their having eaten of the grain of the land, and no longer did there come to be manna…"

45. Wagenaar, *Origin*, 139–44.

Teruah

As month I, month VII is marked by a pair of sabbatical festivals, Teruah and Kippurim. Contrary to Passover and Massot, Teruah (Blast) does not get a narrative description of its first occurrence. It is cursorily mentioned in Lev 23:24 (Pg) and in Num 29:1 (Ps). The significance of Teruah is thus easily overlooked. It only involves the blowing of trumpets as a festival of remembrance, a *shabbaton zikaron*, literally, a "minor Sabbath of remembrance." What is remembered on Teruah? Since Exod 12:2 sets Passover in month I, the blast of trumpets on 1 VII cannot signal the New Year of the sabbatical calendar.[46] Falling on the fourth day of the week like 1 I, 1 IV and 1 X (see Table 1), Teruah commemorates the creation of the calendar (Gen 1:14), but this does not explain why it is called a *shabbaton zikaron*.

The silence over the function of Teruah corresponds to the way the intercalation scheme of the sabbatical calendar is "hidden" in the narrative (see Chapter 2). The administrators of the calendar protect their prerogatives by restricting access to the details of the system to their own circle of initiates. However, for the calendar to be effective and functional, everybody needs to be informed at crucial moments. Hence, the beginning of month VII is announced by the sound of a trumpet to make sure that the entire population keeps apace with the intercalation of the calendar. Although the intercalation rhythm is regular (Table 3), people can easily forget whether the current year is a normal year (52 weeks), a small leap year (53 weeks) or a great leap year (54 weeks), which only occurs every 28 years.[47] The trumpet announces the beginning of the seventh month, regardless of how many weeks were intercalated before. During normal years, the trumpet blows on the morrow of 31 VI (Tuesday) and month VII begins immediately. If the trumpet does not sound on the morrow of 31 VI, everyone knows that the coming week is intercalatory. If the trumpet is heard on the following Wednesday, it means that the current year is a small leap year, with only one week intercalated. However, when the trumpet is heard two weeks after the morrow of 31 VI, it is clear that the year is a great leap year with two intercalated weeks before month VII begins. With this simple system, the entire population keeps track of intercalation without having to understand its principles.

46. Ibid., 127.
47. Or 35 years between year 168 and the next great leap year on year 28 of the following cycle of intercalation.

The function of Teruah in intercalation explains why Teruah is referred to as a Sabbath *shabbaton* and is thus equated with the weekly Sabbath in Lev 23:3, 24. The *shabbaton*s are calendar regulators rather than festivals marked with particular rituals. The abandonment of the sabbatical calendar shifted the trumpet calls to the beginning of the lunar month (Num 29:1–6).[48]

Yom haKippurim (Leviticus 16; 23:26–31)

The Day of Purgations is the last of the four yearly holy days of the sabbatical calendar. It has never been attributed to Pg. Yet, it fits the sabbatical calendar and the theology of Pg. Its presentation as a day of humiliation corresponds to its description in Lev 16. Like Lev 23, ch. 16 has received a number of additions which blur its unique atonement system. It is often believed that the secondary feature is the burdening of the he-goat with Israel's sin, since the slaughter of a ram, bull and goat for YHWH are similar to other sacrificial procedures in Leviticus.[49] However, the mention of the sacrifice of the bull in v. 3 being duplicated in vv. 6 and 11 suggests that it frames an original core. This core deals exclusively with two goats as reproduced below.[50] In Pg, the "scapegoat" ritual is more likely to be the original element. I identify the following narrative in line with Pg's theological profile:

> [Lev 16:2aα] YHWH said to Moses, "Speak to Aaron your brother: [5]'From the congregation of the sons of Israel he will take two he-goats for sin [7a]he will take the two he-goats, [8]Aaron will draw lots over the two he-goats, one for YHWH and one for the expelled guilt. [9]Aaron will present the goat which the lot designated for YHWH and he will make it sinful. [10]He will make the goat designated for the expelled guilt stand alive in front of YHWH as purgation through him by sending it for the expelled guilt to the wilderness. [21]Aaron will lay his two hands on the head of the live goat and confess on it all the transgressions of the sons of Israel. All their wrongdoings and all their sins he will transfer them onto the head of the

48. P. E. Miller, "Karaite Perspectives on Yôm Terûâ," in Chazan, Hallo and Schiffman, eds., *Ki Baruch Hu*, 537–41.

49. Against, M. Noth, *Das dritte Buch Mose: Leviticus* (Göttingen: Vandenhoeck & Ruprecht, 1962), 107.

50. T. Seidl, "Levitikus 16—'Schlussstein' des priesterlichen Systems der Sündenvergebung," in *Levitikus als Buch* (ed. H.-J. Fabry and H.-W. Jüngling; BBB 119; Berlin: Philo, 1999), 219–48; K. Koch, *Die Priesterschrift von Exodus 25 bis Levitikus 16* (FRLANT 71; Göttingen: Vandenhoeck & Ruprecht, 1959), 92–96. This core is considered as the centre of the Torah; see R. Rendtorff, "Leviticus 16 als Mitte der Tora," *BibInt* 11 (2003): 252–58.

goat. Through a man of that time, he will send it to the wilderness. [22]The
goat will carry all their transgressions to an isolated land. He will send the
goat in the wilderness, [29]and it will be for you an everlasting ordinance in
month 7 on the 10th of the month. You will humiliate your lives and you
will do no work. [34]It will be an everlasting ordinance for the purgation of
the sons of Israel from all their sins once a year. It will be done as YHWH
commanded to Moses.'"

Although the casting of lots was a common procedure,[51] Lev 16:8
spells out a unique procedure in biblical sacrifices,[52] which sets this ritual
apart and connects it with land allotment (Num 34:13). The canonical
text integrates the day of purgations within the overall sacrificial system
by adding a number of sacrificial victims which lend to this unique rite a
flavour of conventional sacrifice. Yet, a fundamental problem remains:
the sending of the goat "for azazel" to the wilderness either duplicates or
completes the expiatory sacrifices.[53] If it is necessary to complete the
overall expiatory procedure, one has to invent blood-resistant sins which
can only be removed by the scapegoat.[54] If it duplicates the sacrificial

---

51. W. Hurowitz and V. A. Hurowitz, "Urim and Thummim in Light of a
Psephomancy Ritual from Assur (*LKA* 137)," *JANES* 21 (1992): 95–115.

52. R. E. Gane, *Ritual Dynamic Structure* (Piscataway, N.J.: Gorgias, 2004),
19–20.

53. R. E. Gane, *Cult and Character* (Winona Lake: Eisenbrauns, 2005), 25–42,
presents a summary of scholarly positions.

54. M. Douglas, "The Go-away Goat," in Rendtorff and Kugler, eds., *The Book
of Leviticus*, 121–41 (129) asks what and whose sins are loaded onto the live goat,
but does not answer. She insists that the goat is not victimized as is the case in the
Greek *pharmakos* rite, but transforms the goat into an envoy of peace to surrounding
people. The azazel would atone for human weakness in general; see M. M. Kalisch,
A Historical and Critical Commentary on the Old Testament: Leviticus (London:
Longman, Green, Reader & Dyer, 1867–72), 2:174. For overlooked, unknown or
not yet atoned sins, see J. H. Kurtz, *Sacrificial Worship of the Old Testament*
(Minneapolis: Klock & Klock, 1980), 386; S. Kellogg, *The Book of Leviticus* (New
York: Funk & Wagnalls, 1900), 257–59. For sins that are stored in the sanctuary
until their removal on the Day of Atonement, see A. Rodríguez, *Substitution in
the Hebrew Cultus* (Berrien Springs: Andrews University Press, 1979), 136, 219,
305–7. Milgrom, I, 162 explains the azazel ritual as dealing with the sins of brazen
sinners who are barred from offering sacrifice and thus their sins remain unpurified
and penetrate the sanctuary. The debate has reached a level of fantastic refinement
which proves the incoherence of the biblical sacrificial system; see J. Sklar, *Sin,
Impurity, Sacrifice, Atonement* (Sheffield: Sheffield Phoenix, 2005), and Roy Gane,
Review of Jay Sklar, *Sin, Impurity, Sacrifice, Atonement, RBL*. Online: http://www
.bookreviews.org] (2006). Far from being an impediment, the incoherence supports
the system, since it requires the intermediary of specialists—namely, the priests

system, blood sacrifices are superfluous. When the transgressions of the entire people of Israel are taken away by one live goat once a year, there is no point in sacrificing animals throughout the year, apart from feeding priestly families. Conversely, if the blood of an animal expiates human sins, why is the goat for azazel sent away without shedding a drop of atoning blood, although the laying hands on the head of an animal is invariably a prelude to its sacrifice?[55]

To avoid these questions, exegetes postulate the existence of a demon named Azazel which needs to be pacified by the offering of a goat which is thus designated "for Azazel" (לעזאזל, Lev 16:8, 10).[56] No evidence of such demon is ever likely to surface because "azazel" is not a name but a *faʿaʾil* verbal form of root עזל, which is always compounded with the preposition ל (so LXX).[57] In the framework of Pg, the variant עזזאל transmitted by SP, 11QT 26.13 and 4Q180 1.7–8 is secondary, because Pg never uses El for God.[58] Even if an angry demon had to be pacified, why does YHWH require a sacrifice as well? If YHWH and Azazel are both to be pacified, why not sacrifice two goats, one for YHWH and one for Azazel? The fate of the two goats is crucial. The goat designated for

of ancient Israel and the exegetes of modern academia who both make a more comfortable living out of it than if they had to breed the sacrificial animals by themselves.

55. Lev 3:2, 8, 12; 4:4, 15, 24, 29, 33; 8:14, 18, 22.

56. The paradox of the demon who has to be pacified by the gift of a goat which carries the sins of the children of Israel has long been noted; see M. Noth, *Leviticus* (trans. J. E. Anderson; London, SCM, 1965), 124; D. P. Wright, *The Disposal of Impurity* (Atlanta: Scholars Press, 1987), 69–73. For C. Calum, *Illuminating Leviticus* (Baltimore: The Johns Hopkins University Press, 2006), 44, the silence over what happens to the goat sent to the wilderness reflects the hocus-pocus explanation given to Jacob about Joseph who in fact was not devoured by a wild beast. A more traditional approach is to be found in A. Pinker, "A Goat to go to Azazel," *JHS* 7 (2007). Online: http://www.arts.ualberta.ca/JHS/abstracts-articles.html#A69.

57. According to E. A. Knauf (oral communication), the Egyptian etymology ʿdꜣ ("guilty, injustice," opposed to maat) + dr/l ("to keep away, eliminate, dispose of") proposed by M. Görg, "Beobachtungen zum sogenannten Azazel-Ritus," *BN* 33 (1986): 10–16, is problematic since Egyptian *d* normally becomes Canaanite *ṣ*. See J. Hoch, *Semitic Words in Egyptian Texts of the New Kingdom and Third Intermediary Period* (Princeton: Princeton University Press, 1994), 437. B. Janowski, "Azazel," *DDD*, 128–31, offers a Hurrian etymology derived from a root only known in Akkadian, ʿzz ("to be angry"), but accepts that azazel should not be translated as a proper noun. See M. Dietrich and O. Loretz, "Der biblische Azazel und AlT *126," *UF* 25 (1993): 99–117.

58. See J. C. R. de Roo, "Was the Goat for Azazel Destined for the Wrath of God?," *Biblica* 81 (2000): 233–42 (235).

the expelled guilt is merely led away. It is *not* sacrificed and there is no indication of a procedure to offer it to the postulated angry demon.

The purpose of the "scapegoat" is to remove the people's sins by carrying them far away to an isolated land in the wilderness (Lev 16:22). This goat is a vehicle, not a victim. As for the goat designated for YHWH, it is assumed that it is sacrificed. In fact, Lev 16:9 states only that once the goat is designated by the lots—Aaron "makes it a sin" (ועשהו חטאת), which is usually translated as "he will offer it as a sin offering." However, the two meanings of חטאה (sin or sin-offering) allow a sacrificial and a non sacrificial reading.[59] The goat is declared guilty but it is not necessarily sacrificed. Since the goat for azazel is also designated as a חטאה, even the staunchest defenders of the sacrificial system have to admit that חטאה can have a non-sacrificial meaning.[60]

If the חטאה does not imply sacrifice for the goat for azazel, the same applies to the goat for YHWH. It makes more sense if the goat for YHWH simply stands in front of Aaron while its fellow is led away. In this case, the goat for YHWH embodies the condition of the sons of Israel under Pg's unconditional *berît*, precisely because nothing happens to it, although it is declared guilty. Whereas its sacrifice removes it from the scene and renders the expelling of the second goat redundant or in need of a desert demon, the ritual closes adequately when the guilty goat passes through the ritual unscathed. Neither goat is killed. The sins of the people are removed by the second goat, while Israel, like the first goat, remains alive in front of YHWH. In this way, the original scapegoat ritual puts an end to all scapegoating procedures such as lynchings, pogroms and any execution of victims to diffuse violent tensions within a community, including Jesus' crucifixion.[61] That is the point of the whole ritual, which is lost when either goat is sacrificed. This reading reflects Pg's notion of purgation already present in the Flood narrative. The scapegoat purges the congregation of the sons of Israel of an entire year's worth of transgressions (v. 22), just as the Flood purged the violence of the ante-diluvian generations. The absence of impurities from the list of transgressions (עונת פשעים חטאת) Aaron transfers onto the goat is the exact reflection of the absence of the pure/impure animal distinction and of the absence of a concluding sacrifice in Pg's Flood narrative.[62] It confirms

59. To prevent non-sacrificial readings, B. A. Levine, *In the Presence of the Lord* (Leiden: Brill, 1974), 102, maintains that the term for sin was misvocalized by the Masoretes.

60. Gane, *Cult*, 258–61, especially n. 64. There is even a bloodless חטאה in Lev 5:12!

61. See Watts, *Ritual and Rhetoric*, 176–83.

62. Gane, *Cult*, 258.

that the original version of the ritual functioned outside the clean/unclean categories and that these categories were inserted later with the addition of the sacrifice of the ram and bull (v. 6).

Beyond the analogy with Gen 9, the azazel rite recovers the "very good" of Gen 1, a condition never put in jeopardy but requiring regular purgation to maintain creational stasis.[63] Aaron's words are as efficacious as Elohim's in Gen 1. The azazel ritual expresses Pg's understanding of ritual purgation in strict coherence with the creation and Flood narrative. Therefore the azazel ritual abrogates sacrifices instead of concluding the sacrificial system of Lev 1–15.[64]

Instead of sacrificing the goats to purge sins, Lev 16:29 insists upon the self-humiliation of the sinner, a further indication of the rejection of the efficacy of atonement by blood. That sins are removed by the azazel ritual should not be interpreted as cheap grace. Sin is dangerous and requires purgation. Compared to the Flood, the Day of Purgation is dry but nevertheless cleanses. Passover blood protects Israel temporarily, until the azazel rite accomplishes the yearly and general purgation. The goat for azazel is the negative or mirror image of the Passover lamb.[65] Blood is shed for the Passover meal, but Kippurim is a day of humiliation, possibly of fasting, during which sins are removed bloodlessly. This is consistent with the concession to kill animals for food rather than to atone human sins. It also coheres with the strenuous protest that YHWH needs no feeding (Ps 50:8–14; Isa 1:11). Hence, although sins are removed on Kippurim, blood is shed on Passover, in the context of a family meal where the priestly function is accomplished by anyone able to slaughter and prepare the lamb. The specific priestly role is limited to the transfer of the people's sins onto the goat once a year. This is a sharp

63. W. J. Houston, "Towards an Integrated Reading of the Dietary Laws of Leviticus," in Rendtorff and Kugler, eds., *The Book of Leviticus*, 142–61 (160), demonstrates the fallacy of Jacob Milgrom and Mary Douglas's attempts to reconcile the dietary laws with Gen 1, but his own solution is hardly more convincing. He claims that "all are good, but each for its own purpose. Some are fit for human food, following the concession made by God in Gen 9:3; others are not, though they have their own functions in the divine economy."

64. Zoroastrianism displays a similar reservation towards animal sacrifice; see A. de Jong, "Animal Sacrifice in Zoroastrianism," in *Sacrifice in Religious Experience* (ed. A. I. Baumgarten; Leiden: Brill, 2002), 127–48; W. F. M. Henkelman, "Animal Sacrifice and 'External' Exchange in the Persepolis Fortification Tablets," in *Approaching the Babylonian Economy* (ed. H. D. Baker and Michael Jursa; AOAT 330; Münster: Ugarit-Verlag, 2005), 137–66.

65. Suggested in a discussion with Helen Jacobus.

limitation of the priestly role in line with the non-cultic nature of the wilderness Residence.[66]

These correspondences demonstrate the consistency of the four yearly festivals within the sabbatical calendar. The goat for azazel is the corner-stone of Pg's ritual system, leading to the shelving of holocausts and sacrifices. They were soon reintroduced through the insertion of fifteen long chapters of sacrificial cuisine into the Pg narrative, blunting the audience's ability to note that if azazel is able to do what the text claims it does, all sacrifices are not only redundant, they are criminal in the eyes of the Elohim of Gen 9. Yet, to suggest that the goat for azazel renders all sacrifices redundant is criminal in the eyes of priests who would lose their prebend.[67] To shore up priestly prerogatives, Lev 6:19, 22 (Ps) warns that priests *have* to eat the flesh of sin offerings in order to digest sins,[68] suggesting that the gastric juices of the laity are unable to perform the task.

To conclude, the analysis of the four festivals regulated by the Sabbath leads to the integration of parts of Lev 23 in Pg. A large part of Gen 12 is also attributed to Pg since it is congruent with the understanding of days limited to daytime in Gen 1 and the rejection of sacrifices in Gen 9. The insistence upon the celebration of Passover at night and the celebration of Massot on the *morrow* of Passover demonstrate the coherence of this text with the gift of manna in Exod 16* and the description of the Passover and Massot festivals in Josh 5:10–12. These texts are integrated into Pg as well. Teruah, described in Lev 23 as a *sabbaton* like the Sabbath, helps the entire population to keep up with the intercalation of the sabbatical calendar. The description of the Day of Atonement in Lev 23 isolates a non-sacrificial core within Lev 16 which conforms to the Pg elements in Gen 9. The network of chronological and theological links with Genesis is thus reinforced. But this is not the end of the story. Leviticus 25 mentions two more cycles beyond the yearly cycle.

---

66. M. Görg, "Das Menschenbild der Priesterschrift," *BK* 42 (1987): 21–29 (28).

67. Watts, *Ritual and Rhetoric*, 72, notes: "Leviticus and Numbers authorized the economic claims and religious authority of Aaronide priests, but they hid this reality by foregrounding the selfless ideal represented by the ʿōlāh. They therefore pictured the regular priestly services as consisting mostly of ʿōlôt offerings (Num 28–29), though their days must actually have been spent dealing mainly with the people's šĕlāmîm."

68. Milgrom, I, 637; Gane, *Cult*, 91–105; B. D. Bibb, "Nadab and Abihu Attempt to Fill a Gap," *JSOT* 96 (2001): 83–99 (92–93).

Chapter 6

SEVENTH YEAR AND JUBILEE AS NEXUS
BETWEEN TIME AND LAND (LEVITICUS 25*)

The presentation of yearly festivals in Lev 23 is followed by the description of greater cycles in ch. 25, reflecting the two distinct *zukru* festivals attested at Emar. Emar's yearly *zukru* started at the full moon of the autumn equinox, in the month of Zarati and closed on the seventh day. This was a modest festival compared the larger *zukru* that took place every seven years, starting from the fifteenth day of SAG.MU, the month called "Head of the year," and lasting seven days. Although the king provided most of the offerings, he was apparently absent from the ceremonies.[1] The heptadic rhythm of the *zukru*, its celebration outside the city and the absence of the king make it particularly interesting in the context of Pg.[2] The *zukru* reveals that major festivities took place outside the city, away from temples, even in the context of Bronze Age urbanization. If there were vibrant religious and cultic activities taking place in the countryside outside Emar, the impact of the destruction of Jerusalem and its temple upon the religious life of Judeans has obviously been exaggerated. It should not come as a surprise that Pg describes elaborate festival cycles that require neither temple, altar nor priest:[3]

> [25:1*] YHWH said to Moses: [2]"Speak to the sons of Israel and you will order them 'When you enter the land that I am giving to you, the land will stop a Sabbath for YHWH. [3]Six years you will sow your field, six years you will prune your vine and you will gather its produce, [4]but the seventh year will be a minor Sabbath for the land, a Sabbath for YHWH. Do not sow your field. Do not prune your vine. [5]Do not harvest the after-growth. Do not pick the grapes of your uncut vine. It will be a Sabbath minor for the

1. Fleming, *Time*, 73–74.
2. C. Carmichael, "The Sabbatical/Jubilee Cycle and the Seven-Year Famine in Egypt," *Biblica* 80 (1999): 224–39.
3   M. Steiner, "Two Popular Cult Sites of Ancient Palestine. Cave 1 in Jerusalem and E 207 in Samaria," *SJOT* 11 (1997): 16–28.

land. [6]The Sabbath of the land will be your food, for you, for your slave, for your maid, for your hireling, for the resident migrating with you, [7]for your cattle and for the wildlife that is in your land all its produce will be for food.'"

As Lev 23:3 deals with a minor Sabbath made of a week of days, Lev 25:3 presents another *Sabbath sabbaton*, a minor Sabbath of a week of years. The seventh year is often referred to as the "sabbatical" year, although the text does not call it so.

The Seventh Year

The seventh year is a Sabbath for YHWH *and* for the land. Time and land are thus intimately linked. After concerning Elohim (Gen 2:2) and humankind (Lev 23:3), the Sabbath now applies to the land. In Lev 25:2, "sabbath" is used as a verb—"The land will sabbath a Sabbath for YHWH"—which, on the false premise that "Sabbath" means "rest" (Gen 2:2), has been used to claim that it involves the resting of the land every seven years. Before the introduction of chemical fertilizers, fallow years in the Levant are documented as close as every two years, depending on rainfall levels. On the Syrian desert fringe, fields could even lie fallow two out of three years, while fallowing in coastal areas was rare.[4] The sabbatical year applied uniformly to the entire realm, which indicates that it has nothing to do with fallowing rhythms since Yehud has half a dozen environmental niches receiving vastly different rainfall levels.[5] While land rotation can be read into Exod 23:10–11,[6] Lev 25:2–5 envisage a general cessation of cultivation on the same year across the entire area rather than the rotation of fallow plots.[7] One year without sowing and pruning vines does not imply, however, that the people remain idle. Humans stop work on the weekly Sabbath and on Kippurim

4. J. Weulersse, *Paysans de Syrie et du Proche-Orient* (Paris: Gallimard, 1946), 153.

5. C. E. Carter, *The Emergence of Yehud in the Persian Period* (JSOTSup 294; Sheffield: Sheffield Academic Press, 1999), 100–113.

6. Milgrom, III, 2154; E. Otto, "Der Ackerbau in Juda im Spiegel der alttestamentlichen Rechtsüberlieferungen," in *Landwirtschaft im Alten Orient* (ed. H. Klengel and J. Renger; Berlin: Dietrich Reimer, 1999), 229–36 (232).

7. Milgrom, III, 2153. The stoppage for the land is not a consequence of the presence of the sanctuary. This notion is fundamental for Jan Joosten's study of the HC and may be correct for the HC, but not for Pg. The Residence, not the temple, is first set up in the wilderness, not in the land, so the special care of the land derives from creation, not from the presence of a hypothetical sanctuary that is never mentioned in Pg.

(Lev 23:3, 28), but the Sabbath for the land does not apply to humans.[8] Instead of a year-long holiday for the sons of Israel, the sabbatical year is "food for them" (v. 6). The pious notion that they should use their free time solely to worship YHWH should be resisted.[9] Leviticus 25:4 distinguishes between land (ארץ) and field (שדה). The prohibition of sowing and picking only applies to fields and vineyards, while vv. 6–7 explicitly state that the land provides the food during the sabbatical year.[10] Aftergrowths are allowed for human and animal consumption, without any distinction of species, social status and ethnicity. This concession is sometimes attributed to a later redaction that turns the concern for the land into a humanitarian concern for the poor, as is the case in Exod 23:10–11 and in Deuteronomy.[11] Yet, concern for food is constant in Pg (Gen 1:29; 9:3; Exod 12:4; Josh 5:10–12) and the integration of wildlife reflects Pg's all-embracing view of creation. Hence, the sanctioning of eating what grows naturally does not contradict the ban on harvesting in vv. 5 and 11. Contrary to Exod 23:11, Lev 25:4 does not include olive trees in the banned harvesting activities. Hence, olives, almonds, pomegranates, pistachios, figs, carobs and honey are tended and gathered as usual.[12] The yields of olives and almonds, Yehud's main traditional cash crops, would hardly decline during the sabbatical year compared to regular years if they have been well tended the previous year in anticipation. People could easily survive the absence of grapes since wine was a luxury, but the same cannot be said about the grains which they were prevented from sowing. The ban on sowing forced people to rely on their herds and flocks, to concentrate on animal products, trading the surplus with neighbouring provinces against the grain that was not produced that year. Yet, spontaneous growths on fallow plots would not provide enough

---

8.   Stackert, *Rewriting*, 120.

9.   Against J.-F. Lefebvre, *Le jubilé biblique* (OBO 194; Fribourg: Editions universitaires, 2003), 82–83.

10.   A. Schenker, "Der Boden und seine Produktivität im Sabbat und Jubeljahr," in *Recht und Kult im Alten Testament* (OBO 172; Fribourg: Universitätsverlag; Göttingen: Vandenhoeck & Ruprecht, 2000), 123–33.

11.   K. Grünwaldt, *Das Heiligkeitsgesetz Leviticus 17–26* (BZAW 271; Berlin: de Gruyter, 1999), 325. K. Elliger, *Leviticus* (Tübingen: Mohr, 1966), 344; R. Kilian, *Literarkritische und formgeschichtliche Untersuchung des Heiligkeitsgesetzes* (BBB 19; Bonn: P. Hanstein, 1963), 122–23, 35; Milgrom, III, 2156–60; A. Cholewiński, *Heiligkeitsgesetz und Deuteronomium* (Rome: Biblical Institute, 1976), 111.

12.   Schenker, "Boden," 100, 103. Today, olive trees are seriously trimmed every 3 to 5 years, with minor yearly pruning of dead wood and suckers. Therefore, the crop would be little affected even if the sabbatical prohibitions applied to olive trees. Thanks to Mr Mikhail Elias and Mrs Maruzella Abboud.

fodder for the flocks and herds, especially since they would have been enlarged in anticipation of the sabbatical year by reducing culling on the sixth year. Animals would have to be led further away from the villages than was the case in normal years to find fodder in uncultivated areas which were plentiful in under-populated Palestine. Pasturing of larger herds and flocks further away was the first stage of a process leading to the clearance of new fields. Once the animals, in particular the goats, had cleaned up the vegetation that covered tracks of uncultivated land further away from the villages than usual, the manpower freed from labour-intensive ploughing and harvesting was mobilized to clear stones, built terraces, walls, wells and canals. The new fields were then allocated to new settlers and put in cultivation the following year. This understanding of the ban on sowing grain on the seventh year reveals the secondary nature of Lev 25:18–22, which attributes survival to the observation of YHWH's statutes.

The ban on sowing on the seventh year was a highly practical eco-nomic measure, leading people to retain the mode of life celebrated in the patriarchal stories. The centrality of the Abraham paradigm in Pg, with its herder-in-tent lifestyle that characterized the mode of survival in Yehud after the destruction of Jerusalem and of the coastal cities, reinforced mobility, discipline and output. Obviously, this would not be conducive to cult centralization and focus on Jerusalem, two features that are foreign to Pg. On the contrary, it is consistent with the Passover and the azazel atoning system, which almost completely dispenses with priestly personnel and can be practised anywhere without any cultic structure. What the seventh-year operations did not dispense with was a central administration to enforce the ban.

The Jubilee

The seventh and last holy day of the sabbatical calendar is the Jubilee, falling on the Day of Atonement of every forty-ninth year. The mastery of the sabbatical calendar extends beyond the setting of festival dates, making possible the regulation of certain accounting procedures and of the entire life of the province, in which religion, politics and the econ-omy are in the hands of a small group of literati.

On the 49th year, the *shofar* is sounded twice, on Teruah (as every year) and again on Kippurim, half-way through the forty-ninth year. The Jubilee is not a year, but a particular point within the forty-ninth year, a point coinciding with the day of Kippurim. The etymology of the word *yobel* ("Jubilee") has nothing to do with the ram's horn blown on the

Jubilee, but denotes abundance.[13] The importance of the Jubilee is underlined through the verb "sanctify" (קדשׁתם, Lev 25:10), used for the last of seventh occurrence in Pg.[14] The sons of Israel are to sanctify the fiftieth year, in line with Pg's notion of holiness applying only to time, not to places or persons.[15] This sets the Jubilee as the crown of the sabbatical calendar, just as the seventh day Sabbath is the crown of creation. Whereas the Sabbath is declared holy by the creator, it is a human prerogative to make the Jubilee holy.

The forty-ninth year is a sabbatical year, as is clearly indicated by the repetition of the ban on sowing from v. 4.[16] Yet, the first Jubilee actually occurs during year fifty, counted from the year of the arrival of the sons of Israel in Canaan at the beginning of month I of year 1.[17] Joshua 5:10–11 make it clear that the first year the sons of Israel spent in the land was like a sabbatical year since they ate the produce of the land which they did not sow. Hence, forty-nine years later is year fifty since their arrival in the land. By this device, Pg adheres strictly to the wilderness fiction and presents the problem from the vantage-point of the audience which is about to enter the land. This is the most straightforward explanation for the problem of the 49th year = 50[18] and is supported by the Samaritan calendar.[19] This solution reveals the secondary nature of the imaginary question of how to survive three years without crops, a problem arising once the Jubilee is considered as falling the year *after* the sabbatical year

13. See Akkadian *(w)bl* ("to bring"), in connection with abundance and fertility "to bring tribute, booty, sacrifice, to escort the bride"; see *HALOT*, 2:383. In Arabic, the adjective *wâbil* means "abundant," and is used in particular to refer to an "abundant rain"; see C. Denizeau, *Dictionaire des parlers arabes de Syrie* (Paris: Geuthner, 1935), 548. Alternatively, *wbl* might also mean "overproduction of food leading to pathological bloating, dyspepsia"; see A. Nehmé, ed., *Al-Mounjid* (Beyrouth: Dar el-Machreq, 1975), 885. The same meaning occurs with the inverted *balāwī* ("much, abundance"); cf. *balāʾ ḥasan* ("favour, blessing, grace," Quran 8:17). See Wehr, 1046.

14. Gen 2:3; Exod 25:8; Lev 23:2, 4, 27; 25:10, 12.

15. Lefebvre, *Jubilé*, 98, 103–4.

16. So A. Schenker, "The Biblical Legislation on the Release of Slaves," *JSOT* 78 (1988): 23–41 (25).

17. R. North, *Sociology of the Biblical Jubilee* (Rome: Pontifical Biblical Institute, 1954), 132; Lefebvre, *Jubilé*, 161–63.

18. R. S. Kawashima, "The Jubilee, Every 49 of 50 Years?," *VT* 53 (2003): 117–20, suspends the counting of the Sabbatical cycle during the Jubilee Year and restarts it on the following year in order to keep the Sabbatical and Jubilee cycles in proper alignment. Other solutions are discussed in G. C. Chirichigno, *Debt-slavery in Israel and the Ancient Near East* (JSOTSup 141; Sheffield: JSOT Press, 1993), 318.

19. Powels, "Calendar," 713–14.

and with a restrictive reading of v. 5, which understands it as forbidding all farming operations.

On the day of the Jubilee, a release is proclaimed that results in the return of everyone to his tenure and family. Since the word for "release," דרור derives from the same root as the one used for Mesopotamian *andurārum* edicts (2400–1600 B.C.E.), the release occurring on the Jubilee has been understood as a cancellation of debts.[20] Mesopotamian debt cancellations were carefully planned to maximize their ideological effect at the smallest cost to the palace.[21] Their effectiveness depended on their unexpectedness, but they often seem to have occurred at the onset of reigns as new monarchs wished to gain the goodwill of their subjects. Were the Jubilee equivalent to the *andurārum*, the forty-nine years of a Jubilee cycle would correspond to a very long reign and would thus be less favourable to the poor than the ancient parallels since it would only happen twice per century.[22] This casts doubts on modern interpretations of the Jubilee that consider it as a panacea to the economic problems of the Third World.[23] However, the *andurārum* edicts only waived arrears on emergency survival loans for food and seeds. It certainly benefited food producers, farmers and herders, the majority of the population from whom the king sought support at the onset of his reign[24] as the burden fell on the lenders, although some concessions were made to alleviate their losses. Ammi-ṣaduqa's edict is silent on the return of land, as is Deut 15, which also deals explicitly with the waiving of debts (שמטה).[25] Interpreters often claim that the return of alienated land was self-understood,[26] since Solon's *seisachtheia* (removal of a load) included the

20. See Ammisaduqa's Edict of 1646 B.C.E. in *CoS* 2:362–64, and F. Kraus, *Königliche Verfügungen in altbabylonischer Zeit* (Leiden: Brill, 1984).

21. J. P. J. Olivier, "Restitution as Economic Redress," *ZABR* 3 (1997): 12–25.

22. Diodorus Siculus 5.9 reports that the men of Lipara (Sicily) divided the land of the island into holdings which after 20 years were redistributed by drawing lots; see R. J. Buck, "Communalism on the Lipari Islands," *CP* 54 (1959): 35–39; M. Austin and P. Vidal-Naquet, *Economie et société en Grèce ancienne* (Paris: Colin, 1972), 260–61. Fifty years is the maximum period of enslavement on account of debts in Nuzi document; see B. L. Eichler, *Indenture at Nuzi* (New Haven: Yale University Press, 1973), 34.

23. A. Rainer, "Der Kampf gegen die Schuldenkrise—das Jobeljahrgesetz Levitikus 25," in *Der Mensch als Hüter seiner Welt* (ed. R. Albertz; Stuttgart: Calwer, 1990), 40–60; J. Milgrom, "Jubilee: A Rallying Cry for Today's Oppressed," *Bible Review* 13, no. 2 (1997), 16, 48.

24. J. J. Finkelstein, "Ammisaduqa's Edict and the Babylonian 'Law Codes'," *JCS* 15 (1961): 91–104.

25. E. Otto, "Programme der sozialen Gerechtigkeit," *ZABR* 3 (1997): 26–65.

26. M. Weinfeld, *Social Justice in Ancient Israel* (Jerusalem: Magnes, 1995), 167.

release of pledged property besides remission of individual debts and manumission of debt slaves.[27] In fact, Lev 25 deals extensively with land, but never mentions remission of debts. Again it may be argued that it is implied in the דרור, but it is perilous to jump to conclusions and claim that remission of arrears is part of the package. All other attestations of דרור in the Bible concern the release of slaves (Isa 61:1; Jer 34:8–20) or land (Ezek 46:17), never the waiving of debts. Moreover, *andurārum* edicts did not cancel every type of debt. The "fine print" of the edict specified that only debts with dates of repayment that had not expired were forgiven. Overdue debts were excluded from the release. Otherwise debtors would have been in the position of delaying repayments in view of an impending *mešarum* or *andurārum* edict.[28]

Contrary to *andurārum* edicts, the Jubilee falls on a date fixed in advanced and known to everyone concerned. Had the Jubilee entailed cancellation of debts, the risk of having debtors postpone repayment until the Jubilee would have become institutionalized practice. Borrowers would have every interest in delaying repayment of debts, with the obvious consequence of closing all access to credit, unless clauses against the Jubilee were added into the loan contracts. Therefore, claiming that debts were cancelled on the forty-ninth year defeats the logic of the Jubilee since the Jubilee provides lender and borrower with exact knowledge of the date of the next release. This is the crucial difference with Mesopotamian edicts, and for this reason these edicts do not correspond to the Jubilee. Hence, the meaning of the stipulated return of each person to his or her tenure has nothing to do with debt cancellation. It is commonly assumed that the return in Lev 25 restores an equilibrium that was upset by insolvency. Leviticus 25 would describe the gradual destitution of indentured farmers who lost their land and ended up as slaves until their debts were waived, allowing their physical return onto the land from which they had been alienated.[29] Since Lev 25 does not mention debt release, this assumption must be challenged. The דרור of the Jubilee is not the שמטה of Deut 15, in spite of the fact that the LXX renders both as ἄφεσις.[30] The Jubilee principle is that after forty-nine years the original distribution of tribal land is re-established. At this point, several notions need clarification: antichresis, land tenure and why debts did not automatically alienate farmers from their tenure.

27. Austin and Vidal-Naquet, *Economie*, 236–39.

28. Olivier, "Restitution," 20.

29. Milgrom, III, 2191–98.

30. Used also to render יובל; see J. W. Wevers, *Notes on the Greek Text of Leviticus* (Atlanta: Scholars Press, 1997), 406.

Land Tenure

Leviticus 25:10, 13 put special emphasis on the return to one's own tenure (אֲחֻזָּתוֹ). It must be clear that tenure is not freehold property (see Lev 25:23). The traditional system of land tenure that prevailed in the Levant until the Mandates was very different from the modern European concepts of land ownership, which revolutionized the prevailing tenure system that Islam had preserved. Since Islamic law is based on the same premise as Lev 25, namely, that the State in the name of the divinity claims formal ownership to the entire land (Lev 25:23), the Ottoman legal treatment of land tenure offers the best comparison available[31] to avoid reading Lev 25 in the light of modern categories.

Living in a world where the remotest piece of land is duly measured, classified and registered under the name of its legal owner, modern readers have difficulties imagining how the ancient land tenure system functioned.[32] The *musha* (Arabic "shared") tenure system offers the closest available example to the situation alluded to in Lev 25 and elsewhere in the Bible. This system is presented as transitional between a semi-nomadic mode and the fully divided property system, but nomadism is not relevant here.[33] Private property was recognized for livestock, tents, personal equipment, garden, terraces and homes. However, arable land was not privatized. The statement by YHWH that "the land is mine" (Lev 25:23) is the theological justification of the inalienability of the land. The divinity as the owner of the land is a common oriental concept.[34] Therefore, each village shared out the arable land it controlled between its families in proportion to the number of male members (*dhukūr*) or of ploughing teams (*feddān*).[35] Each unit received long and

---

31. D. Zeʾevi, *An Ottoman Century* (Albany: State University of New York Press, 1996), 122–29.

32. Traditional practices can be baffling when viewed with modern eyes. In certain villages in today's Ghana, a piece of land may be bought and held in full ownership according to State law, while according to the local chief, the owner is merely renting land that belongs to the tribe. Hence, land is bought from the State and simultaneously rented, and no one objects to the contradiction.

33. S. Atran, "Hamula Organisation and Mashaʾa Tenure in Palestine," *Man* 21 (1986): 271–95 (275). For an update on the phenomenon of pastoral nomadism as a function of urban societies; see E. Marx, "The Political Economy of Middle Eastern and North African Pastoral Nomads," in *Nomadic Societies in the Middle East and North Africa* (ed. D. Chatty; Leiden: Brill, 2006), 78–97.

34. M. Bauks, "Die Begriffe מוֹרָשָׁה und אֲחֻזָּה in Pg," *ZAW* 116 (2004): 171–88.

35. Y. Firestone, "The Land-equalizing mushâʿ Village," in *Ottoman Palestine* (ed. G. G. Gilbar; Leiden: Brill, 1990), 91–130 (92–94); B. Schaebler, "Practicing

narrow non-contiguous strips from the different cantons controlled by the village, reflecting the different types of soil available. Risk rather than gains was thus spread between the different families so that if one area suffered from excessive moisture or drought, other strips established on different soil types, different sun exposure and gradient may fare better.[36] To early Western observers, the strict egalitarian principle that governed the *musha* system of land tenure seemed absurd, at first.[37] As the layout of strips was occasionally modified, observers deduced that farmers had no interest in improving land that was not their own. Strips were redistributed by drawing lots to keep up with demographic changes and to make sure that the same strips were not always allotted to the same families. Newborn males and returnees were automatically granted a portion of their family's share.[38] There was no need or possibility to register individual claims of land ownership.[39] Land was *de facto* available to any male who claimed it from his family tenure.[40] For this reason, Lev 25 and

Musha: Common Land and Common Good in Southern Syria Under the Ottomans and the French," in *New Perspectives on Property and Land in the Middle East* (ed. R. Owen; Cambridge, Mass.: Harvard University Press, 2001), 241–311; D. Schloen, *The House of the Father as Fact and Symbol: Patrimony in Ugarit and in the Ancient Near East* (Winona Lake: Eisenbrauns, 2001).

36. C. Kramer, *Village Ethnoarchaeology* (London: Academic Press, 1982), 35; Atran, "Hamula," 275.

37. See A. Nadan, "Colonial Misunderstanding of an Efficient Peasant Institution," *JESHO* 46 (2003): 320–54, and K. W. Stein, "Rural Changes and Peasant Destitution: Contributing Causes to the Arab Revolt in Palestine, 1936–1939," in *Peasants and Politics in the Modern Middle East* (ed. F. Kazemi and J. Waterbury; Miami: Florida International University Press, 1991), 143–70, for a very negative view of the *musha*. Drawings of actual divisions are given in Weulersse, *Paysans*, 99–108, and A. Latron, *La vie rurale en Syrie et au Liban* (Beyrouth: Institut français de Damas, 1936), 192–94. Strips could reach several kilometres in length, while being on a few furrows wide, cutting across any obstacle. Harvest had to be started on the same day from the same side by everyone to avoid mistakes. Mandate authorities admitted that this system reflected certain logic and did not always attempt to reform it.

38. D. Warriner, "Land Tenure in the Fertile Crescent in the Nineteenth and Twentieth Centuries," in *The Economic History of the Middle East 1800–1914* (ed. C. Issawi; Chicago: University of Chicago Press, 1975), 71–78 (75); Weulersse, *Paysans*, 99–108. Ruth 4:3 expressly mentions Naomi's land share (חלק השדה), not a particular field.

39. To this very day, no cadastre has been established in the mountains of South Lebanon (Cazas of Hasbaya, Marjayoun, Bint-Jbail); see Jean Kilzi, online at http://www.geometre-expert.fr/content/file/liban5.pdf.

40. See the widow of Shunem 2 Kgs 8:1–6. The book of Ruth plays on the more complicated case of a widow that had not borne sons, coupling two separate

the whole of Pg are based on the notion of אחזה, from √אחז ("to grasp, seize"), hence the notions of "hold" and land holding. Ownership of land was not only unnecessary, it was blasphemous. As Lev 25:23 states, the land belonged to the divinity, although in practice the position of users was hardly more precarious than the position of modern owners.[41] Uncultivated land, "dead" land in Arabic, could be put under cultivation by anyone with no need to secure any kind of title of ownership.[42] Population growth (Pg's multiply and fructify) had direct effect on the system. As the number of shares increased, their relative size shrank, unless the amount of cultivated land increased proportionally to make sure that the village managed to produce its own food requirements and the surplus required to pay taxes. In this regard, regular land clearing operations on the seventh year would keep up with demographic increase, whether natural or through the arrival of new settlers.

No Alienation of Land Through Debts

Leviticus 25:10, 13 insists upon a return taking place on the Jubilee. The "return" is a stereotyped expression attested from the Sumerians to the Ptolemies.[43] The return decreed in Lev 25:13 cannot mean the physical return of indebted farmers onto the land they owned and then lost precisely because land was not owned and so debts could not lead to loss of land ownership.[44] Studies of Egyptian farming of the second

issues—namely, Naomi's tenure and Ruth's marriage, which the Kethib–Qere in Ruth 4:7 understands in opposite ways; see Z. Zevit, "Dating Ruth," *ZAW* 117 (2005): 574–600.

41. G. Gerleman, "Nutzrecht und Wohnrecht: zur Bedeutung von ʿḥzh und nḥlh," *ZAW* 89 (1977): 316–17; J. A. Fager, *Land Tenure and the Biblical Jubilee* (JSOTSup 155; Sheffield: JSOT Press, 1993), 89.

42. Islamic law grants *ihya al-mawat*, a right of use of dead land to whoever cultivates it; see B. Doumani, *Rediscovering Palestine* (Berkeley: University of California Press, 1995), 164. Note also *wadʿ yad*, "placing of the hand," and the discussion in S. Altorki and D. P. Cole, "Land and Identity Among Awlad ʿAli Bedouin: Egypt's Northwest Coast," in Chatty, ed., *Nomadic Societies*, 634–53 (641).

43. Weinfeld, *Justice*, 159. Compare the Neo-Assyrian pledge *šapāru*, literally "to send," and *kammusu*, "to dwell," to designate the possessory pledging of a person, as well as *uṣu*, "to bring out," for the release of the pledge; see K. Radner, "The Neo-Assyrian Period," in *Security for Debt in Ancient Near Eastern Law* (ed. R. Westbrook and R. Jasnow; CHANE 9; Baltimore: The Johns Hopkins University Press, 1999), 265–88 (269–71).

44. Albertz, "Der Kampf gegen die Schuldenkrise," 41.

millennium B.C.E. as well as studies of Ottoman Palestine suggest that the notion of debts alienating farmers from their land is flawed. The system was indeed rife with debt, but debts did not alienate farmers from their tenure. Successive years of crop failure, a pattern occurring every decade or so, would force farmers to borrow seeds. Since all farmers shared the same hardships, they were unable to help each other.[45] The only people in a position to help farmers were merchants who could end up "owning" entire villages,[46] or rather a share of their crops since farmers were rarely in a position to repay the entirety of their loans. Theoretically, merchants would find themselves at the head of pseudo-estates (Gen 47:13–26). A similar phenomenon is observable four millennia earlier at Bronze Age Nuzi (near Kirkuk) where creditors acquired large estates through being adopted by hundreds of their indebted "fathers." The adopted son absorbed land and consolidated his estate by inheriting his fathers' land. Yet, even in such case, "fathers" were not dispossessed. They remained on the spot and carried on cultivating "their" land.[47]

The same principle applies to nineteenth-century C.E. Transjordan. In spite of the Ottoman Land Law requiring the registration of land titles, the extension of credit and the subsequent formation of estates did not alienate farmers from the land.[48] When the British established a formal credit system in Mandate Palestine, they were surprised that farmers did not turn away from the "usurious" merchants and borrow from the banks. This apparent paradox has a simple answer. Debts were beneficial to both parties.[49] In bad years, the creditor kept "his" villages alive by supplying seeds, further increasing debts. In good years, his position of creditor afforded the merchant with exclusive access to the surplus at a price well below market price,[50] because he avoided competition with other

45. *Pace* M. Chaney, "Bitter Bounty," in *The Bible and Liberation* (ed. N. K. Gottwald and R. A. Horsley; Maryknoll: Orbis, 1993), 250–63 (258–59), who postulates that the formation of latifundiae in eighth-century B.C.E. Israel led to the breakdown of bartering and reciprocal interest-free loans among villagers and its replacement by credit granted by urbanite landlords.

46. Warriner, "Tenure," 77.

47. C. Zaccagnini, "Land Tenure and Transfer of Land at Nuzi," in *Land Tenure and Social Transformation in the Middle East* (ed. T. Khalidi; Beirut: American University Press, 1984), 79–96 (87).

48. E. L. Rogan, *Frontiers of the State in the Late Ottoman Empire* (Cambridge: Cambridge University Press, 1999).

49. A. Nadan, "The Competitive Advantage of Moneylenders over Banks in Rural Palestine," *JESHO* 48 (2005): 1–39 (31).

50. Prices follow a seasonal cycle. In spite of improved transport facilities in Mandatory Syria, prices would increase by 30 to 50 per cent a few months after the

merchants which would have worked in favour of the farmers. During bumper harvests, the price of abundant produce sank proportionally because small tenants did not have the physical and financial ability to store and wait, hence further reducing their ability to repay loans.[51] For this reason, merchant-moneylenders showed little interest in the recovery of securities since it would have terminated their preferential access to surplus. Merchants only sought to get loans repaid in grain at the harvest. The aim was not complete repayment, however, since the objective was to continue securing exclusive access to a steady and cheap supply of agricultural produce.

In these conditions, were farmers helpless victims? Farmers were willing partners in a deal that secured a precious source of grain and seeds in times of dearth.[52] Foreclosure through the expulsion of indebted farmers would have broken the relationship and would have been detrimental to both parties. Hence, neither debts nor latifundialism, if such a notion is at all appropriate, led to destitution. Landlordism was nothing more than a credit operation.[53] As long as the economy was not integrated into a market which turned land into a commodity, farmers worked "their" land, whatever their financial situation. This is the

beginning of the harvest. Prices would then peak at sowing time and again at the end of winter. Smaller farmers on the brink of starvation bore all the brunt of the price low since they were desperate to sell produces immediately; see Latron, *Vie*, 124–25. At Nuzi (middle of the second millennium B.C.E.), the value of one homer of barley fluctuated between half a shekel of silver and four shekels; see Eichler, *Indenture*, 15 n. 29.

51. In Africa and other developing regions, a new idea is being developed to overcome this very problem, one which is based on the principle of a finance house buying produce from growers at a discount but with a clause entitling the seller to buy back the produce at the same price at any moment. The produce is kept in a bonded warehouse or silo by a third party and checked for quality and quantity by an independent inspector. The finance house issues fixed-interest warrants backed by the assets they have purchased and are keeping in store. These warrants are sold to investors worldwide. As soon as the farmer reclaims his goods, the warrants are redeemed. The farmer reclaims and sells his goods on the commodity market when the prices appear the most favourable to him. Everyone benefits: the farmer gets the best prices for his goods, the warrant buyers get good fixed interest, the finance house makes a margin sufficient to cover its costs with a reasonable margin (which the farmer pays) and the warehouse and inspection companies get business too.

52. Doumani, *Palestine*, 161. During the Islamic era, cheapness was maintained by advanced purchase through *salam* contracts by which money was advanced for future delivery of a set amount of produce at the time of harvest regardless of the market price at the time of delivery. See ibid., 131–36.

53. Warriner, "Tenure," 77.

fellah's ultimate concern. Patronage is established,[54] and the creditor provides security to his farmers in case of famine while gaining exclusive access to surpluses during good years. The creditor has no interest in removing indebted farmers from the land.[55] Hence debts did not lead to slavery and dislocation. This only happened once land became a commodity, either due to its scarcity following demographic pressure or due to major transformation of the economy following irrigation for the production of cash crops and the integration of the local economy into an international market.[56] None of these factors were prevalent in Palestine before the Ptolemaic era. Leviticus 25 reflects a system in which land was not a commodity and debts did not lead to foreclosure and loss of land. The principle of land inalienability in Lev 25:23 was faithfully transmitted through Islamic law to the Ottoman Empire, which considered most arable land *miri* land (State land). The notion of private land ownership is excluded *de jure* when the land is YHWH's or the sultan's. For this reason, Pg consistently refers to land tenure which regulates land use and dispenses with ownership. Tenure is inalienable and cannot be lost through debts precisely because it is not ownership.

The question, then, is: What kind of return is implied by the Jubilee if debts did not remove tenants from their land? The answer is provided in Lev 25:14–16:

> When you pledge something or someone to your fellow do not cheat each other. The number of years until the Jubilee will regulate the amount secured by the pledge. The amount will be proportional to the years until the Jubilee since what you are pledging is only the produce.

54. B. Lang, "The Social Organization of Peasant Poverty in Biblical Israel," in his *Anthropological Approaches to the Old Testament* (Sheffield: Almond, 1985), 83–99.

55. R. Westbrook, "Patronage in the Ancient Near East," *JESHO* 48 (2005): 210–33.

56. Increase in the value of agricultural produce strengthens the desire to own or at least control land; see C. Isawy, *An Economic History of the Middle East and North Africa* (New York: Columbia University Press, 1982), 138. In developing countries today and in recent history, farmers fall into the hands of traders who supply the inputs, take a pledge on the land (in biblical times a pledging assign or antichretic pledge), buy the farmers' crops (deducting the value of the inputs from the sale price) and then sell the produce at a profit because they are able to transport, store and market in optimal conditions, all of which the farmers cannot do. The farmers fall into this pattern of dependency and the merchants maintain a delicate balance between the extent to which they can exploit the farmers and their need to ensure the farmers earn just enough to keep the system going.

The return of each one to his tenure implies that the Jubilee marks the maturity of antichretic loans presented here as buying and selling to a fellow Israelite. Much confusion has risen from too narrow an understanding of these verbs. The root מכר should not be restricted to selling since it covers all aspects of business transactions, as does the Assyrian *tamkāru*. As explained above, merchants were also lenders. For this reason, מכר is better rendered here as "to trade." It is clear from Lev 25:23 that ארץ לא תמכר cannot mean "the land you will not sell" since the Israelites as tenants are not the owners of the land (YHWH is the owner). Nevertheless, exegetes often postulate the selling of freehold properties without realizing that it contradicts the notion of tenure. Trading or bartering[57] tenure is not equivalent to selling land, but corresponds to pledging shares of usufruct.[58]

The next word (צמתת) in the crucial phrase והארץ לא תמכר לצמתת is rendered as "the land shall not be sold in perpetuity" (NRSV), following Vulgate's *perpetuum*. However, the LXX's εἰς βεβαίωσιν ("guarantee, certainty, absolutely, consolidation") conveys no temporal sense. It is a technical expression in contracts denoting what guarantees a sale.[59] Milgrom chooses the sense of silence attested by Lam 3:53, and translates the crucial phrase as "the land shall not be sold beyond reclaim," in accordance with *HALOT*, which argues that cognate languages allow two meanings in Hebrew, either "to destroy," or "to silence." The link between "silence" and "reclaim" is tenuous and is dictated by the need to harmonize this verse with the next ones dealing with redemption.[60] Yet,

---

57. Syriac *mkr*, "to barter, betroth, espouse"; see J. Payne Smith, ed., *A Compendious Syriac Dictionary* (Winona Lake: Eisenbrauns, 1998), 272.

58. J. P. Weinberg, "The Word *ndb* in the Bible," in *Solving Riddles and Untying Knots* (ed. Z. Zevit, S. Gitin and M. Sokoloff; Winona Lake: Eisenbrauns, 1995), 365–75 (373) argues that the people not deported to Babylonia were organized by "community named by toponyms." However, this could simply be the result of tradition by which village communities are characterized by a strong bond with their place of origin and from which every male expected to inherit some kind of right of land use should he need it, quite independent of actual ownership categories; see Doumani, *Palestine*, 156–57. The place of origin also had important repercussions on one's status, rights and duties. For Egypt, see R. Taubenschlag, "Citizens and Non-citizens in the Papyri," in *Opera Minora* (Warsawa: Państwowe wydawnictwo naukowe, 1959), 211–22.

59. P. Chantraine, *Dictionnaire étymologique de la langue grecque* (Paris: Klincksieck, 1968), 172. Wis 6:18; *3 Macc* 5:42: D. Pralon, "Le style de Léviticus des Septantes," in *La Bible d'Alexandrie 3* (ed. P. Harlé and D. Pralon; Paris: Cerf, 1988), 47–81.

60. Milgrom, III, 2184.

unredeemable sales are designated as *ana dārâti* in Susa,[61] and as *ʿolam* at Ugarit, Elephantine and Wadi Daliyeh.[62] The common meanings of √צמת as "to draw together, pull together, assemble, collect, bundle, transfer real estate"[63] make better sense here, and I translate the entire phrase as "the land must not be traded as freehold because the land is mine." This verse forbids the transfer of land leading to the formation of consolidated estates (collections). When land is pledged for antichretic loans, loans are secured by pledging the usufruct or the yield of a number of land shares for a given time as stipulated in Lev 25:14–16,[64] while the land itself remains inalienable. The idea is that credit operations must not allow creditors to take permanent control of arable land.

The LXX renders Lev 25:23 differently, "the land will not be sold as surety," forbidding the use of land which the Hebrew text allows. This reflects a much harsher economic situation where indenture did lead to seizure of land and the transfer of debtors to slave markets. The Zeno papyri attest the transfer of numerous Palestinian slaves whose land was turned into *kleroi* granted to Greek settlers.[65] The *Letter of Aristeas*

---

61. R. Westbrook, *Property and the Family in Biblical Law* (JSOTSup 113; Sheffield: Sheffield Academic Press, 1991), 106.

62. See D. M. *The Samaria Papyri from Wadi Daliyeh* (DJD 28; Oxford: Clarendon, 2001), 31.

63. *HALOT*, 3:1035–36. On *ṣamata*, "transfer of ownership," at Ugarit, see R. Westbrook, "Social Justice and Creative Jurisprudence in Late Bronze Syria," *JESHO* 44 (2001): 26 n. 7. On Assyrian *simtu*, "to befit, belong," and *šimtu*, "ownership mark, branding iron," and *šīmtu*, "original amount, principle," see *CAD* 15:281, 17:10–11, 19. On Levantine Arabic *smt*, "price," or *ṣmt*, "to cheat a buyer on price or quality," see Barthélemy, *Dictionnaire*, 356, 445. On Samaritan *ṣmt*, "to assemble, collect, gather," see A. Tal, *A Dictionary of Samaritan Aramaic* (HdO 1/50; 2 vols.; Leiden: Brill, 2000), 2:735–36, and *ṣimmūt*, "meeting, conjunction?," see Powels, "Calendar," 734. On Maghribi Arabic *msāmta*, "contiguity," and *ṣmt*, "to become solid, firm, to coagulate, to thicken," used for cheese, concrete, boiled eggs and cooked wine, see A.-L. de Prémare et al., *Dictionaire Arabe–Français* (Paris: L'Harmattan, 1996), 6:182, 8:101.

64. K. Veenhof, "Old Assyrian Period," in Westbrook and Jasnow, eds., *Security for Debt*, 93–160 (128). A variety of unspecific words were used in connection with pledges: *šapartum*, from a root designating "to manage, administer, direct"; *erubbātum* or *erābum*, from a verb "to enter." A. Skaist, "Emar," in Westbrook and Jasnow, eds., *Security for Debt*, 237–50 (237–38), suggests *amēlūtu, mazzazānu, maškanu, qātātu*.

65. *CPJ* 1:128–30 reports a failed attempt to seize a pledge. Also PCZ 59093 and 59804; see X. Durand, *Des Grecs en Palestine au IIIème siècle avant Jésus-Christ* (Paris: Gabalda, 1997), 224–33. The traffic flourished already in the Late Bronze Age; see I. Márquez Rowe, "How Can Someone Sell His Own Fellow to the Egyptians?," *VT* 54 (2004): 335–43.

mentions the freeing of over 100,000 Jewish slaves as part of a bargain leading to the translation of the LXX (*Let. Aris.* 12–27). Whatever the historicity of the bargain, it can safely be assumed that slavery was a major issue at Alexandria at the time of the translation, and it is not surprising to find that Lev 25:23 LXX is more restrictive than its Hebrew *Vorlage*. Before the Ptolemaic era, however, the pledging of the usufruct of the land was not threatening. In fact, it was the only way to secure credit.

Antichresis

Once מכר and צמת are understood as referring to pledging and mortgaging the products of the land rather than to the sale of the land itself, the Jubilee does not imply the return of ex-land owners to their land but as the term of all credit operations. In theory, antichretic loans imply the use of the mortgaged property by the mortgagee in lieu of interest payments. It is a contractual term whereby a borrower (obligor, obligator, debtor) temporarily transfers (assigns) possession of goods or property to a lender (creditor) who retains the yield (revenues, interest, usufruct) derived from the assets (goods, land, animal or person)[66] during the tenor (period) of the debt (loan, obligation) up until the reimbursement (refund, maturity) of the debt.

Mesopotamian contracts distinguish two types of pledges. Possesory pledge (or pledging assign) is the most common in case of subsistence loans.[67] The lender uses the land in question rent-free in exchange for an interest free loan.[68] When the borrower defaults, the land remains under

---

66. Verses 47–54 apply to people the principle of land pledges in antichretic loan arrangements, in exact parallelism to vv. 14–28. As other productive assets, people and animals could be pledged as land was. In the absence of early reclaim, all pledged persons were released from their obligations of service on the Jubilee since the loan calculated on the basis of the remaining years until the Jubilee was fully reimbursed by then.

67. R. Westbrook, "Old Babylonian Period," in Westbrook and Jasnow, eds., *Security for Debt*, 63–92 (66). Antichretic pledge does not appear to be used for commercial loans; see Veenhof, "Old Assyrian Period," 100, 133.

68. Examples at Ugarit are discussed in I. Márquez Rowe, "The King's Men at Ugarit," *JESHO* 41 (2002): 1–19. The *mazzazânu*-pledges at Nuzi are discussed in Eichler, *Indenture*, 89, who translates one text as follows: "(27'–29') Concerning the interest on his capital, he stationed house, field, orchard, (or) domestics as a *mazzazânu*-pledge (39'–38'). When he brings the capital, he may enter his house; when he brings the capital, he may stand in his field; when he brings the capital, he may claim (?) his orchard; when he brings the capital, he may take his slave girl; when he brings the capital, his slave may return to him."

the control of the lender, unless it is redeemed by the borrower's kin. In hypothecary pledge (or hypothecate assign), the land is surety for a loan with interest; its use remains in the hand of the borrower unless he defaults. At that moment only, the creditor takes control of the pledged item. In practice, both types have similar consequences since in most cases the lender asked the borrower to work the pledged land in exchange for a portion of the yield.

The legal distinction between hypothecary and possessory pledge was irrelevant to peasants whose relationship to the land remained the same. From his point of view, the *fellah* considered the land as his own, based on the simple fact that he used it.[69] The creditor's share of the crop ranged from one-fifth to four-fifths of the produce depending on the fertility of the land, on who provided seeds and traction and who paid the taxes. In practice, pledge of land use is a kind of land lease.[70] The Jubilee system regulates loans and entails the reimbursement of the principal by small tenants who, having little else to offer, pledge their tenure and through their work pay back the loan by setting aside a portion of the yield. Since the size of the loan is tied to the number of harvests until the Jubilee, both parties have the assurance that principal and interests will be paid in full.[71] When entering into any capital loan arrangement, borrower and lender, knowing exactly when the next Jubilee will be, fix the size of the loan accordingly. This requires understanding the "count of years after the Jubilee" (v. 15) as the number of years *until* the next Jubilee.[72] The fewer years to run, the lower the loan, because there are fewer harvests ahead. The number of years left to run before the next Jubilee determines the maximum value of loans corresponding to a fair "return" (yield in harvests) on that capital. The mathematics is extremely simple and the

69. Doumani, *Palestine*, 156–57. In Islamic law, the notion of ownership corresponds to the right to use.

70. Radner, "Neo-Assyrian Period," 271. In modern practice, a farmer approaches a merchant to borrow seed, tools, food, etc. The lender takes as a pledge the use of all or part of the tenure land of the borrower and pays himself back by keeping all or part of the produce that the land yields. In addition, he will require the borrower to work for him, full or part time. When the loan has been fully repaid (in kind), the lender returns the pledge to the borrower and ceases to receive any of the produce that the land yields. Ancient practice differed only by accepting the slaves or kin of the borrower as pledge besides land.

71. R. J. D. Knauth, "Debt Release: Cancelled, Suspended or Completed?," forthcoming in *ZABR*. Knauth shows that the debt was paid off by the beginning of the Jubilee. Prior to that, it was possible to redeem the debt-slave and/or property with an amount pro-rata in relation to the number of years left until the Jubilee.

72. Milgrom, III, 2178.

fact that every transaction is limited in time delineates clearly each party's interest and obligations. The Jubilee provides a yardstick for the term of the loan and for the usufruct of the pledged item. The value of the loan is easy to determine (in number of years of average yield); borrowing and lending cannot exceed the remaining years left before expiration of the contract (date of the next Jubilee). In such a system, it would be a foolish lender indeed who would make funds available to a borrower over and above the value of the expected yield (in number of harvests). There may be minimal shortfalls if the yields have been poor, but that is the risk the lender is taking.[73]

The whole point and beauty of the Jubilee is that it regulates credit through the pledging assign mechanism and thus eliminates the need for debt cancellation because the size of loans is proportional to the number of harvests that can be realized on the usufruct of the land pledged to secure the loan before the full usufruct is returned to its tenant. Borrowers worked the land they had pledged since they had no other foreseeable resources. The Jubilee is highly practical since farmers rarely need to borrow for long tenors (i.e. for periods beyond one year or two at the most). Today, a farmer would indeed borrow over a longer period to finance the acquisition of machinery, buildings and so on, but in biblical times (as in developing countries today), the vast majority of farmers were small-holders whose main concern was to find the resources to cultivate the next crop. So, a small-holder would need finance to procure seed, to buy oxen to pull his plough, to acquire a few basic implements to dig, hoe and harvest. Admittedly, the cost of oxen might have to be spread over more than one year, but the other costs can all be amortized within the growing season.

Taking into account the seventh years, the longest a farmer would need to borrow is seldom likely to stretch to more than two, maybe three years. Unless the Jubilee is less than three years away or there occurs some unforeseen event (drought, pests, natural catastrophe, raids and plundering) which might prevent him from repaying his loan, the whole notion of debt remission is an abstract concept that cannot concern the farmer. The Jubilee does not deal with such emergencies. The שמטה of Deut 15 takes care of those *force majeure* emergencies by releasing arrears due on survival loans to small farmers, as was the case in Mesopotamia,[74] but on a seven-year basis. With the Jubilee-linked scale

73. The risk that the security may remain unproductive is different from default: Westbrook, "Old Babylonian," 69.

74. Sale documents often state clearly whether the sale was completed during a year of famine or war; see C. Zaccagnini, "War and Famine at Emar," *Orientalia* 64

based on the residual value of the usufruct or produce of the land, the borrower is released from having to work for the lender on the assigned land because the "lease" has come to an end at the Jubilee since the debt is paid back fully through the assign mechanism. The use of the pledged land reverts to the family to whom it was originally allocated. A royal office responsible for the preservation of order and stability through *mišarum* and *andarārum* edicts[75] is not necessary. Note that there is no suggestion of duress. Credit is an essential ingredient to a healthy economy. Credit is regulated by the calendar. The horn blown on 10 VII of the 49th year signals that all contracts have reached their term.[76] Such proclamation on the day of Kippurim sets the Jubilee on a par with the Flood and the azazel ritual,[77] as a purgation of the economy.

The calendar is blind to individual and political considerations. Removed from the hands of the king who used it for prestige or to quench social crisis,[78] the cyclical Jubilee establishes a mathematical basis for the exact calculation of loans, which is in sharp contrast to the ethical position encouraged by Deuteronomy. Taking into account personal situations, family links, moral and religious obligations develops networks of clients and obligees, while a mathematical economy sets the basis of an impartial justice that needs not favour the poor (Lev 19:15 Ps). Rather than showing kindness to the poor, it curbs clientelism. For this reason, the fear of YHWH, the promise of security and prosperity in exchange of observance of divine laws (Lev 25:17–22; 26)[79] are unmistakable marks of Deuteronomistic theology (Deut 15:6) and are secondary additions to the Pg text.

(1995): 96–100, which indicates recognition of particular conditions for redemption. Tablet TBR 65:6 from Emar states than the sale of a paternal house was done during a year of famine. Westbrook, "Justice," 24–27, is unable to explain why the final clause states that if the buyers say to the sellers, "I do not take your house," the buyers have no claim to the silver (ll. 14–16). The contract anticipates what the two parties had agreed upon, namely, that the buyers would leave the sellers in the house, probably in order to work the land around it for them.

75. C. Simonetti, "Die Nachlaßedikte in Mesopotamien und im antiken Syrien," in *Das Jobeljahr im Wandel* (ed. G. Scheuermann; Würzburg: Echter, 2000), 5–54.

76. Likewise, share-cropping contracts in Mandate Syria expired on 14 September; see Latron, *Vie*, 57.

77. R. S. Kawashima, "The Jubilee Year and the Return of Cosmic Purity," *CBQ* 65 (2003): 370–89.

78. Y. Amit, "The Jubilee Law—An Attempt at Instituting Social Justice," in *Justice and Righteousness* (ed. H. G. Reventlow; JSOTSup 137; Sheffield: JSOT Press, 1992), 47–59 (52).

79. Lohfink, "Abänderung," 129–36.

Pg's notion of sanctity applied exclusively to time is delineated through cycles of weeks, years, weeks of years and weeks of weeks of years.[80] Humans stop on the Sabbath, as did Elohim. The seventh year is a stop for the land, freeing the *fellahin* to clear uncultivated land, increasing production and reducing the threat of famine. The Jubilee is not a year but a point set on the day of Kippurim every seventh sabbatical year to mark the maturity of all loans and the return of all pledges. The very good of creation is restored periodically by a set of practical measures that belong neither to utopia nor to a nostalgic attempt to restore an original state of purity. Chaos is ever present, but it is not menacing, as long as each purgation cycle is completed. The azazel ritual enacted yearly on the Day of purgations expels sins. On the same day, every 49 years, all pledges return to their owners. The sabbatical calendar is the thread that runs through Pg and provides a coherence that culminates in Lev 25. The description of the regular land-clearing operations of the sabbatical year and the financial system of the Jubilee is the practical application of the principles enunciated in the Creation story and the Flood narrative. The themes of time and land announced in Gen 1:1 find their most concrete explanation in the sabbatical year and the Jubilee. The Jubilee is the nexus of the sabbatical calendar and of the land; the land is understood here in a most down-to-earth way as the food-producing soil.

Recapitulation

The first five chapters of this study have sought to demonstrate that a number of Priestly passages in the Pentateuch are better understood when they are read in the light of the sabbatical calendar. With exactly 52 weeks, the value of this calendar is upheld in the books of *Enoch*, *Jubilees* and in some Dead Sea Scrolls. The use of the sabbatical calendar in the Bible is usually considered unlikely. In my view, however, it is undisputable.

Chapter 1 recovers the significance of the Sabbath as the crown of creation. The main thrust of Gen 1 is the sanctification of the seventh day and the rejection of the lunar calendar.

Chapter 2 maintained that the Sabbath is the first unit of a complete calendar which with an elaborate intercalation scheme. Hinted at with

---

80. Kawashima, "Jubilee Year," 386. Sabbatical years are mentioned in 1 Macc 6:49; *Ant.* 12.9.5, 378; 14.10.6, 202, 206 (remission of tribute by Julius Caesar); 14.16.2, 475; 15.1.2, 7.

Enoch's age, the two stages of intercalation are concealed in Abraham's lifespan and the size of the curtains of the Residence.

Chapter 3 spelled out the validity of the sabbatical calendar hypothesis by testing it in the Flood narrative, the classical chronological conundrum of the Bible. The validity of the hypothesis is confirmed by its ability to account for several difficult points and to solve the *crux interpretum* of Shem's age two years after the Flood (Gen 11:10).

Chapter 4 exposed the overall chronology of the Pg document in seven eras, all based on the sabbatical calendar.

Chapter 5 applied the principles of the sabbatical calendar to the festival calendar presented in Lev 23 and put it in relation to narratives explaining the origin and meaning of Pesaḥ, Massot and Yom Kippur. The function of Teruah is tied to the intercalation of the sabbatical calendar. It informs the population whether or not the current year is a leap year and how many weeks are intercalated.

The study continued in the present chapter with the sabbatical year and Jubilee in Lev 25. It was in this chapter that a new understanding of the sabbatical year was offered. The Jubilee was not a long holiday, but a Sabbath for the land which frees manpower for major land-reclaim projects. The Jubilee is explained as the term of all financial operations rather than as a system of debt-release. An obvious outworking of the sabbatical calendar, the seventh year and the Jubilee are the nexus of the themes of time and land mentioned in Gen 1:1, the incipit of Pg.

The importance of such analysis for the exegesis of the Pentateuch is limited, until the sabbatical calendar is brought in relation to Priestly passages. I postulate that the Priestly document (Pg) is built upon the sabbatical calendar, presenting in narrative form its creation and intercalation (Gen 1; 5–9; 25; Exod 36), its festivals (Exod 12; 16; Lev 16; 23; Josh 5) and its practical economic applications (Lev 25). The sabbatical calendar provides an external criterion for the identification of Pg and its isolation from Priestly material. Thanks to the sabbatical calendar, Pg's theological profile is more sharply defined. Many additions can be identified and explained as calendrical or theological alterations of Pg and its sabbatical scheme. Pg thus becomes an exegetical tool to sort "Priestly" texts between Pg and Ps. The delimitation of Pg, however, is far from being an established fact. Part II of this study tries to clarify the contours and the end of the Priestly narrative.

Part II

LAND AS A MAJOR THEME OF THE PRIESTLY DOCUMENT

Chapter 7

THE LAND IN GENESIS

The first section of Pg's narrative, now part of the book of Genesis, is structured as a list of Toldot (תולדות), a difficult concept formed from ילד√, meaning "to give birth, to be born." The Toldot introduce the presentation of the offspring of a particular ancestor and the narration of events more or less connected with that figure. The LXX renders the term Toldot as "genesis," which has the advantage of retaining the ambiguity of the Hebrew and requires no further translation since it has passed directly into European languages.[1] The formula "these are the Toldot" (אלה תולדות) occurs twelve times in the Pentateuch, eleven times in Genesis.[2] There is a twelfth Toldot in Num 3:1, which is usually excluded from Pg, and a last one in Ruth 4:18 for Perez. The structuring function of the Toldot formulae makes them ideal hooks on which redactors can add material, as happened in the case of Esau, who has two Toldot formulae (Gen 36:1, 9), and in Num 3, where Aaron and Moses' Toldot appear in the context of the census enumerating the twelve tribes of Israel.[3] There is general agreement that two of the Toldot formulae are secondary, but not over which ones.[4]

1. S. Tengström, *Die Toledotformel* (Uppsala: C. W. K. Gleerup, 1981), 58.
2. B. Renaud, "Les généalogies et la structure de l'histoire sacerdotale dans le livre de la Genèse," *RB* 97 (1990): 5–30; P. Weimar, "Die Toledot-Formel in der priesterschriftlichen Geschichtsdarstellung," *BZ* 18 (1974): 65–93.
3. See the discussion in D. T. Olson, *The Death of the Old and the Birth of the New* (Chico, Calif.: Scholars Press, 1985), 98–114.
4. W. Eichrodt, *Die Quellen der Genesis von neuem untersucht* (Giessen: Töpelmann, 1916), 20–23, 52–54; O. Eissfeldt, "Biblos Geneseōs," *Kleine Schriften* III, (Tübingen: J. C. B. Mohr, 1966), 459; J. Scharbert, "Der Sinn der Toldot-Formel in der Priesterschrift," in *Wort–Gebot–Glaube* (ed. H. J. Stoebe; Zürich: Zwingli, 1970), 45; Tengström, *Toledotformel*, 32–34, and Renaud, "Généalogies," 7, consider Gen 36:9 original. P. Weimar, "Struktur und Komposition der priesterschriftlichen Geschichtsdarstellung," *BN* 23 (1984): 81–134 (88 n. 28), prefers Gen 36:1.

Excluding Ishmael and Esau's Toldot, Tengström displays the common bias, which favours Isaac against Ishmael and Jacob over against Esau. In this regard, Pg is strikingly different; it never depreciates Ishmael or Esau and for this very reason it has provoked strong redactional reactions. Ishmael and Esau's Toldot clearly continue the process of land distribution in Northern Arabia and in Edom (Gen 25:12–15; 36:40–43). The least invasive solution is to reduce the present list of twelve Toldot to ten by simply removing Num 3:1 and Esau's second Toldot (Gen 36:9).[5] The most cogent argument in favour of an original list of ten Toldot is the internal evidence provided by the lists of ante- and post-diluvian ancestors in Gen 5 and 11 which are ten generations deep.[6] Since the Toldot of the skies and the land (Gen 2:4a) are placed as a postscript, rather than as a title and since they are followed immediately by a second Toldot in Gen 5:1, the whole of Gen 2:4 has sometimes been considered post-Pg.[7] Yet, the first Toldot had to be positioned as a postscript because placing it at the beginning of the narrative would have prevented imitating the absolute beginning of *Enuma eliš*: "When on high." The cluster "on the day of YHWH's making…" (ביום עשות יהוה) in Gen 2:4b cannot belong to the same layer as v. 4a since Gen 1 insists that heavens and land were created by *Elohim* in *seven* days. For this reason, the Toldot of the skies and of the land in Gen 2:4a have to be retained as the conclusion of Pg's Creation narrative. These Toldot, as the other Toldot, share a common concern for seed and land.

Elohim Created the Land (Genesis 1:1)

The Creation narrative in Gen 1:1–2:4a deals with the separation of day/night, above/below, wet/dry and with the calendar (see Chapter 1). Right at the outset, the land (הארץ) is mentioned next to the skies. Most translations render ארץ as "earth," presenting Gen 1:1 as the origin of the planet earth and of the entire universe. Yet, Hebrew has a variety of words to denote the universe or the world in a broad sense (עולם, חבל). If the skies (rather than the heavens) and the land are indeed a *merismus*

---

5. Pg's Toldot remain the fundamental structural element of the book of Genesis in its final form; see Hieke, *Genealogien*, 241–51.

6. Lohfink, "Priestly Narrative," 151 n. 38.

7. T. Stordalen, "Genesis 2,4: Restudying a locus classicus," *ZAW* 104 (1992): 163–77 (173); see D. Carr, "BIBLOS GENESEWS Revisited," *ZAW* 110 (1998): 159–72. Yet, the juxtaposition of two similar elements does not imply that they collide.

for the entire creation,[8] אֶרֶץ stands for the element "earth" rather than for the planet of the same name. This point is confirmed by the next verse, where the land and the waters are already two separate entities, indicating that the land does not include the waters. Pg consistently distinguishes the land from the waters.

The *merismus* "skies and land" compounds the furthest (skies) and the closest (land), or better, the unbound with the measured. This may seem strange to modern readers who are accustomed to reading Gen 1 as cosmology. At first sight, the cosmological reading of Gen 1 is supported by parallel in the title phrase of *Enuma eliš* (I:1) which is rendered as "When on high no name was given to heaven, nor below was the netherworld called by name…"[9] However, the word translated as "netherworld" is *ammatum*, literally a cubit rather than the expected *dannatum*, "firm land, ground, bottom of a foundation pit," or *erṣetum*, "land, territory, netherworld, district, quarter of a city, soil, ground."

The use of *ammatum* insists that the matching member to the heavens is first and foremost the measurable plot of land.[10] With אֶרֶץ, Gen 1 parallels this concept exactly, focusing more on agriculture than on the cosmos. In spite of the dictionaries' claims of the contrary, Hebrew *ereṣ* and Akkadian *erṣetum* do not convey a cosmic sense.[11] These words do not even encompass the entire dry land, in spite of v. 10, which equates אֶרֶץ with יבשׁה. Dry land includes two large sub-categories, the uncultivated steppe between settlements used for grazing (מדבר) and the cultivated or domesticated land, itself divided as arable land, gardens, terraces, courtyards, middens, wine presses, threshing floors, rural or urban houses. The use of each category of land is regulated by particular regulations (see Lev 25). Of course, the existence of legal accuracy does not prevent looser usage of the term elsewhere. Yet, the import of אֶרֶץ in Gen 1:1 is lost when it is equated with the entire cosmos or the planet earth. Right from the outset, the words בראשׁית and אֶרֶץ state the central

8. See the discussion and bibliography in Bauks, *Amfang*, 107–9.

9. *CoS* 1:111.

10. *The Babylonian Theodicy* (line 58) also pairs the heavens with *ammatum*. W. G. Lambert, *Babylonian Wisdom Literature* (Oxford: Clarendon, 1960), 305, justifies its translation as "earth" by drawing a dubious parallel with Hebrew אדמה. *Ammatum* belongs to the technical language of the Kudurrus; see D. Charpin, "Chroniques bibliographiques 2," *RA* 96 (2002): 169–91 (178). Thanks to Antoine Cavigneaux for this reference.

11. The examples supplied by *CAD* in support of the cosmic sense of *erṣetu* are rather weak since they concern "foundations, insemination, rivers, produce, signs," and all pertain better to soil than to the planet.

themes of the entire Pg composition: time (or rhythm) and land. Obviously, scholars keen to prove that Pg ends before the sons of Israel enter the land of Canaan do not stress the point.

All mentions of the land within the creation story confirm that every occurrence of the word *ereṣ* is territorial rather than planetary. After the initial verses, the land appears on day 3 (four times) as the agent of germination of the vegetation, clearly linked with seeds. On day 4, one of the functions of the luminaries and of the stars on the surface of the dome is to bring light on the *land*.[12] On day 5, the land hosts the multiplication of birds who fly over the *land*. The seven mentions of the land on day six refer to the creation of land animals, which come forth from the *land* as the plants did. Land is the territory where terrestrial animals, birds and humans live, the necessary habitat for their seed to multiply.

Human multiplication is also the theme of Adam's Toldot in Gen 5, a multiplication stalled by the Flood. The Flood is not caused by overpopulation but by the filling of the *land* with violence (Gen 6:11), which rendered the land unsuitable for multiplication. After the Flood, Elohim gives a sign of the ברית, which he establishes between him and the *land* (Gen 9:13), not simply with Noah and his sons.

One Land—One People: Genesis 10

The Toldot of Noah's sons introduce the so-called Table of Nations in Gen 10 which contains 73 (MT) or 75 (LXX) names. The identification of J and P elements in this chapter is undisputed thanks to the clear structure of the Pg text. P distributes the descendants of Noah's sons across the surface of the then known lands:[13] Japheth's sons and grandsons to the north and the Mediterranean islands, Hamites to the south and Semites to the east, from the vantage point of a narrator standing in Canaan. The presentation of each group is closed by a summary (Gen 10:5, 20, 31) stressing the neatness of the arrangement whereas each family inhabits its own land and speaks its own language. Post-diluvian multiplication is depicted as a harmonious spread over the land which fosters individuation,

---

12. Such light may also be divinatory, enabling weather forecast and foretelling of future events; see B. Halpern, "Assyrian and pre-Socratic Astronomies and the Location of the Book of Job," in *Kein Land für sich allein* (ed. U. Hübner and E. A. Knauf; Fribourg: Universitätsverlag; Göttingen: Vandenhoeck & Ruprecht, 2002), 255–64.

13. Blenkinsopp, *Pentateuch*, 88. H. Cazelles, "Table des peuples, nations et modes de vie," in *Biblica et semitica* (ed. L. Cagni; Napoli: Istituto universitario orientale, 1999), 67–79.

a principle reflecting the separation of elements of creation rather than the violence of the antediluvian situation.

After a series of plural forms of the word "land" (e.g. "in their lands"), the conclusion in Gen 10:32 returns to the singular to note that all the families of Noah's sons spread in the land. Translations of the singular as "earth" while the plurals in the previous verses are rendered as "lands" muddle Pg's careful use of vocabulary. Land and day are precise categories. As the day does not include the night (separated on day 1), the land does not include the sea (separated on day 3). Hence our modern notion of "the earth" is improperly broad. Pg's Table of Nations uses ethnography to write geography. The various ethnic groups portion out the land of Gen 1:1 into their lands, each one with its particular dialect. The scarcity of grandsons, in particular among Semites, underlines how precarious the process is. Once the land of Gen 1 is shared out into lands, the focus shifts to one of those lands and its relation to the last un-landed human group.

Abraham: Burial Tenure

The Toldot of Noah's sons (Gen 10:1–32) are followed by Shem's, which, contrary to the previous Toldot, do not mention land at all, thus stressing the abnormality of a landless group. Shem's Toldot close with the birth of Abram, Nahor and Haran (Gen 11:26). The next verse introduces Terah's Toldot (Gen 11:27–25:10), which focus upon Abraham. Abraham has no Toldot of his own, since his lineage is under threat of extinction. Terah's Toldot depict a catastrophic scenario. Haran, Abram's brother, is the first human to die before his father, leaving three orphans behind. Nahor marries one of his orphaned nieces. Abram takes care of his orphaned nephew since his wife is the first recorded barren woman. Terah is the first man to move away from the land of his birth and thus leaves Iscah, Nahor and Milcah behind (Gen 11:28–32). This first immigrant group moves out of Ur and settles in Haran until Abram, Sarai and Lot leave Terah and depart for the land of Canaan. This particular land bears the name of a sonless ancestor of Gen 10:6. Abram is thus called to move to a land bereft of its original male occupants. The whole of the Torah as it now stands preserves Pg's notion by never referring to a land of Israel, an expression that first appears in 1 Sam 13:9.[14]

Separation continues as Abram stays in Canaan while Lot settles the towns of the Kikkar (Gen 13:11). In the land of Canaan, Abraham buys a

14. Y. Leibowitz, *Peuple. Terre. Etat* (Paris: Plon, 1995), 161. The first occurrence is in 1 Sam 13:9.

burial tenure from the sons of Heth (Gen 17:17–20). What Abraham buys and what he then owns (לאברהם למקנה, Gen 23:18) is not land tenure that Abraham's seed will eventually receive for free. Abraham only buys a burial tenure (אחזת־קבר, Gen 23:20) because the land of Canaan is not empty at this point of the narrative. That the land is settled by Hittites rather than by Canaanites does not allow Abraham to claim land ownership. These Hittites are the legal settlers in the land of Canaan, maybe through marrying daughters of the sonless Canaan (see Gen 28:1), and thus the Hittites are the people of the *land* (Gen 23:7–10; 27:46). The mention of the trees in the field where the burial cave stands has been use to exclude Gen 23 from Pg because the divine promise (Gen 17) is not compatible with the requirement to buy land.[15] This line of argument misses Pg's precise legal categories. Burial tenure is not equivalent to land tenure, and tenure is *not* ownership. What is bought and then owned is the right of use (usufruct) which is duly transferable to the holder's legal heirs. Abraham buys the right to access the cave whenever he and his heirs have a dead body to dispose of. The Hittites sell the right of access to the cave, which seems to include the right for Abraham and his group to camp in front of the cave and for their herds to park and graze in and in the shade of the trees during burials and, by extension, during yearly burial-site rituals. However, the transaction does not modify Abraham's legal status in relation to the land of Canaan, which remains the land of his sojourns (Gen 17:8). Although Elohim promises to give him the entire land of Canaan, Abraham remains a migrant and resident (גר ותושב, Gen 23:4). Each actor's legal stand *vis-à-vis* access to land is carefully delineated.

Ishmael: Villages and Burial Tenure

That Ishmael has a Toldot of his own (Gen 25:12–17) while Abraham has none is a thorn in the flesh for Ps, which devotes chapters to the dismissal of Ishmael from the line of the "elects" (see Gen 21:8–21; 22). Yet, Pg clearly grants access to the land of Canaan to Ishmael, although the names of his offspring reflect a North Arabian proto-Bedouin political confederation.[16] As promised in Gen 17:20, Ishmael fathers twelve *rulers* (נשיאם, Gen 25:16) organized according to their ethnic groups

15. See Blum, *Komposition*, 441–46, referring to "Kauf der Höhle" and to "Übereignung des Landes."

16. E. A. Knauf, *Ismael* (Wiesbaden: Harrassowitz, 1989), 49; A. K. Grayson, *Assyrian and Babylonian Chronicles* (TCS 5; Locust Valley, N.Y.: J. J. Augustin, 1975), 106–10.

(לאמתם), villages (בחצריהם) and enclosures (בטירתם).[17] Although "vil-lage" and "enclosure" stem from roots conveying notions of fenced off areas, Lev 25:31 (Pg) explains that they still belong to the rural category where freehold is excluded in opposition to urban centres where houses are freehold possession (see Chapter 6). Non-urban location is crucial since it indicates that the Ishmaelites have no permanent settlements (משבים), in contrast to Esau's settlements in Transjordan (Gen 36:43) and those Jacob and his sons have in Egypt and in Canaan (Gen 31:1; Lev 23:3, 31). Ishmael retains legal access to the land of Abraham's sojourns (Gen 17:8), but since the Ishmaelite names sketch North Arabia, Pg's Ishmael keeps a foot on both sides of Wadi Arabah. For this reason, Ishmael is never said to move away from Canaan. Ishmaelites move back and forth but retain a stake in rural Canaan by having Ishmael buried at Machpelah with his father Abraham. The text does not mention Mach-pelah explicitly and only claims that Ishmael was "added to his people" (Gen 25:17 // 25:8, ויאסף אל־עמיו). However, rejecting the obvious fact that Ishmael's "people" refers to Abraham, whose bones rested in Machpelah (Gen 25:9), entails that Isaac was not buried in Machpelah either since Gen 36:29 uses the same expression for Ishmael and for Isaac's burials. Both Abraham's sons inherited their father's burial tenure at Machpelah.

Esau: Tenure in Edom

Isaac's Toldot (Gen 25:19*–35:29*) display seven occurrences of the word ארץ[18] in spite of the fact that it is mainly concerned with Esau and Jacob's marriages. Matrimony has major repercussions on access to land. Hence Rebekah insists that Jacob marries an Aramean cousin rather than a daughter of Canaan as Esau did. Jacob is thus sent away to Aram and returns just in time to join his brother and bury their father Isaac (Gen 35:29). Esau's Toldot follow immediately (Gen 36:1–43). The main thrust is Esau's departure from the land of Canaan as a consequence of his polygamy (see Gen 28:9) and the large offspring it entails. Isaac's group is split up into two clans. Esau's migration follows Lot's (Gen 13:6). Canaan is consistently presented as a land at the limit of its sup-porting capacity since it is already full of Hittites married to Canaanite women (Gen 23; 27:46; 28:1, 6). Esau's migration is total, leaving nothing behind. The land of Esau's destination is in front (מפני, Gen

17. Another rare word (see Num 31:10; Ezek 25:4; Mic 2:12; Ps 69:26; 1 Chr 6:39) attested mainly through Arabic *ṭawâr*.
18. Gen 27:46; 28:4; 31:18; 33:18; 35:6, 12 (×2).

36:6) of Jacob, a purposefully vague location. The SP and LXX transmit a *lectio facilior* which adds that it is away from Canaan,[19] which leaves open whether this entails the eastern side of Wadi Arabah.[20] The mention of the land of Canaan as the provenance of Esau's wealth just before the verb of departure does suggest that the mysterious land is *not* Canaan (רכש בארץ כנען וילך אל־ארץ). This is the main point. Since grazing grounds in the land of Canaan are insufficient to support both groups, Esau moves away voluntarily without animosity so as to make room for Jacob.[21]

The twelve Edomite sheikhs or tribal leaders (אלופים) denote a different social structure than that which existed among the Ishmaelites (Gen 25:12–17).[22] They head clans (משפחות) rather than ethnic groups (אמים, Gen 25:16), though the narrator's main interest is to stress the geographical distance which separates the Edomites from Canaan. Esau's departure could have been told after Jacob's descent into Egypt and the sons of Israel would still have entered an empty Canaan. For Pg, however, it is crucial to get rid of potential Edomites while Jacob is still in the land in order to de-legitimize later Edomite claims in Canaan. Esau's sons live in vague "places" (מקמות) compared to Ishmaelite villages and enclosures. The names of some Edomite sheikhs correspond to actual cities, farming tribes and Bedouin tribes in Transjordan, but Oholibamah (meaning "wherever my tent is") is a pun denoting the impossibility of locating Edomite territory.[23] The location of the mountain of Seir where Esau is said to have settled (Gen 36:8) is ambiguous. If Seir stands for the eastern side of the Rift Valley, Pg claims the entire Judean Negeb for the Judeans. If Seir is south of Hebron, Pg simply wants to secure the territory north of Hebron. In any event, there are certainly no forsaken firstborn sons[24] in Pg since Esau's descendants own land tenure away from Canaan (Gen 36:43), presumably through intermarriage with Ishmaelite cousins.

Contrary to Abraham, Sarah, Ishmael, Isaac and Jacob, Esau is not buried at Machpelah: he has no death notice, no lifespan. He is gone for good. Whereas Ishmael's burial at Machpelah is suggested by the

19. E. A. Knauf, "Genesis 36,1–43," in *Jacob* (ed. J.-D. Macchi and T. Römer; Geneva: Labor et Fides, 2001), 291–300 (294 n. 18).

20. Ibid., 295.

21. Lohfink, "Original Sins," 100–101.

22. See Knauf, "Genesis 36," 291–300.

23. Ibid., 297.

24. R. Syrén, *The Forsaken Firstborn* (JSOTSup 133; Sheffield: Sheffield Academic Press, 1993).

statement that he was gathered to his people, Esau's is not gathered to his people. When it comes to Esau, Pg's ecumenism[25] is exhausted because the group behind Pg had problems with the Edomites of their time. Pg allows Rebekah to unleash a tantrum against Esau's wives (Gen 27:46). Then Pg becomes ambiguous about the location of Esau's land tenure and completely silent about the location of his tomb. Land tenure, women and tombs are crucial issues.

Jacob: Tenure in Egypt

The last of Pg's ten Toldot are Jacob's (Gen 37:1*–50:13*). Contrary to expectations, Esau's departure does not lead to Jacob's final settlement in the land of Canaan but to a move to Egypt as Pg integrates the older traditions of the Exodus. The seven mentions of the word ארץ[26] in Jacob's Toldot refer to both Canaan and Egypt. Pg is as silent over the reasons for Jacob's departure from Canaan as it is concerning Abram's departure from Haran. Jacob gets hold of tenure in the land of Goshen, in the land of Egypt (Gen 47:27). This is the first occurrence of the "land of Egypt" in Pg, as Jacob settles there with his family (compare Gen 46:7). Pg is careful to distinguish the land which welcomes, feed and enables Israel to multiply, from the Egyptians (see Exod 1:13). Jacob's burial at Machpelah (Gen 50:51) ends the Toldot series and concludes the first part of Pg. The generational theme is exhausted once the sons of Israel have filled the land of Goshen (Gen 47:27; Exod 1:7). The second part of Pg is devoted to the attribution of a land to Jacob's sons, who remain the last landless group of Elohim's creation when they are enslaved by Pharaoh.

Summary

This brief overview of the Toldot reveals that the land theme is prominent. In Gen 1:1, Elohim created the land, not the planet earth. The Toldot of the heavens and the land focuses on the land as an agricultural rather than a cosmic entity. Land is what makes seeds sprout. The second Toldot introduces Adam's lineage. Although it does not describe the geographical distribution of antediluvian humanity, Gen 5 concludes with the filling of the land with violence which corrupts the land itself

---

25. A. de Pury, "Abraham: The Priestly Writer's 'Ecumenical' Ancestor," in *Rethinking the Foundations* (ed. S. L. McKenzie, T. Römer and H. H. Schmid; BZAW 294; Berlin: de Gruyter, 2000), 163–81.

26. Gen 37:1 (×2); 47:27 (×2), 28; 49:30; 50:13.

(Gen 6:11–12). The Toldot of Noah and his sons introduces a list of people which are in fact toponyms mapping out the various lands of the known world during the Persian era (Gen 10). Shem's Toldot heads another list of generations parallel to that of Adam. It ends like Gen 6:10 with the birth of triplets but presents no geography. The land theme becomes the lack of it. Terah's Toldot opens with the death of a son before his father and Sarai's sterility (Gen 11:28, 30–31). From then on, all Toldot are marked by the problem of the land resulting in migrations. Terah leaves Ur for Haran; Abram leaves Haran for Canaan; Lot separates from Abram; Esau moves away to Seir; Jacob goes to Paddan Aram due to a lack of suitable spouses to bear his offspring and then gets land tenure in Egypt. Who gets tenure where is the constant preoccupation of the second part of Pg in Genesis since the fulfilment of Elohim's call to be fruitful and multiply requires securing land to feed everyone's offspring.

Chapter 8

THE LAND IN EXODUS AND LEVITICUS

If the presence of the land theme in Genesis is inescapable, it might be considered less prominent in the following books, which are set for the most part in the wilderness. The first half of the book of Exodus still takes place in Egypt, however. The Exodus is caused by the enslavement of the sons of Israel, which is specified as brutal (פרך). The hard slavery (עבדה קשה) renders the lives of the sons of Israel bitter (וימררו), their breath shortened (קצר רוח), which prevented them from hearing their liberator (Exod 6:9). These elements mirror the violence that caused the Flood. Whereas the Flood was sparked off by a land filled with violence (Gen 6:11), the Exodus is caused by Egyptian brutality. The response to this violence is the escape of the slaves, a theme that has proved pregnant throughout history. Yet, liberation is a beautiful but hollow concept if it is not followed by the acquisition of land. Pg insists more on land than on liberation:

> Exod 1:7*The sons of Israel fructified. They teemed. They multiplied. The land was filled with them. 13Egypt enslaved them with brutality. 14They embittered their lives with a hard labour in mortar and brick and every kind of toil in the fields; brutal was the forced labour by which they enslaved them. 2:23*It lasted many days. The sons of Israel groaned because of the labour. They cried out. An outcry went up to the Elohim because of the labour. 24Elohim heard their groaning. Elohim remembered his treaty with Abraham, with Isaac and with Jacob. 25Elohim saw the sons of Israel. Elohim knew. 6:2 Elohim spoke to Moses. He ordered him, "I am YHWH, 3I let myself be seen by Abraham, Isaac and Jacob in El Shaddai, but by my name YHWH I was not known to them. 4Nevertheless, I will validate my treaty with them to give them the land of Canaan, the land of their sojourns in which they sojourned. 5Moreover, I have heard the groans of the sons of Israel, whom Egypt is enslaving. I have remembered my treaty. 6Therefore, order to the sons of Israel: 'I am YHWH, I will bring you out from under the burden of Egypt, I will deliver you from their slavery, I will redeem you with an outstretched arm and by great judgments. 7I will take you as my people; I will be your Elohim.

> You will know that I am YHWH your Elohim who is bringing you out
> from under the burden of Egypt. [8]I will make you enter the land which I
> swore to give to Abraham, to Isaac and to Jacob. I will give it to you as
> inheritance—I am YHWH.'" [9]Moses said so to the sons of Israel; but they
> did not hear because of the shortened breath and hard slavery. [10]YHWH
> said to Moses: [11]"Enter, speak to Pharaoh King of Egypt so he will send
> the sons of Israel out of his land!" [12]Moses said to YHWH: "If the sons of
> Israel did not listen to me, how will Pharaoh listen to me, since I am
> uncircumcised of lips?"

Liberation is hardly liberating if the manumitted slaves are not given the
physical means to fend for themselves. In this key passage, Pg presents
YHWH who appears for the first time as the one who will accomplish the
land grant promised by El-shaddai to Abraham and Jacob. Deliverance,
redemption, outstretched arm, oath, inheritance are nice theological pies
in the sky if they do not materialize through the control of a concrete
territory from which the ex-slaves can produce their daily bread. Land
remains the aim of the entire Exodus, which only ends when the sons of
Israel enter the land of Canaan.

It has been argued that the gift of the land was already accomplished
in Gen 17:8.[1] Hence, the need to realize the land promise—"I will give
you..." (Exod 6:8)—is downplayed in order to escape the conclusion
that any Exodus narrative ending before the entry into the land of Canaan
in Joshua is incomplete. Promise is equated with accomplishment. Such
a ploy is acceptable if one does not cultivate one's daily food. However,
the Pentateuch was not written in a modern university, but in a farming
economy where promises of land fill no stomachs.

The cycle of plagues (Exod 7:1*–14:29*), culminating with the death
of every Egyptian first-born, removes the sons of Israel from the *land* of
Egypt, a land rendered lethal in spite of its fertility by the hard slavery
imposed by Pharaoh. YHWH hardens Pharaoh's heart (קשה, Exod 7:3) as
the direct consequence of Pharaoh's hardening of the Israelites' conditions. The parallel displays Pg's notion of divine justice which does not
lash out in self-righteous wrath but treats an evil by the same evil (Gen
6:13; Num 14:28).

Once they cross the sea, the sons of Israel find themselves in the
wilderness, presented not as another land but as a no-land. This notion is
the mirror image of the Flood, which Pg treats as a chronological gap
(see Chapter 3). Pg has YHWH miraculously feeding the sons of Israel

---

1. The gift would even be confirmed by Gen 28:4; 35:12; Num 20:12; 27:12.
However, W. H. Schmidt, *Exodus* (BKAT 2; Neukirchen–Vluyn: Neukirchener
Verlag, 1974), 274–76, claims that v. 8 cannot be removed from vv. 6–12.

throughout the wilderness period with manna thereby removing the wilderness from the ordinary steppe roamed by herders and underlining the importance of the land through its absence: "they ate manna until their arrival to the limits of the *land* of Canaan" (Exod 16:35). The designation of manna as bread (Exod 16:15), the absence of quails,[2] of accompanying flocks and of sacrifices in Pg's wilderness narrative set the wilderness outside geography with a vegetarian diet reflecting the antediluvian era. Wilderness is outside space as the Flood was outside time. In the wilderness, space is replaced by presence as YHWH fills the Residence (Exod 40:34) to make the absence of land bearable. global

The absence of the land is further developed through the wilderness theme which Pg uses consistently to keep the land in the sights of the entire narrative. In Lev 16, the key to Pg's atonement system (Chapter 5), the goat for azazel is led away by "a man of my time" (איש עתי), understood as "a man ready to go."[3] Such translation collapses the wilderness fiction and turns the description of the azazel ritual as an order to be accomplished immediately in the wilderness by Aaron. However, the accomplishment formula is missing. It is replaced in Lev 16:34a by a *weqatal* form (והיתה) denoting future accomplishment. Leviticus 16:34b begins with a narrative form with Moses in the position of object of the command rather than subject of the action: "It was done according to what YHWH commanded Moses" (ויעש כאשר צוה יהוה את משה). Neither Moses nor Aaron is performing the ritual.[4] It was accomplished later by the "man of my time" when goats were available. This mysterious man could not be one of those standing in the wilderness since the goat "for azazel" could not be driven to the wilderness (המדברה) by people who themselves stood in the wilderness. As Passover was first performed in the land of Egypt, the day of purgations (Lev 23:26) had to wait until arrival in the land of Canaan. Similarly, the second Passover is prepared immediately upon arrival in the land of Canaan (Josh 5:10). Therefore, no festivals were celebrated and no rituals were performed in the wilderness because they were prescribed for performance in the land (Lev 23:3, 31). The "man of my time" signals that Eleazar (Num 20:28) will be the one transferring the sins of the people on the goat for azazel.

Matthias Köckert sets the end of Pg in Lev 16:34, considering that the laying out of the principles of the cult and the Day of Purgation among

---

2. Frankel, *Murmuring*, 111–13.
3. Following the LXX's ἑτοῖμος, "ready." Milgrom, I, 1045, translates "a man in waiting," but admits that the *hapax* remains unresolved.
4. The Syriac version puts the verb in plural to suggest they did. The LXX cuts the phrase differently and translates by a passive form "Once a year it shall be done…"

the people provides a satisfying closure to the entire Pg narrative.[5] In this view, the congregation remains stranded in the wilderness, ordered to perform a ritual which they are unable to perform, while the synoptic presentation of the festivals of the sabbatical calendar stands seven chapters further on.

Land Tenure as Security

The integration of large parts of Lev 25 into Pg on the basis of the coherence of the seventh year and Jubilee cycles with the sabbatical calendar raises the importance of the land to the same level to that of the calendar. If the demonstration of the calendrical coherence of Pg examined in Part I is accepted, the importance of the land in Lev 23 and 25 is overwhelming. The festival calendar is framed by two mentions of "your settlements" (Lev 23:3, 31) as the place where the festivals will be celebrated. The so-called sabbatical year is a Sabbath for the land, not for the farmers. It is interpreted above (Chapter 6) as a mechanism mobilizing the entire workforce to reclaim large tracts of land. Land is again the main topic of the Jubilee system, regulating credit with the goal of preserving land tenure from the encroachments of private estates.

Compared to the lofty ideals of contemporary studies of the subject, this analysis presents tough measures for facing concrete economic challenges. Enough seeds need to be saved rather than eaten in prevision of the next year's campaign. If not, they have to be borrowed. At what rate? Which assets will secure the loan? This is the concern of the redemption clauses in Lev 25:25–28. The root מוך, meaning "to be short, sink, weaken," does not necessarily imply destitution. The shortage can reflect problems of cash-flow, a common predicament for farmers before the harvest. Funds are obtained through antichretic pledge (see Lev 25:15–16 and Chapter 6). Because land tenure is concerned, the principle of tenure inalienability is reinforced by granting the right to reclaim the land pledged by relatives before the maturity of the loan. Relatives are directly concerned by any pledging of land in their village. Since land is not held in full property by individual farmers, any mortgaging of land necessarily endangers the overall capacity of the family circle to feed itself and to pay its taxes. Hence, the redeeming party is bound to be a brother of sorts. The redemption process only makes sense within the family circle since debts do not concern individuals but families. Regress

---

5. M. Köckert, *Leben in Gottes Gegenwart* (FAT 43; Tübingen: Mohr Siebeck, 2004), 105.

would turn an individual released by someone outside his direct family into the debt slave of his redeemer with little or no practical advantage to either party.[6] In Mesopotamia also, redemption of property lost during commercial activities was allowed,[7] although the redemption rights seem to apply only to antichretic pledges for non-commercial loans.[8] In a healthy economic system, shares of land tenure were constantly traded, resulting in large variations of the actual surface cultivated by individual families and in the proportion of the harvest each family retained for its own needs. Leviticus 25 protects land tenure by allowing reclamation before the general return of pledges on the Jubilee. If, however, no reclaimer intervened, the pledge (person, animal, land or harvest shares) remained under the control of the creditor until the Jubilee, unless the borrower himself was able to reimburse the loan earlier (Lev 25:26–28).

Urban Property

While tribal land was not privatized, Lev 25:29–31 set houses within walled urban centres in a category different from arable land and village dwellings. Urban real-estate is not tenure but freehold property (צמתת, Lev 25:23), as was still theoretically the case in the Ottoman Empire during the seventeenth century.[9] Therefore, urban property can be permanently alienated and it is not affected by the Jubilee.[10] The exclusion

6. Radner, "Neo-Assyrian Period," 266, 284.

7. Weinfeld, *Justice*, 167. K. R. Veenhof, "Redemption of Houses in Assur and Sippar," in *Munuscula Mesopotamica* (ed. B. Böck, E. Cancik-Kirschbaum and T. Richter; Münster: Ugarit-Verlag, 1999), 599–616, notes that during the Old Assyrian era, the city of Assur passed an edict allowing debtors to recover property sold under duress to pay back loans if half the sale price could be paid back immediately. The remaining arrears would be reimbursed in three instalments.

8. Westbrook, "Old Babylonian," 100; Veenhof, "Old Assyrian Period," 133; K. Abraham, "Middle Assyrian Period," in Westbrook and Jasnow, eds., *Security for Debt in Ancient Near Eastern Law*, 161–222 (181).

9. Mufti Şeyhülislam Ebüssuud Efendi, quoted in Ze'evi, *Century*, 131. See also Doumani, *Palestine*, 156. Kramer, *Village*, 63 n. 9, notes: "Lands inside cities are *mulk* [freehold property]. Their owners can sell them, give them away as presents, or dedicate them as *waqf*s. When they die, the whole area passes into the hands of their heirs. *Miri* lands [state owned] are those cultivated areas in villages, which each cultivator is allocated for his own use. They cannot be sold, given away or dedicated as *waqf*s. When [the cultivator] dies, if he has sons they continue using the land. If not, the land is reassigned to the *sipahi's tapu*."

10. Again, the sale of such houses does not imply destitution. It is of course possible that an urban house can be sold to pay debts. For this reason limited redemption rights are granted, rights which are valid for one year after the sale date.

of urban space from tenure regulations is significant for determining the outlook of the writers of the text. The fact that tribal tenure is protected by the Jubilee does not contradict the suggestion that these verses were written within the walls that set the property of the group which commissioned the text beyond the reach of Jubilee regulations and the protection of tribal tenure.[11] Sale of an urban house clearly indicates the existence within the polity of Pg of a class of merchants who own houses in towns or in walled farmsteads in the countryside, in contrast to the rural population. These merchants would be in close contact with the administration that is presupposed by the land reclaim operations during the seventh year. The mobilization of the entire male population would require an efficient administration able to plan projects, distribute food and prevent sowing in the villages. Some of the reclaimed land would be granted to the members of the civil and military authorities so that they could support themselves on estates, on the basis of the land-for-service system.[12] Land grants require that enough free land is available to be bequeathed without reducing the surface of tenure land available in the villages. Leviticus 25 demonstrates full awareness of the intricate issues at play and presents state of the art solutions to the question of land management at the province level. Theologically, the concern over land and credit management ensues naturally from the Exodus. As YHWH redeemed the sons of Israel from Egypt (Exod 6:6), land and people must remain redeemable, either through advance reimbursement of loans or at the Jubilee which marks the term of all loans. While credit is necessary for boosting the economy, tenure land must be protected to ensure that the sons of Israel do not fall into economic slavery.

According to Lev 25:23, the land of Canaan remains the exclusive property of YHWH. This principle entails that residents in Canaan are either tenure holders (sons of Israel and non-Israelites) or chattel-slaves (non-Israelites, Lev 25:44–46). Robert Kawashima highlighted the organic link between Creation, Flood and the Jubilee, thus paving the way for the attribution of parts of Lev 25 to Pg.[13] The Jubilee is the application of Pg's notion of pollution and purgation in the economic realm. The Flood cleansed the violence that prevailed among the first generations. The Reed Sea purged Egypt of its oppressive Pharaoh. The

---

11. *Pace* N. C. Habel, *The Land is Mine* (Minneapolis: Fortress, 1995), 99, who claims that the sympathy of the audience is not with the urbanites.

12. Military estates can be identified in Idumea (the military border facing Egypt and Arabia) by the place names Beth-marcaboth and Hazar-susim (1 Chr 4:31), a point made by E. A. Knauf (personal communication).

13. Kawashima, "Jubilee Year," 370–89.

azazel ritual purged the sins and transgressions of the sons of Israel on a yearly basis, but did little to combat economic distortions. The Jubilee purged the economy and held at bay the chaotic forces of slavery, hunger, landlessness and anarchic credit operations. Hence, access to land must be guaranteed to all while not preventing credit. An Israelite may sell his labour, the labour of his slaves, his crops, pledge the usufruct of his tenure, but ownership of the land and of the sons of Israel cannot be transferred. While credit is essential for the economy, loans must not exceed the productive capacity of the land that secures them. Elohim is able to grant non-conditional *berîts* and to wipe out sins yearly without compensation. Yet credit involves inter-human relations which require accountability. In the interests of borrowers and lenders, debts must be repaid and not waived. Rather than restoring the rights of returnees,[14] the sabbatical year and the Jubilee protect tribal tenure from the encroachments of private estates (Isa 5:8; Ezek 46:16–18; Mic 2:2) and encourage the development of estates on dead land. The importance of land management in Leviticus is easily missed since the book is now dominated by a large amount of sacrificial cuisine.

14. G. Robinson, "Das Jobel-Jahr," in Daniels, Glessmer and Rösel, eds., *Ernten, was man sät*, 471–94; Amit, "Jubilee Law," 47–59; M. M. Morfino, "Il corno del clamore' che annuncia liberazione," *Theologia & Historica* 9 (2000): 9–75. However, this idea is rejected by J. S. Bergsma, "The Jubilee: A Post-exilic Priestly Attempt to Reclaim Lands?," *Biblica* 84 (2003): 225–46, and H. G. M. Williamson, "Comments on Oded Lipschits, *The Fall and Rise of Jerusalem*," in *In Conversation with Oded Lipschits: The Fall and Rise of Jerusalem* (ed. D. Vanderhooft; Winona Lake: Eisenbrauns, 2005), *JHS* 7 (2007) article 2, 36–38, online: http://www.arts.ualberta.ca/JHS/abstracts-articles.html#A63.

Chapter 9

THE LAND IN NUMBERS AND DEUTERONOMY

Census and Land Allotment (Numbers 1)

The book of Numbers opens with a census list that gave the Greek name to the book. I consider references relative to the itinerary, the Tent of Meeting, the Levites and Joseph as secondary, leaving the following text for Pg:

> [1:1] YHWH spoke to Moses on day one of the second month of the second year since their coming out of the land of Egypt: [2*]"Levy the head of all the congregation of the sons of Israel by clans, paternal dynasties, reckoning by name every male on their roll-call [3*] from twenty years old and over, every one going out with the army in Israel. You will muster them by their armies, you and Aaron. [4]Take with you a man per tribe, each one a chief of his paternal house." [5]These are the names of the men that stood with them:
>
> For Reuben: Elizur ben Shedeur
> [6]For Simeon: Shelumiel ben Zurishaddai
> [7]For Judah: Nahshon ben Amminadab
> [8]For Issachar: Nethanel ben Zuar
> [9]For Zebulun: Eliab ben Helon
> [10]For Ephraim: Elishama ben Ammihud
> For Manasseh: Gamaliel ben Pedahzur
> [11]For Benjamin: Abidan ben Gideoni
> [12]For Dan: Ahiezer ben Ammishaddai
> [13]For Asher: Pagiel ben Ochran
> [14]For Gad: Eliasaph ben Deuel
> [15]For Naphtali: Ahira ben Enan.
>
> [16]These were the ones called by the congregation, leaders of their paternal tribes. They were heads of thousands of Israel. [17]Moses and Aaron took these men who were marked out by name, [18]with the entire congregation assembled on day one of month two. They registered themselves according to their genealogy along their tribes by paternal dynasties by the count of names from twenty years old and over by their roll-call. [46*]Total: 603,550.

The accumulation of units and sub-units (clans, *beit-ab*, roll-call, male, adult) underlines the thoroughness of the census, compared to the rough estimate (600,000) given in Exod 12:40.[1] Setting the date of the order on a Friday gives an urgency that justifies the call of assistants, given the size of the task to be accomplished before the impending Sabbath, which has now been set as a day of compulsory cessation of work (Lev 23:3). Since none of the theophoric names is constructed with YHWH, the list coheres with Pg's notion of progressive revelation of the divine names. None of Moses' contemporaries bear a Yahwistic name since YHWH's name was revealed for the first time to Moses (Exod 6:2–3). The immediate aim of the census is expressed by a form of ילד√, a hint to the Toldot series in Genesis, the name of which derives from the same root. Boys become men upon registration at age twenty on the tribal roll-call, which entitled them for a share of their family's land tenure.

The aim of the census has been understood as preparation for war since muster (פקד) and armies (צבא) belong to military vocabulary.[2] However, Pg creates its own notion of armies in Gen 2:1, de-astralizing the heavenly host by including every creature of the skies and of the land. Then Exod 12:41 states that YHWH's armies are the sons of Israel. Hence the armies mentioned here are not military. The next Pg passage devoted to the land renders soldiers redundant.

Exploring an Empty Land (Numbers 13–14)

Numbers 13–14 have attracted intense redactional activity. That doublets and repetitions indicate redactional activity has been contested,[3] although in this case, the traces are so blatant that redactional activity is hard to deny.[4] The spies go from Paran to Lebo-hamath or only as far as Hebron and return to Paran or Kadesh. Reports are given in Num 13:27–30 and in vv. 32–33. Caleb alone is acquitted in Num 14:24 but with Joshua in v. 30. This has given rise to the supposition that Pg took over an older

---

1. On the basis of the 600,000 males who crossed the Sea (Exod 12:40), Num 1 permits a rough increase of 9 males per day in the desert, or 10 when the 54 Sabbaths are removed, suggesting that parturients observed the sabbatical idleness of Lev 23:3: ([603,550–600,000] / 380 days)–54 Sabbaths = 10.89. This ten-fold increase reflects the ten Toldot of Genesis and the ten generations of the lists in Gen 5 and 11.

2. J. R. Spencer, "PQD, the Levites, and Numbers 1–4," *ZAW* 110 (1998): 535–46.

3. G. Wenham, *Numbers* (Leicester: Inter-Varsity, 1981), 124–26.

4. Olson, *Death*, 28, 132–33.

Calebite narrative,[5] or that a *Grundschicht* received three *Fortschreibungen* each focusing on a particular figure: Aaron and the congregation, Caleb, or Joshua.[6] I identify the following Pg narrative:

[10:11] On the twentieth of the second month of the second year, [13:1] YHWH said to Moses: [2]"Send some men and they will tour the land of Canaan, which I am giving to the sons of Israel, one per paternal tribe, all of them leaders you will send. [3a]Moses sent them from the Wilderness of Paran according to YHWH's command, [3b]all of them were heads of the sons of Israel. [4]These are their names:
for the tribe of Reuben, Shammua ben Zaccur
> [5]For the tribe of Simeon, Shaphat ben Hori
> [6]For the tribe of Judah, Caleb ben Jephunneh
> [7]For the tribe of Issachar, Igal ben Joseph
> [8]For the tribe of Ephraim, Hoshea bin Nun
> [9]For the tribe of Benjamin, Palti ben Raphu
> [10]For the tribe of Zebulun, Gaddiel ben Sodi
> [11]For the tribe of Manasseh, Gaddi ben Susi
> [12]For the tribe of Dan, Ammiel ben Gemalli
> [13]For the tribe of Asher, Sethur ben Michael
> [14]For the tribe of Naphtali, Nahbi ben Vophsi
> [15]For the tribe of Gad, Geuel ben Machi."

[16]These are the names of the men that Moses sent to tour the land. Moses called Hoshea bin Nun Yehoshua. [17*]Moses sent them to tour the land of Canaan. He ordered, "Go up this way in the Negeb! Go up the mountain, [18]check the land and the people settled on it. Are they strong or weak, few or many? [19]And the land in which they are settled, is it good or bad? What are the cities into which they are settled, are they in camps or in fortresses? [20]Is the land fat or lean, is there wood in it or none? You will strengthen yourselves and take some of the fruit of the land. These were the days of first grapes. [21]They went up. They toured the land [23]They entered as far as a wadi of grapes. They cut there a cane and a single bunch of grapes. It was carried with a yoke for two. They also took some pomegranates and figs; [24]that place they called Wadi Eshcol because of the bunch of grapes which the sons of Israel cut there. [25]They returned from touring the land at the end of 40 days. [26*]They came back to Moses, to Aaron and to the whole congregation of the sons of Israel. They reported to the entire congregation. They showed them the fruit of the land. [32]Then, they slandered the land which they had toured for the sons of Israel: "The land we toured is a land eating its inhabitants!" 14:1a The entire congregation rose. They raised their voice. [1b]The people cried that night. [2]All the sons of Israel lamented against Moses and Aaron. The whole congregation declared: "If only we had died in the land of Egypt or

5. See the overview in ibid., 133–38.

6. B. R. Knipping, *Die Kundschaftergeschichte Numeri 13–14* (Hamburg: Kovac, 2000), 486–91.

in this wilderness! [3b]Is it not better for us to return to Egypt?" [4]They said to each other "Let us choose a head. We better return to Egypt." [5]Moses and Aaron fell face down in front of the general assembly of the sons of Israel, [6]but Joshua bin Nun and Caleb ben Jephunneh, from those who had toured the land, tore their cloaks. [7]They said to the entire congregation of the sons of Israel: "The land we toured is a very very good land." [26]YHWH said to Moses and Aaron: [27]"Until when will this bad congregation lament against me? I have heard their lamentation against me. [28]Order to them, 'As surely as I live, announcement of YHWH, I will do to you just as I have heard you saying: [29*]in this wilderness your corpses will fall, all your musters, all your numbers from twenty years old and older who lamented against me. [35]I am YHWH, I have spoken. I will surely do this to this entire bad congregation ganging against me. In this wilderness they will be perfected. Here they will die [38]except Joshua bin Nun and Caleb ben Jephunneh."

YHWH orders the sending of twelve men to tour the land. Each one is the head of his tribe (Num 1:16 // 13:3). The list of names in vv. 4 to 16 is usually rejected from Pg, but given Pg's propensity for lists, the consensus should be challenged.[7] As in the list of censors (Num 1:4–15), Levi is not mentioned, Joseph is redundant, Judah holds no prominent position and there are no Yahwistic names included in the Exodus generation until Moses changes Hoshea's name into Joshua. Compared to the twelve theophoric names in Num 1, this list holds only three theophoric names,[8] none of them constructed with Shaddai. This deficiency explains the surveyors' failure to interpret correctly the reality they saw in Canaan.

Moses' instructions to the scouts (Num 13:18–20) are usually excluded from Pg and attributed to J, although the beginning of the J spy story is supposed to have been dropped when P's was inserted.[9] It is more economical to consider most of the non-Pg elements in Num 13–14 as Ps. The route to be followed by the surveyors is described in the broadest terms (from the Negeb to the mountain) since Canaan is a *terra incognita* to the sons of Israel who came out of Egypt.[10] The possibility that the

---

7. For some suggestions on the function of name lists and magic squares, see G. J. Brooke, "4Q341: An Exercise for Spelling and for Spell," in *Writing and Ancient Near Eastern Society* (ed. P. Bienkowski, C. Mee and E. Slater; LHBOTS 426; London: T&T Clark, 2005), 271–82.

8. Gaddiel, Ammiel, Michael (vv. 10, 12, 13).

9. See Campbell and O'Brien, *Sources*, 153.

10. Their forefathers had last been in Canaan 413 years before the Exodus to bury Jacob in Machpelah (Gen 50:13 says 17 years after Jacob's *eisodos*; Exod 12:40 says 430 years in Egypt).

Canaanites may be strong (חזק) recalls YHWH's strengthening of Pharaoh's heart (Exod 7:13). The surveyors are exhorted to strengthen each other (והתחזקתם) and bring back a sample of the fruit of the land. The mention of fortresses is a hint to the pre-Pg conquest tradition by which Pg intentionally misleads its audience into thinking that the land is well defended and that YHWH's host was mustered to attack it (Num 1:3). The surveyors return at the end of forty days with a huge grape cluster and other fruits as legal proof of the fertility of the land. The question is how to interpret such fertility. Does it mean that the land is good or bad (טובה רעה)? The whole passage is built upon this question (see Num 14:3, 7, 27, 35).

The explorers' report (דבר) in Num 13:26b becomes a slander (דבה, Num 13:32), a law-suit and a maligning report that distorts the reality, especially in legal contexts.[11] Whereas YHWH brought Israel out of Egypt, the scouts bring forth slander against Canaan. The prospect of eating the fruit of land is turned into fear of being eaten by the land. The introduction of giants in the last part of the verse destroys the parallelism. These giants align Pg's episode with Joshua's military conquest. The giants break Pg's logic based on the scouts' misinterpretation of the grapes and other fruits brought back by the surveyors, which are tokens of the land's fertility. According to Pg, the slander of the land consists of the mistaken inference that such a fertile land must be eating its inhabitants because it is so obviously empty. With the insertion of the giants, however, the Israelites' fear is amply justified. The slander of the land is not slanderous anymore. On the contrary, it is the justification of YHWH's sanction, which becomes unjustified since he has no more reason to blame the people. Being afraid of giants is no more of a sin than is being hungry in the wilderness (Exod 16). The failure to recognize the giants as a later addition warps the understanding of the rest of Pg.[12] In most cases, the contradiction is not noted,[13] or the presence of a mighty population in the land leads to the conclusion that Pg presupposes a military conquest under the leadership of Joshua.[14] For Pg, the land is both fertile (Num 13:23, 26) and anthropophagous (Num 13:32).

11. Gen 37:2; Jer 20:10; Ezek 36:3; Ps 31(Eng. 32):14; Prov 10:18; 25:10.

12. Lohfink, "Original Sins," 111, considers the giants as "an expanded motif from the old sources that is not precisely covered by the naming of the sin as 'slander of the land.'"

13. R. Achenbach, "Die Erzählung von der gescheiterten Landnahme von Kadesch Barnea," *ZABR* 9 (2003): 56–123 (98–99).

14. Schmidt, *Studien*, 223; N. Rabe, *Vom Gerücht zum Gericht* (Tübingen: Francke, 1994), 410–13. C. Levin, *Der Jahwist* (FRLANT 157; Tübingen: Vandenhoeck & Ruprecht, 1993), 376, however, removes the giants at the end of v. 32.

The notion of an anthropophagic land is not unique.[15] In Ezek 36:12–14 it indicates depopulation without implying aridity.[16] In this context, the mission of the explorers was not military but the preparation of an overall land-survey to distribute the available population across the various areas according to their agricultural potential.[17] The combination of fertility and emptiness demonstrates the land's goodness.[18] The "sin" of the congregation is to misinterpret emptiness as adversity. The good empty land is slandered as evil. The refusal to ascribe goodness to a land that is simultaneously fertile and empty renders the congregation bad (Num 14:27, 35) and the Egyptian slavery as good, although Joshua and Caleb affirm that the land is very good (Num 14:7 // Gen 1:31). YHWH hears the complaint of the sons of Israel and acts upon it according to a concept of proportional retribution, as he did in Exod 16:12. YHWH chooses one of the two options suggested by the people in v. 2: death in the wilderness, rather than in Egypt. The plague that strikes the surveyors corresponds to the non-Pg plagues against Egypt (Exod 9:14) and to the plague that struck Korah (Num 17:13 [Eng. 16:48] non-Pg). In Pg, the ten spies simply die of old age in the wilderness, along with the other members of their generation. The same applies to Moses and Aaron who are not mentioned besides Caleb and Joshua as survivors in Num 14:38.[19] Such a simple explanation did not, however, suit the agenda of later redactors.

The giants (Num 13:28–33) reach back as far as Gen 6:1–8 (Ps), and their origins can be traced to the lusty Titans. Since their introduction into Pg's empty land justifies the refusal to enter the land, redactors have added an extra rebellion committed specifically by the leaders of the people. The striking of the rock at Kadesh (Num 20:1–12) constitutes the leaders' original sin[20] and explains why Moses and Aaron did not enter Canaan.[21] YHWH's reproach that Moses and Aaron have not trusted him

15. See the overview of different interpretations of the land eating its inhabitants in Knipping, *Kundschaftergeschichte*, 135–36 n. 272.

16. Contra Frankel, *Murmuring*, 138–39.

17. Ibid., 137, quoting Y. Medan, "A Temporary Weeping and a Weeping for Generations (the Sin of the Spies)," *Megadim* 10 (1990): 21–37 (24–26).

18. A. S. Seale, "Numbers 13:32," *Expository Times* 68 (1956): 28.

19. See K. Schmid, "The Late Persian Formation of the Torah: Observations on Deuteronomy 34," in *Judah and the Judeans in the Fourth Century BCE* (ed. O. Lipschits, G. N. Knoppers and R. Albertz; Winona Lake: Eisenbrauns, 2007), 237–51 (250).

20. Num 20:1–12 // Exod 17 // Num 27:12–14 and Deut 32:48–52. Lohfink, "Original Sins," 112–14.

21. J. Milgrom, *Numbers* (Philadelphia: Jewish Publication Society, 1990), 448: "Down through the ages, the sin of Moses, as described in Numbers 20:1–13, has

(אמן, Num 20:12 Ps) is at loggerheads with Pg's unconditional ברית, which requires no particular display of faith on the human side.[22] The contradiction is confirmed when this lack of trust is explained as the failure to sanctify YHWH in the eyes of the sons of Israel (להקדישני, v. 12), while in Pg sanctity pertains only to time.[23]

The empty land in Num 13:32 renders the military aspect of the great army mustered in Num 1 irrelevant and underlines the civil purpose of the census. Counting the adult males is essential for land allotment, establishing taxes and organizing corvée gangs during the seventh year (Lev 25:2–5). Hence, the land is also the main theme of this part of Pg, as entry into Canaan is looming large on the agenda. However, the slander of the good land prevents immediate entry and requires adequate purgation.

Purging the Congregation Outside the Land
(Numbers 20–Deuteronomy 34)

The land slander pericope ends with YHWH's clearing of Caleb and Joshua. The story moves on directly with Aaron's death:

> [Num 20:22b] The sons of Israel—the whole congregation arrived at Mount the Mount. [23*]YHWH ordered to Moses: [25]"Call Aaron and Eleazar his son and go up with them at Mount the Mount. [26]Strip Aaron of his garments and put them on his son Eleazar. Aaron will be added and die there!" [27]Moses did as YHWH commanded. They went up Mount the Mount in the eyes of the whole congregation. [28]Moses stripped Aaron of his garments. He put them on Eleazar his son. Aaron died there on top of the mountain. Moses came down and Eleazar from the mountain. [29]The entire congregation saw that Aaron had perished. The entire house of Israel wept over Aaron thirty days. [26:1] YHWH ordered to Moses and to Eleazar son of Aaron: [2]"Levy the heads of all the congregation of the sons of Israel from twenty years old and older by paternal house, all those going out with the army in Israel. [3]Moses and Eleazar spoke with them in the steppes of Moab opposite the Jordan of Jericho. [51]These are the muster of the sons of Israel: 601,730. [52]YHWH said to Moses: [53]"Between these shall the land be divided by lots, by count of names. [54]You will increase the inheritance of a large group and

been regarded as one of the Gordian knots of the Bible: the punishment is clear; but what is the crime?" Hecateus of Abdera (*apud* Diodorus Siculus 40.3.1–8) transmits what is probably an older tradition according to which Moses did enter the land. It is likely that his death before reaching the Promised Land originated at the end of the Judaean kingdom, thereby explaining Josiah's untimely death or Jehoiachin's in far-away Babylon in spite of his release from prison.

22. See Pola, *Priesterschrift*, 95–97; Knauf, "Exodus," 76 n. 12.
23. Gen 2:3; Exod 25:8; Lev 23:2, 27; 25:10.

diminish that of a small one. Each area will be proportional to the muster. [55]By lot the land will be divided, by the names of their paternal tribes they will inherit, [56]by drawing lots you will divide inheritance between large and small groups." [63]Those are the musters by which Moses and Eleazar mustered the sons of Israel in the steppes of Moab opposite the Jordan of Jericho. [64]Among those, there was no one from the musters by which Moses and Aaron had mustered the sons of Israel in the wilderness [65]since YHWH had ordered that they would die in the wilderness. So no one was left from them, except Caleb ben Jephunneh and Joshua bin Nun. [27:12] YHWH ordered to Moses, "Go up this mountain of Abarim and see the land I have given the sons of Israel." [15]Moses said to YHWH: [16]"May YHWH, the Elohim of the spirits of all flesh, appoint a man over the congregation [17]who will go out in front of them and will enter in front of them, who will cause them to go out and will cause them to enter, so that YHWH's congregation will not be like sheep without a shepherd." [18]YHWH ordered to Moses, "Take Joshua bin Nun, a man in whom is the spirit, and you will lay your hand on him. [19]Then you will make him stand before Eleazar and before the entire congregation and you will commission him in their eyes. [20]Then you will transfer some of your majesty on him so that the whole congregation of the sons of Israel will listen to him. [21]However, he will be subordinated to Eleazar the priest and will receive guidance from him by judgement of the Urim before YHWH. On his order they will go out, and at his command they will come in, him and all the sons of Israel with him, and the whole congregation!" [22]Moses did according to what YHWH commanded him. He took Joshua. He made him stand before Eleazar the priest and the whole congregation. [23]He laid his hands on him. He commissioned him, as YHWH said by Moses' hand. [34:1] YHWH said to Moses: [2]"Command to the sons of Israel and you will order them: When you enter the land of Canaan, this is the land that will fall to you as share, the land of Canaan as to its boundaries. [3]For you the southern boundary will be from the end of the Salt Sea at the East [5*]and its arrival at the Sea. [6]The seaward boundary will be for you the Great Sea; this will be for you the seaward boundary. [7]This will be for you the northern boundary: from the Great Sea for you it will turn towards Mount the Mount. [8*]From Mount the Mount it will turn towards [11*]the Sea of Kinnereth eastwards. [12]The boundary will go down the Jordan and its arrivals will be at the Salt Sea; this will be for the land as to its boundaries around!" [13]Moses commanded the sons of Israel: "This is the land that you will endow by lot!" [Deut 34:1*] Moses went up from the steppes of Moab to Mt Nebo, the head of Pisgah facing Jericho. YHWH caused him to see all the land. [4]YHWH ordered to him: "This is the land about which I swore to Abraham, to Isaac and to Jacob: 'To your seed I will give it,' I made you see it with your own eyes but you will not enter there!" [5a]Moses died here. [7]Moses was a hundred and twenty years old when he died, his eyes were not dim and his jaw did not tremble. [8]The sons of Israel wept over Moses in the steppes of Moab thirty days. The days of the mourning cries of Moses were perfected.

Aaron dies at "Mount the Mount" (הר ההר), a non-descript name in line with Pg's depiction of the wilderness as a geographical void, an anti-land where mountains have no names. Aaron's body is added (יאסף) but not to his people (compare Num 20:26 with Gen 25:8, 17; 35:29; 49:29, 33), indicating that his bones were given a burial away from Machpelah, in a place which Pg recognizes as an important religious ground. Pg knows the pre-biblical tradition considering *Jabal an-Nabī Hārūn* as a holy mountain and a place of pilgrimage (as it is to this day[24]) and does not condemn it.

The death of Aaron clears the way for the emergence of the generation born in the wilderness through the nomination of Eleazar as successor of his father. This is immediately followed by the mention of the Jordan of Jericho, the first geographical note since the departure from Egypt. Contrary to Mount the Mount, the river has a name since it marks the limit between the "wilderness" and the land. Jericho qualifies the lower course of the river rather than the city of the same name since the land is empty. As the entire Exodus generation dies in the wilderness, a second census is necessary in order to determine exactly the number of lots the land of Canaan has to be divided into. The census reveals a decline of 1,820 adult males compared to the previous count. In spite of the slight decline, the death of the Exodus generation did not jeopardize the prom-ise of offspring.[25] The count is large enough to underline that the manna has proved an excellent staple, but the seriousness of the purgation is not downplayed.

Just as the distribution of manna always met the needs of the people, the new census guarantees the fairness of the land distribution (compare Num 26:52–56 and Exod 16:16–18). The lots and the census indicate that Pg envisages the *dhukūr* type of *mushaʿ* (Lev 25:13), that is a divi-sion according to the number of adult males (see Chapter 6). That the census takes place about forty years after the previous one suggests that the census is to be repeated on a regular basis. The census is essential for the preservation of the egalitarian principle of the *mushaʿ*, adjusting the number of land shares to the exact number of adult males belonging to each village.[26] Hence the wilderness fiction continues to furnish the backdrop of a most realistic land management system.

24. E. A. Knauf, "Supplementa Ismaelitica 14," *BN* 61 (1992): 22–26.
25. Olson, *Death*, 140.
26. R. T. Antoun, *Arab Village* (Bloomington: Indiana University Press, 1972), 22–24, provides a concrete example in twentieth-century C.E. Jordan of a residual *mushaʿ* where demographic variations were not corrected by a census. Families from larger clans and independent families had to join the smaller clans to even up the division of unconsolidated land.

The mention of the steppes of Moab next to the Jordan of Jericho (Num 26:63) raises the sense of anticipation as the actual land becomes visible. The insistence upon the thorough disappearance of the Exodus generation produces suspense since Moses is still alive. Will he make it to the other side?

Before complying with the divine order and ascending Mt Abarim, Moses, who does not want to be outdone by Aaron, asks for a successor of his own (Num 27:15–23). This passage is naturally rejected from Pg by scholars who set the end of Pg before Joshua.[27] If Pg narrates the entrance of the sons of Israel into the land, Joshua's commission as Moses' successor is the natural consequence of Moses' death in the wilderness. Pg obviously takes over the older conquest tradition, but instead of presenting the appointment of Joshua as YHWH's order as is the case for Eleazar, the suggestion to appoint Joshua comes from Moses. Moses presents Joshua as the general who will lead Israel in battle, as if YHWH had overlooked this crucial point. Moses' depiction of Joshua reflects the traditional Joshua, who is a warrior as far back as the tradition can be recovered (Josh 10:12–13 Book of Yashar). In the light of Pg's concept of the empty land (Num 13:32; Josh 4:19), Moses' request is preposterous since Joshua would not even find windmills to attack. YHWH does not need Joshua to guide his people into the land.[28] With this request, Pg puts Moses in an unfavourable light, showing that he misinterpreted the report of the surveyors as much as the rest of the congregation did (Num 14:1–7). Forty years later, Moses was still convinced that such a fertile land could not possibly be empty. This interpretation only makes sense if the "sin" of the leaders (Num 20:1–12) is attributed to a post-Pg redaction, contrary to Lohfink's delimitation. Consequently, Lohfink's notion of original sins should not be accepted wholesale.[29] Moses and Aaron die in the wilderness along with the rest of the wilderness generation and for the same reason.[30]

YHWH's granting of Moses' request is a rare tongue-in-cheek passage in Pg. As a concession to old Moses, YHWH chooses Joshua since he has

---

27. Frevel, *Blick*, 272–83; L. Perlitt, "Priesterschrift im Deuteronomium?," *ZAW* 100 (1988): 65–88 (81–83), reprinted in Perlitt's *Deuteronomium-Studien* (FAT 8; Tübingen: J. C. B. Mohr, 1994), 123–43; H. Seebass, "Die Ankündigung des Mosetodes," in Kiesow and Meurer, eds., *Textarbeit*, 457–67.

28. Frevel, *Blick*, 344.

29. Lohfink, "Original Sins," 106–10.

30. Since they ascribe Num 20 to Pg, M. Noth, *Numeri* (Göttingen: Vandenhoeck & Ruprecht, 1966), 185–87; Perlitt, "Priesterschrift?," 81–83; and Frevel, *Blick*, 283, have to consider Num 27:15–23 as Ps.

spirit already in him, so that Moses may lay *one* hand on him. Moses lays both hands,[31] but to no avail since neither authority nor function are transferred, which stands in contrast to what happened when Eleazar donned Aaron's clothes (Num 20:28). Moses mimics the transfer of office from Aaron to Eleazar and the transfer of the people's sin onto the head of the goat for azazel (Lev 16:21). YHWH suggests that Moses give Joshua some of his majesty (הוד). As no such majesty was ever mentioned before—this is the only occurrence of the word in the Pentateuch—the audience is bound to wonder what majesty there is to transfer. Elsewhere, majesty is attributed to YHWH or to the king (Jer 22:18). Besides having his traditional prophetic status and role handed over to Aaron already in Exod 7:1, Moses is now told that the transfer of his majesty to Joshua is futile since Joshua is subordinated to Eleazar who is the one who takes over Moses' mediating role by being in charge of the Urim. The whole passage deprives Moses and Joshua of their heroic lustre. Although the passage is sometimes rejected from Pg because Pg's Moses does not usually argue with YHWH,[32] the biting irony displayed here is more likely to originate from Pg than from later hands, which tend to harmonize Pg with other traditions which all tend to glorify Moses. I thus attribute Num 27:12–23 to Pg and consider the repetition of the scene in Deut 32:48–52 as secondary. Whereas Pg treated Jacob with contemptuous near silence, Pg turns ironic over Moses' death. This passage derails the icon of Deuteronomic theology and underlines the irrelevance of the warrior for the imminent entry in a land of Canaan, which is as full of enormous fruits as it is empty of Canaanites.

Having appointed his own redundant successor, Moses is told to transmit the last missing piece of information before the land may be entered, the actual limits of the land to be allotted (Num 34:1–12). The description gets vaguer as it proceeds northward, reproducing the actual vantage point of an onlooker standing with Moses on a height opposite Jericho. The extent of the land of Canaan becomes Moses' testament. It is the last instructions he transmits to the sons of Israel before his death.

That Transjordan is excluded from the Israelite patrimony is a *lectio difficilior* which confirms that the description is likely to belong to Pg rather than to later redactions.[33] The text lists a number of points which

31. SP and Syriac harmonize v. 23 with v. 18 by reading ידו ("his hand") instead of MT's ידיו ("his hands").

32. Frevel, *Blick*, 282.

33. H. Seebass, "'Holy' Land in the Old Testament: Numbers and Joshua," *VT* 56 (2006): 92–104 (99).

do not set hard and fast borders on the ground.[34] The use of modern maps opens an unbridgeable gap between the inaccuracy of textual descriptions and the expectations of modern readers.[35] The Jordan Valley and the Mediterranean mark convenient eastern and western limits. The southern limit is overloaded by secondary material from Josh 15:1b, 3,[36] while Pg only mentions natural features because the land is empty. Pg draws a virtual line reaching straight to the Mediterranean (Num 34:5b–6), claiming the southern parts of the kingdom of Judah for the sons of Israel. The northern limit is very problematic (Num 34:7–8a*). The generic "Mount the Mount" is the first landmark from the Great Sea. This Mount does not fit the site of Aaron's grave (Num 20:22), which is located by tradition near Petra on the eastern side of the Rift, over a hundred kilometres south of Moses' vantage point opposite Jericho. This means that the south-eastern corner of Canaan is presented as its north-western one. The only secure point in the north is Lebo-hamath, probably located at Lebweh near Baalbeck in the Lebanese Beqaᶜ. The other places (Zedad, Ziphron, Hazar Enan, Shepham, Riblah) are a fudged version of Ezek 47:15–18.[37] As with the southern limit, it is likely that these town names are secondary. This means that הר ההר is the only northern point between the Mediterranean and the Sea of Galilee. If this הר ההר is the same as Aaron's grave, the description of the northern limit is either a gross mistake or a deliberate act of sabotage which was tentatively improved later by inserting elements from Josh 15 and Ezek 47. Otherwise הר ההר refers to any prominent mountain in the north, such as Mt Hermon or Mt Tabor. The temptation to be more specific should be resisted. These schematic lines do not establish any rights to land, water or pasture. They are a counterpart to the Table of Nations (Gen 10).

Unlike Aaron, Moses is granted a glimpse of the land thanks to its proximity. Compared to Mount the Mount (Num 20:22), Mt Abarim bears something closer to a proper name, although it is still made up for the circumstance, "Mount of the Fords." From there, Moses sees the long-awaited land and dies. Most exegetes who believe in the existence of Pg consider Moses' death to be the end of the document, although it

34. The word גבל is both "boundary" (as in Arabic *jebel*, "mountain") and the territory within the boundaries.

35. N. Lissovsky and N. Naʾaman, "A New Outlook on the Boundary System of the Twelve Tribes," *UF* 35 (2003): 291–332 (320).

36. N. Naʾaman, "Lebo-Hamath, Ṣubat-Hamath, and the Northern Boundary of the Land of Canaan," *UF* 31 (1999): 417–41 (434).

37. Ibid., 435.

leaves the sons of Israel stranded in the wilderness. Jean-Louis Ska recognizes the problem and claims that Pg is better at narrating beginnings than ends.[38] Yet, the end is duly transmitted in Joshua (see Chapter 10). Before discussing it, the Pg material in Deuteronomy should be considered.

The attribution to Pg of the few verses in Priestly style in Deuteronomy depends on one's presuppositions about the Tetrateuch and the Hexateuch, on whether chronology is considered an integral part of Pg or a late redactional element, and on whether or not Num 27:12–14 is accepted as Pg. According to Lothar Perlitt, the vocabulary used in Deut 1:3; 32:48–52; 34:1a*, 7–9 is not typical of Pg but reflects late redactional activity with Deuteronomistic influence.[39] Perlitt, however, does not indicate where Pg ends. Semantics are useful, but are not enough to exclude Pg from Deuteronomy altogether.

In Deut 1:3, the Akkadian numeral עשׁתי, rather than the common אחד for "one," and the announcement of a speech by Moses that seems to presuppose the body of Deuteronomy render this verse suspect. The chronological indication (11 XI) is redundant since the fortieth year can be deduced from the difference between Moses' age when YHWH first spoke to him (80 years, Exod 7:7) and when he died (120 years, Deut 34:7). Accordingly, this verse should not be ascribed to Pg.[40] It bridges the wide gap separating Num 34 and the next Pg element resulting from the insertion of Deuteronomy into Pg's narrative.

The fading away of Pg's strand after Exodus is often interpreted as a proof of its non-existence, when in fact the massive amount of material added into it merely renders it harder to follow. Next to the biting irony displayed in Num 27:12–23, Deut 32:48–52 certainly appears as a timid *sekundäre Wiederholung* by a compiler who shies away from Pg's deriding of Moses.[41] Deuteronomy 32:51–52 can be removed since these verses belong to the "sin of the leaders" (Num 20:1–12 Ps). Like Num 20:24; 27:13, v. 50 suggests that Aaron was added to his people, something that stands in contrast to Num 20:26–28 (Pg). The whole passage is therefore secondary. As for Deut 34:1–9, it is the least disputed Pg passage in Deuteronomy. Deuteronomy 34:1 narrates the accomplishment of the order in Num 27:12, but the geographical indicators do not match. Mount of the Fords becomes Mt Nebo, the head of the Pisgah

38. J.-L. Ska, *Introduction à la lecture du Pentateuque* (Bruxelles: Lessius, 2002), 215; Ska, "Indépendance," 414.

39. Perlitt, "Priesterschrift?," 68–72.

40. Ibid.

41. Ibid., 75–76.

opposite Jericho. The proximity of the land gradually dissolves the notion of a wilderness. As Moses climbs up, the ancient tell of Jericho in the land of Canaan is the first recognizable landmark. Its proximity causes the last stretch of wilderness to be called "the steppes of Moab." There is thus no reason to consider these names as secondary.[42] The combination of the terms "mountain," "head" and "seeing" recall the end of the Flood and cast Moses as a second Noah, whose mission is accomplished when the top of the mountains become visible again (Gen 8:5). Yet Pg reaches back further. On the Pisgah, another made-up name,[43] Moses transcends Noah and becomes the missing onlooker, the one who did not see the land appear as the waters were piled up in one place (Gen 1:9), three days before the creation of humankind. Pg consciously presents the land of Canaan as the accomplishment of the narrative that started in Gen 1:1. The last words, "Gilead as far as Dan," presuppose the settlement of some tribes in Transjordan, which does not belong to the sons of Israel (see Num 34:1–12). The note appearing in SP, "from the Brook of Egypt to the Euphrates," reflects the megalomaniac dream of Gen 15:18.

YHWH's last words to Moses (Deut 34:4) are a reminder of the promise of the land made to Abraham and to Moses himself (Gen 17:8; Exod 6:8). Moses then dies, having accomplished his mission by bringing the sons of Israel to the threshold of the land. Having gone up the mountain alone, Moses dies, though his body receives no burial (against v. 6). Commissioned when he was 80 years old (Exod 7:6), Moses dies 40 years later aged 120 (Deut 34:7). Sent on the 400th day after the Exodus (Num 10:11), the surveyors' slander of the land delayed the accomplishment of YHWH's promise but it does not prevent it. The principle of human responsibility does not compromise the unconditional ברית but balances the unbreakable divine promise with human accountability. The pitfalls of irresistible fate and cheap grace are avoided. The sons of Israel perfected (ויתמו, Deut 34:8) the days of Moses with 30 days of mourning, a detail which serves to equate Moses with the rest of the exodus generation, which was equally perfected in the wilderness (Num 14:35).

---

42. Against ibid., 141.

43. In the light of √פשׂק, the meaning of √פסג (Ps 48:14) could be "to cut, split, divide," referring to the eroded plateau of the area overlooking the Rift East of Jericho, or "to look carefully, to make a list" (*HALOT*, 3:946–47), which would be fitting for Balaam (Num 23:14) and Moses. Also relevant are Syro-Palestinian Arabic *fsḥ* ("to leave, to shirk one's duties") and *fsḥ* ("to make room for those who want to get past"); see Barthélemy, *Dictionnaire*, 607–9.

The majority of scholars place Pg's end at some point towards the end of Deut 34,[44] although Moses' death would be a sad concluding note for Pg.[45] Neither Moses' vitality[46] at the moment of death nor the closeness of the land alleviates this sense of inadequacy. Since the land was promised to Abraham before the promise was reiterated to Moses, there is no reason for the death of Moses to prevent the accomplishment of the promise. The census of the wilderness generation and the description of the land of Canaan as being situated on the western side of the Jordan find their natural conclusion in the actual entry into Canaan. The slight ridicule heaped upon the dying Moses (Num 27) downplays his importance and indicates that life and narrative go on without him. Moses was one link among others, but he is not the end of the story, especially since Pg cancels out the entire Sinai pericope and the covenant linked to it.

44. Noth, *Studien*, 17–19; Elliger, "Sinn," 121–42; R. Rendorff, "Pentateuch," in *Evangelisches Kirchenlexikon* (ed. R. Frick; Göttingen: Vandenhoeck & Ruprecht, 1959), 113; J. Scharbert, "Priesterschrift," *LTK* 7 (1963): 753; R. Kilian, "Die Hoffnung auf Heimkehr in der Priesterschrift," *Bibel und Leben* 7 (1966): 226; O. Kaiser, *Einleitung in das Alte Testament* (Gütersloh: Mohn, 1969), 91–93; Weimar, "Struktur," 81–134; W. H. Schmidt, *Einführung in das Alte Testament* (Berlin: de Gruyter, 1985), 97–98; R. Smend, Jr., *Die Entstehung des Alten Testaments* (Stuttgart: Kohlhammer, 1978), 45; Schmidt, *Studien*, 241–71; E. Zenger, "Priesterschrift," *LTK* 3 (1999): 578–79; E. Cortese, *Josua 13–21: Ein priesterschriftlicher Abschnitt in deuteronomistischen Geschichtswerk* (OBO 94; Fribourg: Universitätsverlag; Göttingen: Vandenhoeck & Ruprecht, 1990), 11; Frevel, *Blick*, 209–10.

45. Perlitt, "Priesterschrift?," 77. Is it more likely, however, that Pg ends before Moses' death?

46. A Samaritan manuscript reads כוה as "strength" instead of "to become inexpressive, blind, dim, colourless" at Lev 13:6. Some Greek manuscripts drop the problematic לחה. My reading of לח ("jawbone" + archaic third person singular pronoun ה) is supported by Vulgate's "dentes illius moti sunt." But see J. H. Tigay, "לא נס כחה 'He Had not Become Wrinkled' (Deuteronomy 34:7)," in Zevit, Gitin and Sokoloff, eds., *Solving Riddles and Untying Knots*, 345–50.

Chapter 10

THE LAND IN JOSHUA

The Conclusion of the Priestly Document

In the Pg narrative, the completion of the days of mourning for Moses is followed immediately by a laconic mention of the crossing of the Jordan on the 10th day of month I (Josh 4:19). Compared to the elaborate crossing described in Josh 3, this is a matter-of-fact note reflecting Pg's notion of an empty Canaan which requires no army, no priests and no spies sent in advance. Although empty, Canaan is not featureless like the wilderness. The sons of Israel camp at Gilgal which marks the destination of the Massot pilgrimage mentioned in Lev 23:6.[1] Gilgal is not a city, but a place in the open-air, the location of a week-long pilgrimage during which the sons of Israel live in tents. Once the lunar calendar replaced the sabbatical calendar, resulting in the shift of the beginning of the year to the autumn equinox, Succoth (Lev 23:41 Ps) replaced the pilgrimage to Gilgal, and Massot was incorporated into Passover.[2] The LXX's omission of the phrase "the sons of Israel camped at Gilgal" is a *lectio facilior*, as are the other variations in this passage, which are all related to the festival calendar.[3] The omission of "until this day" by the LXX is due to the same demotion of the Gilgal pilgrimage and avoids legitimizing a practice which was discontinued when the text was translated.

1. 4QJosh[a] and *Ant.* 5.20 have Joshua building an altar at Gilgal, contrary to the MT, which sets it on Mt Ebal. The LXX has MT Josh 8:30–35 after 9:2, just before the Gibeonite episode; see E. Ulrich, "The Bible in the Making," in *The Bible at Qumran* (ed. P. W. Flint; Grand Rapids: Eerdmans, 2001), 51–66 (62), and DJD 9: 201–3.

2. See the bibliography and discussion in Wagenaar, *Origin*, 21–58, in spite of indiscriminate notions of J and P and the suggestion that the core of vv. 10–12 belonged to the Deuteronomistic History (p. 54). Neh 8:17 states that the festival of Booths is a recent invention.

3. E. Noort, "The Disgrace of Egypt," in *The Wisdom of Egypt* (ed. A. Hilhorst and G. H. van Kooten; Leiden: Brill, 2005), 3–19.

The day after the Passover, the sons of Israel encamped at Gilgal to eat wild grain growing spontaneously in the land of Canaan. The word עבור is unique in the Hebrew Bible, as noted by Noth, who, in his hurry to assert the absence of traces of an independent Pg narrative in Josh 1–12, argues that the passage cannot belong to Pg.[4] In fact, עבור could only be used against Pg if it was typical of non-Pg passages, but since it is a *hapax legomenon*, it proves nothing, apart that it fits the context following the crossing (עבר) of the Jordan.

Upon the cessation of manna, Eleazar and Joshua endow (נחל, Josh 14:1) the land to the sons of Israel. The attribution of a plot of land to each male is the logical conclusion of a three-step operation which started with the census (Num 1) assessing the needs, followed by the evaluation of the available resources by surveying the land (Num 13) delimitated in Num 34, leading to the actual distribution equating resources to needs (Josh 14). Allotment is done by drawing lots, as required in Num 34:13. Although tenure (אחוזה) denotes usufruct rather than ownership, it does not exclude inheritance. Usufruct is heritable and can be mortgaged.[5] General re-allotment after each census corrects demographic fluctuations.

Given the importance of land, one could expect that the lists of towns in Josh 15–19 belong to Pg. This, however, is difficult to reconcile with Pg's notion of an empty land of Canaanites.

The congregation holds a last general assembly at Shiloh—Shiloh being a camp, not a city[6]—to validate the land distribution and to underline the accomplishment of the order to domesticate the land (והארץ נכבשה, Josh 18:1). The root כבש appears elsewhere in the Hexateuch in Num 32:22, 29 with a military sense of subduing the enemies, as is also the case in 1 Chr 22:18. Its mention in Josh 18:1 does not fit a military context and is redundant after Josh 11:23, which marks the end of Joshua's conquest. The claim that Josh 18:1b does not belong to Pg because it is closer to post-priestly texts is disputable.[7] Sandwiched between the allotment of Judah and Joseph and those for the remaining tribes, Josh 18:1 and כבש√ stick out of their present context,[8] though they form a large *inclusio* with Gen 1:28 which is a cogent narrative indicator of the continuation of Pg in Joshua.[9]

---

4.   Noth, *Studien*, 183, especially n. 2.

5.   L. E. Sweet, *Tell Ṭoqaan* (Ann Arbor: University of Michigan Press, 1960), 58.

6.   See I. Hjelm, *Jerusalem's Rise to Sovereignty* (JSOTSup 404; London: T&T Clark International, 2004), 195–210.

7.   Ska, *Introduction*, 215.

8.   Failing to recognize the originality of Pg's theology, Hepner, "Israelites," 167, translates כבש as "to conquer."

9.   Knauf, "Priesterschrift," 113–15.

Michaela Bauks objects that making כבש the key of Pg's peaceful entry into the land is overstretching the semantic field of the term, which is not pacifist.[10] She notes that semantic comparisons are of little avail since nothing excludes the possibility of a late redactional level copying expressions or keywords from the different traditions within the Pentateuch in order to harmonize them. This argument is certainly correct, but it also applies to Noth's objection to Pg's presence in Joshua and to Perlitt's objection about its presence in Deuteronomy. However, the argument has no bearing on √כבש since it occurs too infrequently to be typical of any particular source. After Josh 18:1, the next occurrence is in 2 Sam 8:11. Late harmonizers would have selected a more common expression or they would not be harmonizing at all. It is much more likely that כבש in Josh 18:1 comes straight from the hand of Pg. As for the non-pacifist sense of √כבש, it is highly significant in the context of the settlement into an empty land, that is, a land empty of humans. In spite of the romantic inclinations of modern urbanites who only experience tracts of untamed nature during holidays and thus tend to idealize it, an unsettled land is full of untamed animals and is by definition hostile and unfit for human settlement. Besides the lack of infrastructure, wild animals help themselves to the produce of new fields and gardens, while on occasions they eat the settlers themselves. Hence, the notion of subjugation appropriately conveys the sheer power required to domesticate the land and keep carnivores, weeds, pests and diseases at bay. As was the case in Mesopotamia, the land (ארץ, *erṣetu*) stands halfway between the urban world and the chaotic wild, which the Assyrian king had the sacred duty of keeping in check through hunting and warfare.[11]

Another attempt at downplaying the significance of the Gen 1:28–Josh 18:1 *inclusio* for the delimitation of Pg argues that Gen 1:28 is directed to humanity in its entirety and has nothing to do with Israel's occupation of the land and P's presentation of God's revelation in three steps (*Elohim* for all humankind, *El Shadday* for Abraham's descendants, and *YHWH* for Israel whose mediator is Moses) clearly shows that Pg's main interest resides in God's revelation to his people and not in Israel's occupation of the land.[12]

10. M. Bauks, "'Une histoire sans fin': L'impasse herméneutique de la notion de 'pays' dans l'Oeuvre sacerdotale (Pg). Quelques réflexions suite à la lecture d'un livre récent," *ETR* 78 (2003): 255–68 (260).

11. E. Cassin, "Le lion et le roi," in *Le semblable et le différent: Symbolismes du pouvoir dans le Proche Orient ancient* (Paris: La découverte, 1987), 167–213.

12. T. Römer, "Israel's Sojourn in the Wilderness and the Construction of the Book of Numbers," in Rezetko, Lim and Aucker, eds., *Reflection and Refraction*, 419–46 (424–25).

This claim conveys its own refutation. Because Gen 1:28 belongs to step one of revelation, it obviously cannot refer to Israel's occupation of the land. Yet Israel nevertheless belongs to humanity. Genesis 1:28 is the commission that is gradually fulfilled in the course of Pg. After the initial mishap of the filling of the land with violence (Gen 6:11), humanity begins filling the land (Gen 11), but further crises delay the accomplishment of the initial commission (Gen 11:28–32). The patriarchal narratives are devoted to the occupation of land. Every descendant of Terah is granted a territory (Gen 13:12; 25:16–17; 36:6–8, 43) but Jacob's seed fructifies and fills the wrong land (Gen 47:27; Exod 1:7). A third step is then necessary before humanity, in its entirety, finally fulfils the initial commission (Josh 18:1; 19:51). The entire plot, basic as it is, unfolds through a coherent Pg narrative. Nothing is postulated, every element is there to be seen. Yet, because it endangers his hypothetical tritoteuch, Thomas Römer prefers not to see the evidence.[13] From Gen 1:1 to Joshua, the land is one of Pg's main concerns. While revelation is indeed the daily bread of professors of Theology, Pg reflects the basic concern of people living in agrarian societies, in which even scribes grow most of the food they eat. While the monthly pay-cheque credited to the accounts of tenured professors is conducive to the divorce of revelation from the land, in the ancient Orient, civil servants only received the use of a plot of land which they had to farm to feed themselves and their families.

The coherence of Josh 5:10–12 with calendrical data in the Pentateuch has recently been explained as canonical alignments of the book of Joshua attributed to late editors eager to tie up loose ends and shore up the coherence of their scriptures.[14] In this chicken-or-egg type of debate, one should note that the existence of the postulated "aligners" is hardly supported by the end-product. The number of contradictions and deviations which escaped them does not provide overwhelming evidence against the opposite view, which claims that the coherence of Josh 5:10–12 reflects the coherence of Pg rather than late alignments. Moreover, attributing Josh 5:10–12 to Pg explains why Eleazar, the Residence and the congregation are not mentioned—Pg's Passover requires no cultic specialists.[15] If Josh 5:10–12 was canonically aligned, it is hard to

13. Ibid., 426.

14. See R. Albertz, "The Canonical Alignment of the Book of Joshua," in Lipschits, Knoppers and Albertz, eds., *Judah and the Judeans in the Fourth Century*, 287–303.

15. Contra E. Blum, "Beschneidung und Pesa in Kanaan," in *Freiheit und Recht* (C. Hardmeier, R. Kessler and A. Ruwe; Gütersloh: Kaiser/Gütersloher, 2003), 292–322 n. 98.

explain the lack of traces of the profuse Ps material, in particular the cult and the priesthood. Joshua 5:10–12 and 18:1 are easier to understand as the conclusion of Pg.

With כבש in Josh 18:1, the narrative which began with Gen 1 comes to a suitable end. A good illustration of this point is found in the chart Frevel produced to show that Pg ends at Moses' death (Table 7). Frevel tabulates keys words from Gen 1:28 to show that the *inclusio* opened by Gen 1:28 closes with Exod. 1:7 rather than at Josh 18:1:[16]

Table 7. *Frevel's "Proof"*

	פרה	רבה	מלא	כבש	שרץ
Gen 1:28	yes	yes	yes	yes	no
Gen 9:1	yes	yes	yes	no	no
Gen 9:7	yes	yes	no	no	yes
Gen 17:2	no	yes	no	no	no
Gen 17:6	yes	no	no	no	no
Gen 28:3	yes	yes	no	no	no
Gen 35:11	yes	yes	no	no	no
Gen 47:27	yes	yes	no	no	no
Gen 48:4	yes	yes	no	no	no
Exod 1:7	yes	yes	yes	no	yes
Josh 18:1	no	no	no	yes	no

In fact, the table demonstrates the closing function of Josh 18:1, which supplies the last element of Gen 1:28 that is missing in Exod 1:7, the rare √כבש. The domestication of the land could not be accomplished before crossing the Jordan, while the other components of Gen 1:28 are not repeated since they are already fulfilled in Exod 1. The rejection of this coherent conclusion duly transmitted in the text is based on precarious claims. In favour of a Pg limited to the Pentateuch, it is argued that in Pg the land is only a hope[17] or that Pg has an open end.[18] More subtle, but hardly more convincing, the land in Pg is deemed a conceptual framework within which YHWH's presence may be realized through the cult,[19] or else the land is the literary aim rather than the literary centre of the narrative.[20] The entry of the sons of Israel in Canaan had been part and parcel of the Moses–Exodus tradition for centuries before Pg connected

16. Frevel, *Blick*, 195.
17. Kilian, "Hoffnung"; R. Kilian, "Die Priesterschrift: Hoffnung auf Heimkehr," *Wort und Botschaft* (1967): 226–43.
18. Elliger, "Sinn," 121–42.
19. T. Römer, "Le Pentateuque toujours en question," in *Congress Volume: Basel, 2001* (ed. A. Lemaire; VTSup 92; Leiden: Brill, 2002), 343–74 (354).
20. Frevel, *Blick*, 350–52.

it with the Patriarchs, Creation and the Flood. Moreover, the conclusion of Pg does not exist as a hypothesis. It can be read by everyone who has eyes to see. For once, the king has his clothes on, yet almost everyone claims he is naked. Without Joshua, Pg is left with the *fiat* without the *lux*.[21]

The failure to acknowledge Josh 18:1 as the conclusion of Pg leads Köckert to interpret the missing כבש in Gen 9:1 as evidence of the irretrievable loss of the "very good" of Gen 1 in the aftermath of the Flood.[22] This understanding presupposes some kind of indelible stigma, an original sin too heavy for the goat for azazel to carry away. These notions reflect the stories of the Garden of Eden and of the Tower of Babel, passages which are never attributed to Pg. In Pg, there is no clue to suggest that after the Flood the very good of Gen 1 has been lost.

Various points after Josh 18:1 have been suggested as Pg's conclusion: the allotment of the land (Josh 18:10;[23] 19:27[24] or 19:51[25]), the refuge towns (Josh 20),[26] the Levitical cities (Josh 21:1–42),[27] the return of Phinehas from Transjordan (Josh 22:32)[28] or the deaths of Joshua and Eleazar (Josh 24:29–30, 33).[29] Since I excluded the cult and the Levites from Pg there is no need to go beyond Josh 18:1, except perhaps to integrate the concluding phrase, "They accomplished sharing out the land" (ויכלו מחלק את הארץ, Josh 19:51b). This phrase adds little to the narrative, though it refers back to Elohim's completion of creation in Gen 2:1 and places the land as the last word of Pg.

21. Kawashima, "Jubilee Year," 381.

22. Köckert, "Land," 150–51.

23. H. Seebass, "Pentateuch," in *Theologische Realenzyklopädie*, vol. 26 (ed. G. Krause; Berlin: de Gruyter, 1996), 185–209.

24. A. Kuenen, *Historisch-kritische Einleitung in die Bücher des Alten Testaments hinsichtlich ihrer Entstehung und Sammlung I:1* (Leipzig, 1887).

25. C. Steuernagel, *Das Buch Josua* (Göttingen, 1899); Blenkinsopp, "Structure of P," 275–92.

26. H. Holzinger, *Das Buch Josua* (Tübingen: Mohr, 1901); R. Smend, Sr., *Die Erzählung des Hexateuch auf ihre Quellen untersucht* (Berlin: Reimer, 1912); O. Eissfeldt, *Hexateuch-Synopse* (Leipzig: Hinrichs, 1922); G. von Rad, *Die Priesterschrift im Hexateuch* (Stuttgart: Kohlhammer, 1934).

27. S. Mowinckel, *Tetrateuch–Pentateuch–Hexateuch* (Berlin: Töpelmann, 1964); Driver, *Introduction*, 159; H. Haag, "Priesterschrift," in *Bibel-Lexikon* (ed. H. Haag; Einsiedeln: Benzinger, 1956), 1365–66. G. Fohrer, "Priesterschrift," in *Die Religion in Geschichte und Gegenwart* (ed. K. Galling; Tübingen: Mohr, 1961), 568–69.

28. A. Dillmann, *Die Bücher Numeri, Deuteronium und Josua* (2d ed.; Leipzig: Hirzel, 1886).

29. Nöldeke, "Grundschicht," 1–144.

* * *

Having reached the end of Part II, it is obvious that the significance of the land in Pg cannot be downplayed easily to justify the setting of the conclusion of the narrative before the entrance of the sons of Israel in Canaan. The delimitation of Pg with the help of the sabbatical calendar increases the importance of the land in Pg and turns it into one of its major themes. The technicalities of land tenure and Jubilee-regulated credit hardly support the spiritualization required to claim that the promise of land is as good as land holdings. Such a detailed discussion of land use and credit introduced by a new calendar is unlikely to end before the settling of the sons of Israel in the land of Canaan.

Conclusion

Whereas Part I and II dealt with the themes of calendar and land separately, it is time to bring together the main results of the inquiry. Genesis remains the least controversial part of the Priestly Document, and for this reason it provides a firm basis from which to launch a study of Pg's nature, extent and theology. Creation culminates with the redefinition of the lunar Sabbath into the seventh day, the only element of creation to be blessed *and* sanctified. Genesis 1:1–2:4 is the introduction to Pg and the presentation of the first two units of the sabbatical calendar, the day and the week (Chapter 1).

Pg's Overall Chronology

The sabbatical calendar provides the necessary data for the identification of a seamless chronological framework in seven eras, a framework which coincides with Lohfink's long Pg from Creation to the entry of the sons of Israel into the land of Canaan:

1.	Creation:	1 week
2.	Antediluvian:	600,000 days + 6 years + 6 months + 6 weeks + 59 days
3.	Flood:	36 weeks
4.	Drying out:	7 months
5.	Postdiluvian:	3 cycles of seven 365-day mean years
6.	Wandering:	14 jubilees minus 40 years
7.	Wilderness:	from 400 days to 40 years

The duration of each era carries sabbatical significance. For this reason, the sevenfold structure is more relevant than the bi- or tripartite divisions that have been suggested so far on thematic rather than chronological grounds.[1] The one missing day in the antediluvian era announces the salvation of Noah's family, while Enoch's 365 years signal the necessity of intercalation. Blending sexagesimal negativity with the positive aspect

---

1. O. H. Steck, "Aufbauprobleme in der Priesterschrift," in Daniels, Glessmer and Rösel, eds., *Ernten, was man sät*, 287–308.

of number seven, the Flood lasts 36 weeks followed by seven months of drying out before the land becomes fit again to provide food (Chapter 3).

The Postdiluvian era, the fifth one in Pg's overall chronology, spans from the begetting of Arpachshad two years after the Flood (Gen 11:10) to Abram's 75th year when he left Haran (Gen 12:4). The period is marked by dislocation and reproductive disorders in Shem's line, which the one people/one land principle featuring in the Table of Nations (Gen 9) renders more conspicuous. While the Semites experience problems in obtaining land, there is an overall improvement in the area of the calendar. Postdiluvian life-span are reduced, a hint that the calendar is intercalated and that years are longer. However, the era lasts 1095 years (3 × 365) which indicates that the mean 365-day year obtained with the intercalation of a week every seventh year is only valid for three consecutive cycles. The remaining guidelines for the second stage of intercalation are supplied in the sixth era.

Characterized by the wanderings of Abraham's line, from his departure from Haran (Gen 12:4) to the setting up of the Residence (Exod 40:17), Pg's sixth era indicates by means of Abraham's lifespan and of the dimensions of the curtains of the Residence that after the insertion of a week on years 7, 14 and 21, two weeks are intercalated on years 28, 56, 84, 112, 140 and 168 (Table 3). Although the sons of Israel have lost their land tenure in Egypt, their presence in the wilderness is compensated by the presence of YHWH among them, which is demonstrated by his daily provision of manna (Chapter 6). The duration of the period of wanderings is 14 jubilees, from which 40 years are missing, thus announcing the final era and supporting the claim that Pg does not leave the sons of Israel stranded in the wilderness.

The jubilee, the largest calendrical unit of the sabbatical calendar, is the basis of an elaborate financial system aimed at preserving tribal tenure (Chapter 5). As the previous era completed the elaboration of the intercalation of the calendar, the two festival cycles, the census and the survey of the land of Canaan render the period in the wilderness a crucial moment for setting out the regulations concerning land tenure. Meant to last only 400 days (from the setting up of the residence to the sending of the explorers), the wilderness era finally lasts 40 years due to the misinterpretation of the emptiness of the land (Chapter 8). In spite of the delay, the last Semite branch is finally endowed with land tenure. The celebration of Passover and of Massot in Canaan closes the wilderness era and the entire Pg narrative.

This meaningful chronology, which can only be obtained with the sabbatical calendar, argues in favour of a coherent Pg document from Creation to Canaan. Many will find it hard to accept that a non-sacrificial theological system lies at the core of the Torah. Many will doubt that parts of H in Leviticus could belong to Pg, or that the end of Pg spills over the limits of the Torah. While details of the delimitation presented here can be disputed, the reliability of the chronological framework cannot be dismissed easily since it is based on simple mathematics. None of the numbers are postulated. They are all transmitted in the various textual traditions. To claim that Pg ends before Canaan requires explaining why Pg, which starts with a seven-day week, would amputate this clear structure in seven epochs. Despite the many attempts to find a substitute conclusion, the Pg narrative only finds a suitable end when the sons of Israel, the last family of Adam's sons without a territory of their own, enter Canaan, apportioning and taking possession of their tenure. The celebration of Passover and Massot in Josh 5 only makes sense in the framework of the sabbatical calendar. Hence, the conclusion of Pg, as Lohfink claims, is to be found in Josh 18:1 where √כבש produces a broad *inclusio* with Gen 1:28 (Chapter 10).

In regard to length, my delimitation of Pg is similar to Lohfink's (see the Appendix). The rejection of the Tabernacle material is compensated for by the integration of parts of Lev 23 and 25. Contrary to Lohfink who postulates the presence of a dozen of lacunae where Pg material would have been lost, my delimitation dispenses with lacunae altogether and recovers a continuous narrative thread.[2] The recovery of an unbroken narrative is a token to the validity of my delimitation. It owes much to the demise of J, which allows the attribution of material previously thought necessary for a coherent J narrative besides the Priestly narrative.

The Sabbatical Calendar as Secondary Modification?

Against the use of the sabbatical calendar to identify Pg, it may be argued that calendrical data relative to the sabbatical calendar results from the modification of a pre-existing narrative that had nothing to do with the sabbatical calendar. In this case, the sabbatical calendar cannot support the existence and extent of Pg.

---

2. The only place where a small amount of material may have been lost is between Exod 36:8 and 10 where the subject shifts abruptly from the plural "wise of heart" to an unnamed individual who joins the curtains together. It is possible that the hiatus is deliberate (see Chapter 2).

It is impossible to prove that the sabbatical calendar was imposed upon a previously non-sabbatical narrative from Creation to Canaan, unless this secondary phase did not erase all the evidence of the pre-sabbatical system. One might just as plausibly argue that the non-sabbatical material in the Pentateuch belongs to the de-sabbatization of Pg rather than to a sabbatization of a non-sabbatical Pg. In any case, the non-sabbatical elements of the Pentateuch do not produce a narrative coherence anywhere approaching that of Pg, and this is what brought about the demise of the Yahwist.

Given the unmistakably sabbatical nature of Gen 1, one would have to discover a purely cosmological Creation narrative. Attempts at recovering multiple redactional layers within Gen 1 have sought to isolate "creation by deed" (*Tatbericht*) from "creation by word" (*Wortbericht*),[3] but they have not identified a coherent non-sabbatical Creation narrative under the tight syntactic structure of Gen 1:1–2:4.[4] Hence, it would be necessary to claim that the postulated pre-sabbatical narrative was not introduced by Gen 1. That it would start with Gen 2 is just as unlikely since Gen 2–4 are now increasingly accepted as presupposing Gen 1.[5] Could the non-sabbatical document begin with Gen 5? This is indeed possible since Enoch's 365 years are not specifically sabbatical and can reflect any solar calendar. At this point, one is confronted with the different flood dates produced by the sum of the begetting ages of the antediluvian fathers in the MT, LXX and SP. It is clear that the variations result from systematic alterations rather than from accidental corruptions,[6] but without the criterion provided by the sabbatical calendar, it is virtually impossible to decide which of the three textual traditions transmits the original system. Only the sabbatical calendar permits the recovery of the chronological system which produces meaning within the overall plot of the Pg narrative.

The fact that it is necessary to select dates provided sometimes by the LXX and sometimes by the MT to recover the sabbatical system strongly suggests that each textual family modified Pg's original sabbatical system in different ways and that none of them transmits an originally non-sabbatical chronology. Most, if not all, of the non-sabbatical data

3. C. Westermann, *Genesis 1–11* (London: SPCK, 1984).
4. O. H. Steck, *Der Schöpfungsbericht der Priesterschrift* (Göttingen: Vandenhoeck & Ruprecht, 1975).
5. A. de Pury, "Pg as the Absolute Beginning," in *Les dernières rédactions du Pentateuque, de l'Hexateuque et de l'Ennéateuque* (ed. T. Römer and K. Schmid; Leuven: University Press, 2007), 99–128.
6. Hughes, *Secrets*, 6.

can be explained as conscious modifications of the sabbatical calendar. If this cannot in itself confirm the original connection of Pg with the sabbatical calendar, it at least shows that, if it ever existed, the postulated non-sabbatical narrative cannot be recovered. Rather than postulating a hypothesis beyond evidence, it is more economical to accept that Pg is the architect of a clear and ambitious literary project[7] based on the sabbatical calendar.

This does not negate the fact that Pg used a number of older stories and myths of origin such as the Exodus and Conquest, Abraham, Jacob, but these elements had not previously been connected to a Creation account and a Flood narrative.[8] It is likely that the Pg narrative grew through the work of a chain of scholars who all accepted the sabbatical calendar, but the individual stages of this process are invisible to readers of the finished product because each stage fits the overall project and thus cannot be identified. Only contradicting elements can be recovered and attributed to later redactional phases (Ps). Recycling Passover and Sabbath traditions that did not conform to the sabbatical calendar, Pg transformed the full moon Sabbath into the seventh-day Sabbath and fixed the Passover in the spring. Searching for the original chronological system outside the framework of the sabbatical calendar, Jeremy Northcote identifies eight revisions of a Progenitor chronology which he establishes by choosing the lowest available figures.[9] This simplistic criterion is, however, unable to identify the overall project behind the chronological system of the Pentateuch or account for its subsequent modifications. Pg is the absolute beginning for the study of the formation of the Pentateuch.[10]

The sabbatical calendar is so well imbedded within the Pg narrative that the origin of the sabbatical calendar is likely to be earlier than *1 Enoch*. It coincides with the origin of the Pg narrative written as a manifesto in favour of the sabbatical calendar. The tight fit between story and numbers is much harder to explain if the sabbatical system was imposed onto a narrative that was not designed to support it from the outset. The sabbatical calendar is the *raison d'être* of Pg from its inception. The Astronomical Book of *1 Enoch* does not reflect some "sectarian"

7. De Pury, "Beginning," 101–2.

8. K. Schmid, *Erzväter und Exodus* (Neukirchen–Vluyn: Neukirchener Verlag, 1999), 253–78.

9. J. Northcote, "The Schematic Development of Old Testament Chronography: Towards an Integrated Model," *JSOT* 29 (2004): 3–36, based on the Progenitor chronology of A. Jepsen, "Zur Chronologie des Priesterkodex," *ZAW* 47 (1929): 252–55.

10. De Pury, "Beginning," 99–128.

calendar but the calendar upheld by the narrative that stands at the basis of the Torah. Nor was the Torah modified under the influence of *1 Enoch*. Ps, among other things, introduced components of other calendars (the 150 days in Gen 7:24; 8:3) into the Pg narrative in order to align the Torah with later calendar reforms.

Non-cultic Residence and Bloodless Atonement

Understanding the Residence as providing the last clue for the intercalation of the sabbatical calendar confirms Pola's claim that the Residence belongs to Pg while the Tabernacle is a hallmark of Ps (see the Introduction). Reworking Pg, Ps suppressed the sabbatical calendar and introduced sacrificial theology in order to support the exclusive privilege of a priestly class in collecting meat and other produce. The significance of the size and shape of the Residence for the intercalation of the sabbatical calendar proves crucial for the identification of Pg in Leviticus, in spite of Pola's contention that Pg ends in Exod 40:33b. The non-sacrificial reading of the azazel ritual in Lev 16 is coherent with the postdiluvian authorization of the killing of animals for *food* only (Gen 9:3) and with the non-sacrificial Residence. If neither goat sheds blood while sins are nevertheless carried away, the Tabernacle and its sacrificial gear are irrelevant (Chapter 5). The non-sacrificial reading finds confirmation in the description of the Passover in Exod 12, presented as a *meal* prepared from a lamb anyone may slaughter. Bloodless purgation of sins is fully coherent with the absence of the seven pairs of clean animals from Pg's ark narrative.

The "very good" nature of creation was not lost in the Flood and Pg's postdiluvian world has no room for the unclean animals presupposed by Noah's sacrifice and the impurities of the first half of Leviticus because the Flood purged antediluvian violence in order to sustain creational order. Antediluvian vegetarianism is indeed lost, but Gen 9:3 indicates that all land animals may be killed to be eaten, a directive which excludes the distinction between pure and impure animals and holocausts. For Pg, violence is *the* threat to creational stasis, the only sin Pg ever mentions (Gen 6:11; Exod 1:13–14). The threat is both contained and underlined by post-diluvian meat consumption. Humans kill in order to eat. Instead of atoning for sins, the shedding of blood is a dangerous act of violence now connected with the satisfaction of hunger. The azazel goat safely trots off into the wilderness with a yearly load of sins. Claims that he meets a fatal end in the hands of a desert demon are transparent attempts to re-admit sacrificial theology through the back door.

Ancient parallels certainly show that the use of carrier animals to eliminate ailments did not render sacrifices obsolete. Both notions coexisted as they do in the final text of Lev 16. Yet Pg's silence over sacrifices coheres with its vegetarian ideal, which is reactivated in the wilderness. Eating meat is a concession to the violence of animal slaughter because it provides life-sustaining food. The notion of holocausts is at loggerheads with Pg's coherent systems, as well as with several prophetic texts that record opposition to sacrifice. Milgrom claims that "the prophets did not object to the cult per se but only to its abuse"[11] but how does he know? Interestingly, Jer 7:22 refers directly to the wilderness period: "On the day of my making them (your fathers) come out of the land of Egypt, I did not command them concerning holocausts and sacrifices". Amos 5:25 also claims that there was no cultic apparatus during the Exodus: "Did you present sacrifices and a cereal offering to me the forty years in the wilderness, O House of Israel?" Either Pg follows a tradition transmitted by Amos and Jeremiah, or these texts are later than Pg and refer directly to Pg's presentation of the non-cultic Residence. In any case, a biblical religion without sacrifices and holocausts survived the restoration of the Jerusalem cult and left traces in the Epitome and the Latin version of Josephus's *Antiquities* (18.1.5, 19), which claim that the Essenes "do not offer sacrifices, as employing a different ritual of purification."[12] It is clear that the long chapters of sacrificial cuisine inserted into Pg's narrative did not erase Pg's notion of bloodless atonement. If Josephus was right, the Essenes were merely holding on to the original Torah theology, that is, Pg's.

Priestless Pg?

YHWH's presence among his people is mediated through the erection of the Residence, a doorless structure that underlines the absence of sacrifices. Yet, the absence of sacrifices does not render the priestly office redundant. Benjamin Ziemer notes that there are no priests in Pola's *Priesterschrift*.[13] In my version of Pg, Aaron is granted a role in the azazel rite and in the allotment of the land of Canaan. The function is

11. Milgrom, I, 482.

12. The Greek text states that they "send votive offerings to the Temple, but perform their sacrifices employing a different ritual." See R. T. Beckwith, "The Qumran Calendar and the Sacrifices of the Essenes," *RQ* 7 (1971): 587–91. See also L. S. Tiemeyer, *Priestly Rites and Prophetic Rage* (FAT 2/19; Tübingen: Mohr Siebeck, 2006).

13. Ziemer, *Abram*, 282 n. 23.

hereditary and is taken over by Eleazar who, after receiving his father's garments, is consistently referred to as "the priest" (Num 26:1, 3, 63; 27:19, 21, 22), while Aaron is designated once as Moses' prophet (Exod 7:1). Pg mildly ridicules Moses' request for a successor and makes it clear that Joshua is subservient to Eleazar the priest who is granted divinatory functions by means of the Urim (Num 27:21). Hence, Pg is not entirely priestless, although it unfolds a concept of priesthood which is far removed from what is expected from "Priestly" texts. No priest is required to slaughter the Passover lamb. No blood is shed to remove the sins of the sons of Israel. Yet the transfer of their sins upon the head of the goat for azazel requires the presence of Aaron (Lev 16:21). Because he died in the wilderness, Aaron never actually accomplished the ritual, and for this reason Aaron is only referred to as priest once (Num 26:64), a posthumous mention which makes up the seventh occurrence of the word כהן in Pg. Eleazar would have to accomplish the yearly transfer of the sins of the entire community seven months after the arrival of the sons of Israel in the land of Canaan. Before the first Day of Atonement in the land, Eleazar is responsible for the allotment of the land by drawing lots with the Urim (Num 27:21). In line with the spirit of the Jubilee, the first allotment narrated in Josh 14:1 would be followed by others at regular intervals to ensure an optimal distribution of land tenure after each census of adult males.

Hence, the absence of Aaronid priests and Levites does not mean that the priestly designation is inappropriate for Pg. Eleazar does not sacrifice animals, but he holds a key function in the maintenance of creational stasis. He transfers sins once a year on the goat for azazel and he periodically re-allocates land. Pg militates in favour of a broader notion of priesthood devoted to the combating of violence rather than the generation of more violence through sacrifice, through the sanctification of a particular priestly cast and a particular sanctuary, and ultimately through military endeavours blessed by the clergy. That Pg's priestlessness resonates with the Protestant priesthood of all believers does not turn Pg into a figment of Protestant imagination. The existence of a broad concept of priesthood emerges from the Torah itself and was threatening enough to provoke some angry denunciations. Pg's notion of the priesthood bears some similarities with Korah's. Korah considered that all Israelites share the same degree of holiness by the simple fact that YHWH is among them all (Num 16:3). Pg's Residence also stresses the importance of YHWH's presence in the midst of the sons of Israel, but not to the extent of rendering the Israelites holy. For Pg, the Residence is a sanctuary because its shape and the size reveal some aspects of the intercalation of the calendar, the only category to which Pg attributes holiness. The Residence was eventually subsumed into the Tent of Meeting to cover up Pg's unorthodox view of holiness, and Korah was said to have been swallowed alive into Sheol for daring to criticize priestly prerogatives (Num 16:33).

The Nadab and Abihu episode is another heavy-handed affirmation of the prerogatives of the official priesthood against the claims of unauthorized personnel. The execution of Nadab and Abihu confirms that, in spite of the covering of its Residence with the sacrificial Tent of Meeting, Pg's notion of priesthood was never forgotten. Leviticus 16:1 connects the azazel rite back to the Nadab and Abihu episode in ch. 10, framing the list of regulations concerning pollutions in Lev 11–15.[14] Hence, YHWH's presence among his people, which, according to Pg, only required the erection of the Residence (Exod 40:34 and Chapter 2), is conditioned in the Ps additions by the performance of purification rituals involving sacrifices on a daily basis. The insertion of Lev 11–15 in front of the passage presenting the azazel ritual prepared the fundamental transformation of Pg's bloodless atonement through the insertion of the sacrifice of a bull and a ram in addition to the sacrifice of the goat for YHWH and the mention of priestly clothes, the sanctuary and its cultic gear. From the point of view of a bloodless atonement, these elements are superfluous,[15] though they integrate the azazel ritual within the sacrificial system[16] and provide food to the authorized clergy.

The hecatombs prescribed by the biblical tariffs render the suggestion that Pg envisages a bloodless cult ludicrous, although as late as the second century C.E., not everyone agreed that "without the shedding of blood there is no forgiveness of sins" (Heb 9:22).[17] The sheer number of sacrificial victims prescribed in the Pentateuch suppresses texts suggesting that YHWH does not care about sacrifices, but it does not erase them.[18] The generous biblical tariffs can be read as the measure of the

---

14. Milgrom, I, 167.

15. Görg, "Azazel-Ritus," 15.

16. C. Körting, "Gottes Gegenwart am Jom Kippur," in Blum and Lux, eds., *Festtraditionen in Israel und im Alten Orient*, 221–58.

17. Isa 1:11; 66:3; Jer 6:20; 7:22–23; Hos 6:6; Ps 50:13: A. Destro and M. Pesce, "Forgiveness of Sins Without a Victim," in Baumgarten, eds., *Sacrifice in Religious Experience*, 151–73.

18. Milgrom, I, 483–85, and also his "Concerning Jeremiah's Repudiation of Sacrifice," in *Studies in Cultic Theology and Terminology* (Leiden: Brill, 1983), 119–21.

controversy that raged over the efficacy of sacrifices. That the goat for azazel is not sacrificed remains a thorn in the flesh of the entire biblical sacrificial system (see Chapter 4).[19]

Sacrifice is always part of an economic system. When Jesus urged his disciple to sacrifice (prayer, alms and fast) in private and thus eliminated the social rewards tied to sacrificial procedures (Matt 6:3, 6, 17), he struggled with the impossibility of uneconomic sacrifice. Centuries earlier, the writers of Pg and of some prophetic texts had reached the conclusion that "sacrifice is sacrifice only as the sacrifice of sacrifice."[20] Whereas Isa 61:6 and 66:21 suggest democratizing or globalizing the priesthood,[21] Pg sharply reduced its functions and removed its privileges by discontinuing sacrifice.[22] In the light of later developments that occurred in Judaism, Christianity and Islam, Pg's bloodless atonement was visionary. Although muted by Ps, the presence of Pg in the Torah contributed to the survival of Judaism after the destruction of the temple of Jerusalem by the Romans, while Ps's hecatombs appear as a belated reaffirmation of the traditional sacrificial cults that would sink into irrelevance after Constantine.

19. At the end of a 378-page study, Gane, *Cult*, 379–81, concludes that the Day of Atonement restores the equilibrium that was disrupted as a result of YHWH's year-round forgiveness and the guilt that accrues to him. Forgiveness endangers YHWH's reputation as ruler by creating an imbalance between justice and kindness. Thus it is YHWH himself who needs to be cleared from all the sins he has forgiven in the past year, although the said "forgiveness" was already traded against sacrifices. That the illustrations of this principle of theodicy come from the books of Samuel and Kings and not from Leviticus or the Torah itself suggests that the Day of Atonement is not as well integrated within the larger system of Israelite rituals as Gane claims (p. 36). With W. K. Gilders, *Blood Ritual in the Hebrew Bible* (Baltimore: The Johns Hopkins University Press, 2004), it can be argued that there is no coherent sacrificial system in the Bible.

20. D. K. Keenan, *The Question of Sacrifice* (Bloomington: Indiana University Press, 2005), 2.

21. Tiemeyer, *Priestly Rites*, 284–86.

22. Isolating an original Pg document which contains a certain amount of legal material but no interest in sacrificial matters is liable to be interpreted by the defenders of the antiquity of the ritual system of Judaism as perpetuating Wellhausen's prejudice in seeking the Gospel before the Law; see Weinfeld, *Place*. *Kashrut* and purity system are now seen as foundational to Judaism, but this kind of Judaism is not identical to the various Judaisms practiced at the beginning of the Persian period.

Land and Wilderness

The rejection of Noth's exclusion of legal and ritual material from Pg leads to the integration of most of the Passover material (Exod 12) into Pg. Celebrated for the first time as the last meal in the land of Egypt and for the second time upon entrance in the land of Canaan, Passover keeps the anticipation of the land alive (Chapter 4). Massot, the second festival of the sabbatical calendar, cannot be celebrated immediately after the first Passover because the sons of Israel find themselves in the wilderness. The first Massot festival is thus celebrated in the land of Canaan, after the second Passover. In the wilderness, YHWH responds to the people's legitimate murmurs by providing manna on a daily basis. From then on, the people of Israel know that YHWH is their Elohim.

Pg conceives of the wilderness as a suspension of space and the Flood as a suspension of time (Chapter 3). In the wilderness, Pg merely mentions the pseudonymous הר ההר and Abarim and does not refer to Sinai at all. The Sinai covenant is based upon rewards and punishments and is thus conditioned by human obedience, in sharp contrast to the unconditional ברית with Noah, with the land and with Abraham (Gen 9 and 17). The appearance of the rainbow is not dependent upon human behaviour. Circumcision is irreversible, whereas Sinai belongs to Ps's deuteronomization of Pg through the insertion of itinerary notices structuring a wilderness narrative greatly expanded by the insertion of the Sinai and of the Tabernacle in Exodus, the sacrificial cuisine of Leviticus, the priests, Levites, quails, giants, Kadesh, Meriba, Balaam in Numbers, and the entire book of Deuteronomy before Moses' death. These additions blur Pg's parallel between the Flood and the Wilderness, two periods when the land was rendered invisible. When the waters covered the land and the wilderness tore away the sons of Israel from their Egyptian land tenure, survival was only possible thanks to the miraculous devices of the ark and of the manna. Land tenure is the prerequisite for a healthy life which must be preserved by the use of the adequate calendar-setting festivals at the proper time and regulating land clearance and credit to prevent the loss of land tenure.

Land Management

On the basis of its obvious coherence with the sabbatical calendar, most of Lev 25 is integrated into Pg. This chapter becomes the cornerstone of land and credit management (Chapter 6). As Elohim sanctified the Sabbath, humans are called to sanctify the Jubilee, the largest unit (49 years) of the calendar, which mirrors the smallest unit (the week).

Sanctity is reserved to *rhythms* only. An obvious outworking of the sabbatical calendar and Gen 1, the Jubilee meshes land and sanctity into a tight fabric which belies the utopian qualifications that have been tagged to both Pg and the Jubilee. The release scheduled on the Jubilee is not a release of debts but the release of pledges when all financial obligations reach maturity.

The requirement of a year-long corvée on the seventh year, a novel interpretation of the sabbatical year (Chapter 6), is far more practical and realistic than the long holiday suggested by commentaries. It would have been a pragmatic measure in the Judean context of low demography and abundance of under-developed land. As the price paid by the *fellahin* for the protection of their land tenure, the clearance of large tracts of land every seven years ensured the regular increase of cultivated land, which in turn ensured that their land quota kept apace with increased population. The rest of the reclaimed land would have been used to create new estates. The census lists of the book of Numbers are necessary components of the land management delineated in Leviticus. Rather than the muster of an invading army, these lists guaranteed access to land to all adult males through the *musha'* tenure system. The second census taken at the end of the wilderness era underlines the necessity of regular census-taking to ensure the adequacy of land tenure and demography.

Genesis 1:1 spells out from the outset the land theme which throughout Pg takes on the very specific meaning of arable land. Any setting of the end of Pg before the entry of the sons of Israel into Canaan is therefore unlikely. The promise of the land to the patriarchs, Abraham's purchase at Machpelah and the sending of surveyors make no sense if Pg has no interest in the land and ends before the entry of the sons of Israel into the land of Canaan.[23] In spite of Jacob's *eisodos*, the sons of Israel did not lose their legal rights to tenure land in Canaan. Ishmael's seed also retains a foothold in Canaan thanks to Ishmael's burial in Machpelah.

A Scribal Text-Book

Although a narrative, Pg presents flat characters that do not foster identification by the audience. Scenery is non-existent; the actors are the decor. Emotions are rarely displayed (Gen 27:46; 29:13). Lists of ages, names and regulations interrupt and structure the narrative flow. The plot is minimal. Violence sets off the main crises (Flood, hard slavery, slander),

---

23. Blenkinsopp, "Structure of P," 287; Lohfink, "Priestly Narrative," 136–72. Although Elliger, "Sinn," sets the end of Pg before *Joshua*, he recognized that Pg's central theme was the land of Canaan.

while the minor crises (untimely death and infertility in Terah's lineage, lack of food in the wilderness) are quickly resolved. Lack of land for the sons of Israel provides the only crisis, sustaining narrative tension from Genesis to Joshua. Yet the action unfolds irresistibly with little suspense. Such style reveals the nature of the document, which is designed as a textbook rather than as a captivating story.

A scribal textbook is probably more fitting than the simile with children literature that was once suggested to designate Pg's didactic style.[24] To delineate the intercalation cycle of the calendar through the Flood narrative, the lifespan of ancestors and the size of curtains may seem odd. Yet, Pg constitutes a complete curriculum. Scribes learnt to read and write the artificial Biblical Hebrew which, as every written language, differed from the language spoken by the students. As is still the case in traditional Quranic and Rabbinic schools, students would have written and memorized Pg a section at the time. The class would then read the passage in unison, learning the text and its written appearance at the same time. Genesis 1, the first chapter of the curriculum, is ideally suited to inculcate the jussive and narrative verbal forms. The list of names in Gen 5, the second chapter of the textbook, is similar to the *onomastica* of ancient scribal curricula.[25] Scribes learnt mythology with the Flood narrative and geography with the Table of Nations (Gen 6–10). Then, Gen 11 offered the opportunity to check the students' ability to handle large figures for drawing up ledgers since, in contrast to Gen 5, the list does not supply the figures for the postdiluvian lifespan. And so the scribal apprentices ploughed through Pg, learning calendar intercalation, credit and land management, in preparation for their future tasks in local administration. Time and chronology are central to this didactic narrative which trained the small number of literati of the province. Rather than a repository of variants on different themes used for preaching as suggested by Campbell and O'Brien (see the Introduction), the Pentateuch derives from a basic document composed to train scribes (Pg), a document which was supplemented with Ps additions.

---

24. S. E. McEvenue, *The Narrative Style of the Priestly Writer* (Rome: Biblical Institute, 1971).

25. C. Eyre and J. Baines, "Interactions between Orality and Literacy in Ancient Egypt," in Schousboe and Larsen, eds., *Literacy and Society*, 91–119 (94–103); R. Hawley, "On the Alphabetic Scribal Curriculum at Ugarit," in *Proceedings of the 51st Rencontre assyriologique internationale* (ed. R. D. Biggs, J. Myers and M. T. Roth; Chicago: Oriental Institute Press, 2008), 57–68; P. D. Gesche, *Schulunterricht in Babylonien im ersten Jahrtausend v. Chr.* (AOAT 275; Münster: Ugarit Verlag, 2000).

Because Pg was the standard text-book through which generations of Judean and Samaritan scribes learnt their trade, it was a classic in every sense of the term. For this reason, once the conditions which saw Pg's composition were discontinued, Pg was not discarded but appended with a huge amount of material. It betrayed Pg's fundamentals but retained its basic structure.

Influenced by Pg from the outset of their training, scribes continued functioning in basic Pg categories, albeit to serve a much more elaborate priestly regime.

Pg's Date

The date of P has sometimes turned into an ugly confessional debate. To "prove" the antiquity of Judaism, amulets from Ketef Hinom, houses in Tell el-Farah North and ancient Near Eastern legal and ritual parallels have been adduced to prove that P is pre-exilic.[26] The problem is that parallels are so numerous that much of the Bible can be dated to any time between the Middle Bronze Age and the Hellenistic era. Hence, in spite of strident claims of the contrary, the scales do not lean in favour of a pre-exilic or even a pre-monarchic date for the inception of the Jubilee concept or of P in general.[27] The same can be said about the origin of the seventh-day Sabbath and of the sabbatical calendar.

Although Pg is structured by chronology and calendar, it provides no explicit indication to the time of its writing. The perpetual sabbatical calendar establishes a stable and unchanging rhythm forever. Yet, the parallels with the cosmology of Anaximander and Anaximenes indicate the seventh century as the earliest possible date for the composition of Pg.[28] A date already during the Neo-Babylonian era is not impossible for Pg since the sabbatical calendar derives from the schematic Mesopotamian calendar attested by the Neo-Assyrian MUL.APIN text. During the seventh century B.C.E., Babylon reformed the Ashur hemerologies that counted nine unlucky days every month, reducing their number to five per month (7th, 14th, 19th, 21th and 28th).[29] Even closer to the seven-day

---

26. Milgrom, III, 2241–45; Weinfeld, *Place*, 34–63.

27. Against Milgrom, III, 2242.

28. Halpern, "Israelite Astronomies," 323–52; B. Halpern, "The Assyrian Astronomy of Genesis 1," *Eretz-Israel* 27 (2003): 74*–83*.

29. In the seventh century B.C.E., Babylon reformed the Ashur hemerologies that counted nine unlucky days every month by reducing their number to the 7th, 14th, 19th, 21st and 28th days; see R. Labat, *Nouveaux textes hémérologiques d'Assur*

week of Gen 1, the Old Avestic calendar divides each month into four periods separated by four days (1st, 8th, 15th and 23rd) dedicated to Dadvah Ahura Mazda, the Creator.[30] Although the date of the Old Avestic calendar is not established, its similarities with Gen 1 render a pre-exilic invention of the seven-day week unlikely.[31]

Much confusion remains over the origin of the seven-day week.[32] Mary Boyce believed that the "Semitic week" influenced the Zoroastrian calendar.[33] Since the week attested in the older biblical strata divides the month in to two parts, between the full and the new moon, the direction of influence goes in the opposite direction, from the Zoroastrian calendar to the seventh-day Shabbat of Gen 1. The favourable depiction of Cyrus in Isa 40–45 suggests that the influence of Persia on Judaism surpassed the influence of Judaism on the Persian Empire. Genesis 1 has also been understood as reacting against Darius I's presentation of Ahura Mazda as the creator of heaven and earth.[34] Does Gen 1 reflect a traditional Semitic week which influenced the Zoroastrian calendar or does Gen 1 reacts against Persian propaganda?

Since the brunt of the sabbatical calendar is directed towards the lunar calendar, the introduction of a new calendar was a political statement marking the end of Babylonian rule and showing loyalty to Persian benefactors. A reform of the Babylonian calendar in Yehud makes more sense once the Persians took over the Neo-Babylonian realm, since this would have marked a clear break from the previous overlords. If the parallels with the Old Avestic calendar suggest an early Persian date for Pg and for the sabbatical calendar, the argument remains weak since the date of the Old Avestic calendar is not established. Another problem is that we do not know whether the sabbatical calendar was ever put into practice. The sabbatical calendar is well attested in the Bible and in the

(Paris, 1957), 306–7; E. Puech, "Requête d'un moissonneur du sud-judéen à la fin du VIIème siècle av. J.-C.," *RB* 110 (2003): 5–16 (n. 19).

30. A. Panaino, "Calendars I: Pre-Islamic," in *Encyclopaedia Iranica* (ed. E. Yarshater; London: Routledge & Kegan Paul, 1990), 4:658–68 (661); H. S. Nyberg, "Questions de cosmogonie et de cosmologie mazdéennes," *JA* 219 (1931): 1–134 (128–34).

31. A. Lemaire, "Le Sabbat à l'époque royale israélite," *RB* 80 (1973): 161–85; Sasson, "Time," 183–94.

32. E. Zerubavel, *The Seven Day Circle* (London: Free Press, 1985).

33. M. Boyce, *Zoroastrians: Their Religious Beliefs and Practices* (3d ed.; London: Routledge & Kegan Paul, 1985), 71.

34. J. Bremmer, "Canonical and Alternative Creation Myths in Ancient Greece," in van Kooten, eds., *The Creation of Heaven and Earth*, 73–96.

Dead Sea Scrolls, but nowhere else although a Ptolemaic account of brick-deliveries indicates that the seventh-day Sabbath was a day off for the workers.[35]

It is tempting to adduce the so-called Passover letter from Elephantine as proof that the sabbatical calendar was proclaimed with the support of the Persian administration. However, here the papyrus is fragmentary and the restoration of the crucial passage is based on Exod 12 and Lev 23.[36] Therefore, there is "no evidence for a Jewish calendar at Elephantine as distinct from the Babylonian calendar."[37] Far from being disused by the Achaemenids, the Babylonian calendar was still used in 527 B.C.E. by Cambyses's administration with three months intercalated during an eight-year cycle (octaeteris).[38] This piece of evidence, however, has little bearing upon the date of Pg and of the sabbatical calendar, since Pg may have created its own calendar rather than mimicking Persian models, while the Persian administration may have used various calendars besides the Old Avestic.[39] It is thus difficult to use the sabbatical calendar to date Pg during the reign of any particular Achaemenid monarch. A second factor should be introduced into the discussion.

On the basis of Pg's negative depiction of the Egyptian monarch, the one and only human foe in Pg, Albert de Pury has suggested a very narrow span (535–530 B.C.E.) for the composition of Pg. De Pury argues that Pg must be dated before Cambyses took over the Pharaonic title

35. *CPJ* 1:10.

36. B. Porten and A. Yardeni, *Textbook of Aramaic Documents from Ancient Egypt* (Winona Lake: Eisenbrauns, 1986), A4:1 Cowley 21 (Sachau Plate 6); B. Porten et al., *The Elephantine Papyri in English* (Leiden: Brill, 1996), 125–26. The only relevant elements duly transmitted are the fourteenth day (line 3), a possible mention of purity (הוו דכין, line 5), a prohibition of drinking (line 6) and a sunset (line 7). At line 7, לניס[ן] may not refer to the month of Nisan since only the top right corner of the *samek* is transmitted.

37. B. Porten, "The Calendar of Aramaic Texts from Achaemenid and Ptolemaic Egypt," in *Irano-Judaica* II (ed. S. Shaked and A. Netzer; Jerusalem: Ben Zvi Institute, 1990), 13–32 (32). Also S. Stern, "The Babylonian Calendar at Elephantine," *ZPE* 130 (2000): 159–71.

38. A second reform was introduced by Darius I in 503 B.C.E., consisting of seven intercalary years in a 19-year period: G. R. F. Assar, "Parthian Calendars at Babylon and Seleucia on the Tigris," *Iran* 41 (2003): 171–91 (171).

39. E. J. Bickerman, "The 'Zoroastrian' Calendar," *Archiv orientalní* 35 (1967): 197–207, has shown that the Achaemenids used the lunisolar calendar at least until 459 B.C.E. Between 471 and 401, the Babylonian calendar was still used in Aramaic documents issued by the Persian administration (almost all found at the colony of Elephantine in Egypt).

between 525 and 522 B.C.E.[40] Yet, de Pury admits that the argument is also valid after Egypt rebelled against Persian domination, after 464 B.C.E. The problem, then, is to decide which date is the most likely for the production of Pg.

De Pury also uses Pg's anti-sacrificial approach to shore up an early date of Pg during the reign of Cyrus on the basis of Herodotus (1.131) who claims that the Persians were hostile to sacrifice.[41] The Persian hostility to blood-sacrifice is a complicated matter[42] and there is no evidence for the worship of Ahura Mazda by Cyrus, apart from the Zoroastrian name of his daughter Atossa.[43] Darius I is the first Achaemenid ruler to mention Ahura Mazda in official texts. In favour of an early date for Pg, de Pury also adduces Deutero-Isaiah's "cyromania" and the euphoria following Cyrus's victory over Babylon, which would have spurred the composition of Pg already during Cyrus's reign while the euphoria lasted.[44] The amount of euphoria generated in Palestine by Cyrus's victory is, however, likely to have been very limited since no Persian troops were seen in Palestine before Cambyses's campaign to Egypt. Biblical studies have been plagued by the glorification of Cyrus which distorts the actual position of the little Judean country that never ranked very high on the Persian agenda.[45] The very existence of biblical *cyromania* (Isa 45:1) suggests that Cyrus was a distant quasi-mythological figure precisely because his accession to the Babylonian throne had little impact in Jerusalem. The relevance of the Cyrus cylinder to the people in Babylon was too quickly applied to Palestine to confirm biblical claims,[46] although the only proof of Empire-wide propaganda is the copy of Darius's Bisutun inscription found in Elephantine. The entire Persian era is characterized by unprecedented levels of subordination

---

40. A. de Pury, "The Jacob Story and the Beginning of the Formation of the Pentateuch," in Dozeman and Schmid, eds., *A Farewell to the Yahwist?*, 51–72 (70), and "Beginning," 125.

41. De Pury, "Beginning," 127.

42. De Jong, "Animal Sacrifice," 127–48. Henkelman, "External Exchange," 137–66.

43. M. Waters, "Cyrus & the Achaemenids," *Iran* 42 (2004): 91–102 (99); M. Boyce, *History of Zoroastrianism* (3 vols.; Leiden: Brill, 1982), 2:41.

44. De Pury, "Beginning," 128.

45. P. Briant, "Histoire impériale et histoire régionale," in *Congress Volume: Oslo, 1998* (ed. A. Lemaire and M. Sæbø; VTSup 80; Leiden: Brill, 2000), 235–45.

46. A. Kuhrt, "The Cyrus Cylinder and Achaemenid Imperial Policy," *JSOT* 25 (1983): 83–97, and "Cyrus the Great of Persia: Images and Realities," in *Representations of Political Power* (ed. M. Heinz and M. H. Feldman; Winona Lake: Eisenbrauns, 2007), 169–92.

of Palestine to Tyre and Sidon[47] and as late as 250 B.C.E., well into the Ptolemaic era, the Zenon papyri seem to indicate that Jerusalem still held a position secondary to Amman. Persian operations in Egypt are far more relevant to the study of the history of Jerusalem than Cyrus's conquest of Babylon.

Although it did involve the passage of troups in Palestine, Cambyses's conquest of Egypt hardly had more impact on Jerusalem than Cyrus's conquest of Babylon. The traditional date for the restoration of the Jerusalem cult may be supported by claiming that, in the wake of Cambyses's campaign in 525 B.C.E., the Persian authorities ordered the construction of a small fortress in Jerusalem to defend the southern border of Benjamin against the Kedarites. In this case, an altar may have been restored in Jerusalem.[48] Since, however, Kedar (Gen 25:13 Pg) was allied to the Persians until 387 B.C.E., when Kedar switched sides and joined Achoris during his campaign in Palestine,[49] it is not clear why the Kedarites would want to attack Benjamin in the first place. In any case, the books of Ezra and Nehemiah deplore that little happened during the reign of Darius I, and so it is clear that the turning-point for Jerusalem is to be sought among the series of Egyptian rebellions against Persian rule. Hence, Diana Edelman argues that, instead of ending with Cyrus's accession to the Persian throne, the so-called "exilic" period persisted until 450 B.C.E.[50]

A first rebellion in Egypt took place at the end of the reign of Darius I ca. 486 B.C.E. (Herodotus 7.1.5–8). Since Greek sources only mention it as prelude to Xerxes's expedition in Greece, the reason and extent of the rebellion are undocumented. In 484 B.C.E., Xerxes's first campaign was directed against Egypt, an effort which taxed Persian resources significantly since another four years were necessary before the army would march against Greece, although Darius had already prepared the European campaign before his death.[51]

---

47. O. Tal, "Some Remarks on the Coastal Plain of Palestine Under Achaemenid Rule," in *L'archéologie de l'empire achéménide* (Paris: de Boccard, 2005), 71–93.

48. Axel E. Knauf, oral communication.

49. See A. Lemaire, "Populations et territoires de la Palestine à l'époque perse," *Transeuphratène* 3 (1990): 31–74.

50. Edelman, *Origins*, 334–43.

51. P. Briant, *Histoire de l'empire perse* (Paris: Fayard, 1996), 541; H. Klinkott, "Xerxes in Aegypten. Gedanken zum negativen Perserbild in der Satrapenstele," in *Aegypten unter fremden Herrschern zwischen persischer Satrapie und roemischer Provinz* (ed. S. Pfeiffer; Frankfurt am Main: Verlag Antike, 2007), 34–53.

Twenty years later, early in the reign of Artaxerxes I (465–425 B.C.E.), Inaros led a rebellion backed by an Athenian fleet (460 B.C.E.). For about a decade, the delta slipped out of the Persian's grip, until the Achaemenids reasserted their rule in 454 B.C.E.[52] This challenge led the imperial administration to adopt a new approach to Palestine. Artaxerxes reorganized Yehud by building new administrative structures. Then, and only then, Jerusalem became the administrative centre, with a fortress and a temple.[53] The restoration of Jerusalem is contemporary with the construction of the first phase of the Samaritan temple on Mount Gerizim,[54] and to the first mentions of Mithra and Anāhita in Achaemenid royal inscriptions.[55] On the regional level, the reign of Artaxerxes also corresponds with the formation of an Idumean provincial district[56] and the appearance of a new type of seals in Yehud.[57] At about the same period, the elegant cursive Aramaic script from the Persian chancellery appeared in Palestine. These major changes mark the most important turning point in the area since the burned-land policy of the Neo-Babylonians following Nebuchadnezzar's failure to conquer Egypt.

Pg's demonization of Pharaoh could apply to several candidates before 450 B.C.E. If the Pharaohs who ruled during the neo-Babylonian era are excluded, Psammetichus III is the earliest choice. As the last ruler of the Twenty-sixth Dynasty, Psammetichus was overthrown by Cambyses in 525 B.C.E., after a reign of about one year (526–525 B.C.E.). Setting the formation of Pg during the short reign of Psammetichus enables the connection of Pg with the celebration of the onset of Persian rule over Palestine. The arrival of troops and of a new administration would have been celebrated with a new calendar. However, Psammetichus did not rebel against Persia. He was the legitimate successor of Amasis. Cambyses defeated him and took over his tile. For this reason,

52. L. L. Grabbe, *A History of the Jews and Judaism in the Second Temple Period*, vol. 1 (LSTS 47; London: T&T Clark International, 2004), 291.

53. O. Lipschits, "Achaemenid Imperial Policy, Settlement Processes and the Status of Jerusalem in the Middle of the Fifth Century B.C.E.," in Lipschits and Oeming, eds., *Judah and the Judeans in the Persian Period*, 19–52.

54. Y. Magen, "The Dating of the First Phase of the Samaritan Temple," in Lipschits, Knoppers and Albertz, eds., *Judah and the Judeans in the Fourth Century B.C.E.*, 157–211.

55. P. Briant, *Histoire de l'Empire perse* (Paris: Fayard, 1996), 264.

56. I. Eph'al, *The Ancient Arabs: Nomads on the Border of the Fertile Crescent, 9th–5th Centuries BC* (Leiden: Brill, 1982), 197–201.

57. O. Lipschits and D. Vanderhooft, "Yehud Stamp Impressions in the Fourth Century B.C.E.: A Time of Administrative Consolidation?," in Lipschits, Knoppers and Albertz, eds., *Judah and the Judeans*, 75–93.

the demonization of Psammetichus would be more likely had he usurped the throne.

The second choice is the unknown leader of the Egyptian revolt at the end of Darius's reign, which Xerxes I defeated in 485 B.C.E. In spite of the lack of information concerning the events, it is more than likely that the end of Persian rule was signified by the enthronement of a new Pharaoh. Compared to the two weeks of Bēl-šimānni's rule in Babylon a few years later, this disruption of Persian rule was long enough to produce a Pharaoh whom Persian propaganda could legitimately consider as usurper and demonize without qualms. Since Xerxes appointed his brother Achaemenes rather than Pherendates, the previous satrap of Egypt who was in office in 486 B.C.E., it is possible that the leader of the insurrection was Pherendates himself.[58] This unknown Pharaoh is a better fit for Pg's Pharaoh than Psammetichus, especially if he was a treacherous satrap.

The third choice is Inaros, son of Psammetichus, who resisted Artaxerxes I in the delta for about six years (ca. 460–455 B.C.E.). Setting the production of Pg in the wake of the second Egyptian revolt narrows the time before the formation of the Torah to one generation. This leaves enough time between Artaxerxes and the earliest date of the composition of the Torah (ca. 400 B.C.E.), but a non-violent, uncultic and priestless Pg hardly fits Artaxerxes's effort to develop Palestine by re-establishing fortresses and temples. The production and successful transmission of a work opposing Artaxerxes's policy at the time is highly unlikely. The leader of the 486 B.C.E. rebellion is thus preferable to Psammetichus and Inaros.

Pg's Setting

Out of a corpus of twenty inscriptions attributed to Xerxes, the longest is a trilingual text found in several copies in Persepolis and Parsagadae.[59] After listing the countries belonging to his realm, Xerxes mentions one or several (Babylonian version) rebellious countries which he crushed and whose temple(s) he destroyed because they performed festivals to the *daeva* (evil gods). This information is about the only reference to any particular action in the bulk of Xerxes's highly repetitive and formulaic inscriptions. Although no particular country or temple is specified, it is

---

58. E. Bresciani, "The Persian Occupation of Egypt," in *Cambridge History of Iran*, vol. 2 (ed. I. Gershevitch; Cambridge: Cambridge University Press, 1985), 509.

59. *ANET* 316–17; P. Lecoq, *Les inscriptions de la Perse achéménide* (Paris: Gallimard, 1997), 256–58 (XPh).

clear that the rebellions in Egypt and in Greece marked a radical break.[60] Whereas the reigns of the previous Achaemenid rulers were characterized by continuity,[61] Xerxes initiated a major shift in Persian policies. A century after Xerxes's reign, the Satrap Stela claimed that Xerxes seized sequestered land from the temple of Edjo at Buto in the Nile delta.[62] Apart from such drastic measures, Xerxes probably required local sanctuaries in or close to sensitive areas to convince the administration of their legitimacy, whereas Cyrus and his immediate successors had taken the legitimacy of all sanctuaries for granted by equating local gods with Ahura Mazda.[63] In response to Xerxes's more restrictive policy, Pg depicted a non-cultic residence, remained silent over temples and non-committal towards Bethel[64] rather than, as is commonly claimed, preparing for the revival of the Jerusalem temple.[65] The sabbatical calendar conveniently broke away from Babylon's lunar calendar and Nabonid's lunar theology.[66] Instead of mentioning Ahura Mazda directly, Pg equates YHWH with a generic Elohim who is first and foremost the creator god, as Ahura Mazda was. Pg's linkage of the seventh-day Sabbath with creation would have helped to convince the Persians that YHWH was the local name of the creator god and that no demons were worshipped at the sanctuary which produced Pg.

Hence, Pg reflects an interesting dilemma. While it is unthinkable that such a document was produced away from a temple, the only place having the means to finance scribes and a library of Israelite and Judean texts, Pg systematically downplays the importance of the cult and structure which supported its production. This paradox can be explained in the context of local sanctuaries under threat of being equated with *daeva*

---

60. M. Jursa, "From the Neo-Babylonian Empire to Achaemenid Rule," in *Regime Change in the Ancient Near East and Egypt* (ed. H. Crawford; Oxford: Oxford University Press, 2007), 73–94.

61. J. Wiesenhofer, "Kontinuität oder Zäsur? Babylon unter den Achämeniden," in *Babylon: Focus mesopotamischer Geschichte, Wiege früher Gelehrsamkeit, Mythos in der Moderne* (ed. J. Renger; Saarbrücken: SDV, Saarbrücker, 1999), 167–88.

62. G. Roeder, *Die ägyptische Götterwelt* (Zürich: Artemis, 1959), 97–106.

63. T. M. Bolin, "The Temple of יהו at Elephantine and Persian Religious Policy," in *The Triumph of Elohim* (ed. D. V. Edelman; Grand Rapids: Eerdmans, 1996), 127–44 (138–39).

64. Pg insists that Elohim departed from both Mamre and Bethel and that "he went up from him" after he had spoken to Abraham (Gen 17:22; 35:13); see de Pury, "Beginning," 126.

65. Against ibid.

66. Beaulieu, "Mad King," 137–66.

worship. During the reign of Xerxes, Pg was produced at Bethel or at Jerusalem if one accepts the traditional date for the restoration of the temple of Jerusalem. Since the Torah mentions neither Jerusalem nor Zion, and since Pg mentions Bethel, it is at Bethel rather than at Jerusalem that Pg was written. Although Pg attributes more importance to Mamre and Machpelah, Bethel is the more likely candidate since it was closer to the centre of power which remained in Mizpah until the reign of Artaxerxes.[67]

Given the little we know about Bethel, it is impossible to evaluate how far Pg's Residence reflects the reality at Bethel during Xerxes's reign. Yet it is hard to imagine that there was no sacrificial cult in Yehud at the time. The common notion that exiles carried the scrolls from Jerusalem's temple library to Babylon and produced Pg and other important proto-biblical works there[68] is as unlikely as claiming that the destruction of Jerusalem rendered Yehud templeless.[69] As long as Bethel functioned as a cultic centre, Pg had good reasons to downplay temple, priests and cult, given that the administration was likely to question the validity of the cult of YHWH at Bethel. There is no need to revive the defunct hypothesis of a rebellion in Judah at the time,[70] since the proximity of Palestine with Egypt was close enough for Xerxes's administration to test the loyalty of the elite at Mizpah and Bethel.

As much as the Egyptian rebellion, the Babylonian revolt in 484 B.C.E. also played a role in changing the attitude of the Achaemenids towards the local elite across the realm. In Babylonia, the local knowledge and administrative expertise of the traditional elite had made them irreplaceable until the reign of Xerxes, whereupon they became dispensable and started losing their privileges to less prominent families whose allegiance to the Persian rule was not in doubt.[71] Being in a far more peripheral

---

67. Edelman, *Origins*, 334–43.

68. Claiming that the scrolls were carried to Babylon, T. Römer, *The So-called Deuteronomistic History* (London: T&T Clark International, 2005), 109 refers to Mizpah as the administrative centre of Judah which merely ruled the "peasants and underdogs" remaining in the land. Römer thus reproduces the biblical myth of the empty land by emptying Mizpah and Bethel of everyone skilled in writing and producing ideology.

69. *Pace* J. Middlemas, *The Troubles of Templeless Judah* (Oxford: Oxford University Press, 2005), 133–44, while accepting that the Bethel sanctuary operated throughout the Babylonian era, refers to Judah as "templeless."

70. Julian Morgestein's hypothesis of a catastrophe in Judah in 485 B.C.E. is untenable; see K. G. Hoglund, *Achaemenid Imperial Administration in Syria-Palestine and the Missions of Ezra and Nehemiah* (Atlanta: SBL, 1992), 51–69.

71. Jursa, "Neo-Babylonian Empire," 91.

location, the position of the Benjaminite elite at Mizpah and Bethel was only jeopardized during Artaxerxes's reign when Jerusalem became the new provincial administrative centre. Between Xerxes and Artaxerxes, however, the Benjaminite elite had to make a show of loyalty, and it is in this particular context that Pg's resolute pacifism combined with the demonization of Pharaoh makes the most sense. It distanced Palestine from its rebellious Egyptian neighbour to allay Xerxes's suspicions. The presentation of violence as the cause of the Flood and the peaceful entry into the empty land of Canaan reinforced Pg's pacifist stance, convincing Xerxes's informants that Mizpah and Bethel would not pose a threat to his brother Achaemenes were his rule over Egypt ever to be challenged. Threats were not hypothetical, neither for Achaemenes, who was murdered in 465 B.C.E.,[72] nor for Bethel, which eventually suffered the fate that befell its counterpart at Elephantine in 410 B.C.E. In this way, Pg fits the imperial authorization hypothesis much better than the complete Torah.

The large majority of texts adduced in favour of the existence of such an authorization refer first and foremost to cultic matters.[73] The non-cultic Pg, rather than the entire Torah, would have been more convincing proof that the cult practiced at Bethel was not dedicated to the *daevas*. The aim was to secure on-going worship of YHWH rather than some hypothetic autonomy. Rather than postulating Persian pressure which forced Judean scribes to pen the Torah as a compromise between Deuteronomistic and Priestly traditions no later than Darius I,[74] the political situation prevailing during Xerxes's reign led to the production of Pg as a compendium of Israelite traditions. As the repository of Benjaminite lore and of the scrolls of Jerusalem's library after the destruction of the city, Bethel was the ideal place for the production of such a pan-Israelite compendium. Introducing the Patriarchs with the Mesopotamian motifs of Creation and Flood, Pg lent a cosmopolitan touch to the provincial lore. Pg filtered out the folkloric coarseness that had been the secret of the success of the Jacob cycle and thus dethroned the story-tellers by arranging the disparate traditions preserved in Bethel onto a consistent chronological line which lent a scientific air to the document. Pg reinforced its respectability by crafting a version of (pedantic) high

72. T. Petit, *Satrapes et satrapies dans l'empire achéménide de Cyrus le Grand à Xerxès I* (Paris: Belles Lettres, 1990), 202.

73. P. Frei, "Persian Imperial Authorization: A Summary," in Watts, eds., *Persia and Torah*, 5–40 (37).

74. E. Blum, *Studien zur Komposition des Pentateuch* (Berlin: de Gruyter, 1990), 333–60.

Hebrew which makes Pg the inventor or the first work written in what is now considered Classical Biblical Hebrew. A composition date of ca. 485 B.C.E. provides enough time for Pg to acquire the respectability of tradition before it was deemed worthy of redactional phases characterized by the insertion of the Tent of Meeting as blueprint of the Jerusalem and Garizim temples in the wake of Artaxerxes's preparations, which are to be dated no earlier than 450 B.C.E. Through the editorial procedure of neutralizing by addition rather than by deletion, various legal collections were inserted into Pg's narrative framework.[75] Although the new Samaritan and Judean temples led to Bethel's demise as a cultic centre and negated Pg's templeless vision, the Torah became the foundational document of the two rival centres and thus preserved Pg in its entirety.[76] The preservation of Pg's contents, however, does not imply theological agreement. If the seventh-day Sabbath was retained and is now applied in most parts of the world, the sabbatical calendar was disused, if it ever was put in practice.

The Empty Land in Historical Perspective

Pg's description of a Canaan that eats its inhabitants (Num 13:32) concurs with the archaeological record that reveals a steady demographic decline after the destruction of Jerusalem, not only around Jerusalem, but even in Benjamin, in spite of the transfer of the administrative centre in Mizpah and continuing cultic activities in Bethel.[77] The Babylonian period saw a decline of approximately 70% of the total population of the province, and up to 90% in Jerusalem and its environs. The Judean desert, the Jordan Valley, the western littoral of the Dead Sea, and the Shephelah experienced a similar decline. The Benjaminite region fared better, with a more moderate decrease in the size of the settled area during the Babylonian and Persian periods.[78]

While Babylon applied a burnt-land policy in southern Syria following Nebuchadnezzar's failure to invade Egypt (601 B.C.E.), the coastal route

75. J. Blenkinsopp, "Was the Pentateuch the Constitution of the Jewish Ethnos?," in Watts, ed., *Persia and Torah*, 41–62 (62).

76. See B. Becking, "Earliest Samaritan Inscriptions: A Parting of the Ways?," in Lipschits, Knoppers and Albertz, eds., *Judah and the Judeans*, 213–22.

77. Carter, *Emergence*, 247, estimates that the population of Persian Yehud was about one-third of what it was before the Babylonian conquest. See also H.-J. Stipp, "Gedalja und die Kolonie von Mizpa," *ZABR* 6 (2000): 155–71.

78. O. Lipschits, "The Rural Settlement in Judah in the Sixth Century B.C.E.: A Rejoinder," *PEQ* 136, no. 2 (2004): 99–107.

became once again a vital link in the wake of Cambyses's military operations in Egypt (525–522 B.C.E.). The highlands that were a desolate fringe depopulated by a series of exiles (722, 720, 705, 596, 586, 582 B.C.E.) were suddenly expected to produce agricultural surpluses to feed overland traffic to and from Egypt. The strategic position of Palestine became even more obvious during the reign of Xerxes and culminated with Artaxerxes's large-scale redevelopment projects. Fresh demand created a favourable economic situation, but in an age of manual labour, hands were required to boost the amount of available manpower if the demand was to be met within a few years rather than a few generations. Ruins housing owls and ravens (Zeph 2:14) had to be peopled again, land that lay fallow for half a century would prove very fertile if it could be cleared from the vegetation that covered it.

The wide-scale land clearing operations implied by the seventh-year ban on sowing suggest the presence of an administration strong enough to mobilize entire farming communities and the existence a nearby market capable of absorbing the extra amounts of meat, cheese, wool and leather produced during the sabbatical year, in place of the grain that was not produced. The sabbatical year is a practical response to tax-pressure, a powerful stimulus to increase production.[79] In the absence of chemical fertilizers, the only way to increase yields was to increase the surface under cultivation, which in turn allowed the progressive introduction of new settlers in the areas cleared by those already present.[80] Such operations are similar to the corvée gangs employed on the walls of Jerusalem in Neh 3,[81] except that men are mobilized for the entirety of the seventh year. Some of the land cleared on sabbatical years would be attributed to soldiers and other civil servants remunerated through the land-for-service system.[82]

Achaemenid rulers granted such estates in Babylonia, for specifically military purpose as their names indicate: *bît qašti* ("bow-land"), *bît sisî* ("horse-land"), *bît narkabti* ("chariot-land"). At first, such military tenures were just as inalienable as tribal tenure, although adoption by-passed

79. D. Warburton, "Before the IMF," *JESHO* 43 (2000): 65–131 (120–23).

80. A. Lemaire, "Histoire et administration de la Palestine à l'époque perse," in *La Palestine à l'époque perse* (ed. E.-M. Laperrousaz; Paris: Cerf, 1994), 11–53, identifies hints to such gangs of forced or voluntary works in Idumean ostraca, the book of Nehemiah and in Aramaic parchments from Afghanistan.

81. N. Naʾaman, "From Conscription of Forced Labor to a Symbol of Bondage," in *"An Experienced Scribe Who Neglects Nothing"* (ed. Y. Sefati et al.; Bethesda: CDL, 2005), 746–58.

82. Neo-Babylonian examples in G. van Driel, *Elusive Silver* (Leiden: Nederlands Instituut voor het Nabije Oosten, 2002), 226–73.

the rule of inalienability.[83] Military obligations attached to tenure were increasingly converted into money as the Persian kings relied more and more on mercenaries.[84] As western campaigns led troops further away from home, soldiers were absent from their tenures for longer periods and were unable to manage them. Such military personnel relied more and more on estate managers such as the Murašû family, who ran the estates for them until the reign of Xerxes I (485–465 B.C.E.), at which point the financial power of these intermediaries became a threat as they distanced the crown from its subjects. This is one explanation for the sudden end of the Murašû archives, the court breaking their power by setting up districts made up of a smaller number of military tenures supervised by a provost (*šaknu*) who was not part of the local community and who was regularly transferred from one district to another.[85] The question is whether or not Lev 25 fits the Achaemenid evolution of military tenures in Yehud.

It cannot be assumed that military tenures were granted in Yehud, yet it is likely that some of the medium-size sites of Charles Carter's classification were estates granted by the Persian king. Very small and small sites (1–5 dunams with a population average of 37–87) are not large enough to be considered as estates. Large sites correspond to semi-urban administrative centres (18.5 dunams, with a total population averaging 462.5). The medium-sized sites (5 to 12 dunams, with a total population averaging 212.5) would correspond to the size of estates attributed to individuals in the land-for-service system.[86] It is significant that the medium-sized estates belong to the category which increased the most during the Persian period, in particular in Judah.[87] This suggests that estates were set up mainly in Judah on dead land,[88] some of them around

83. S. Lafont, "Fief et féodalité dans le Proche-Orient ancien," in *Les féodalités* (ed. E. Bournazel and J. P. Poly; Paris: Presses universitaires de France, 1998), 515–644.

84. See Lafont, "Fief," 621–22.

85. F. Joannès, "Pouvoirs locaux et organisation du territoire en Babylonie achéménide," *Transeuphratène* 3 (1990): 173–89 (187); M. W. Stolper, *Entrepreneurs and Empire* (Istanbul: Nederlands historisch-archaeologisch instituut te Istanbul, 1985), 154–56. However, this new set-up did not prevent the power of satraps from rising to the point of challenging the king; see ibid., 630.

86. Carter, *Emergence*, 190, 215–16 n. 5.

87. Ibid., 221 Table 13. Edelman, *Origins*, 328, counts 26 newly established farmsteads or hamlets in Persian Benjamin and 27 in Judah.

88. Some twentieth-century land reforms developed estates on uncultivated land only; see D. Warriner, *Land Reform and Development in the Middle East* (London: Royal Institute of International Affairs, 1957), 8 (Italy) and 101 (Syria).

Jerusalem,[89] while in Benjamin the traditional system declined as people were attracted to the new estates in Judah.[90] This is a reversal of the situation prevailing at the end of the Babylonian era, when the majority of the population was concentrated in Benjamin. During sabbatical years, gangs of Benjaminite workers were sent to develop estates in Judah where most of the dead land was found.

The enforcement of the sabbatical year on the population of Yehud can be understood as the practical response to a drastic rise in demand for animal products. In the light of a well-established phenomenon by which areas on the periphery of major war theatres experience an economic boom resulting from the sudden demand created by the presence of armies nearby,[91] Xerxes's troops mobilized against Egypt in 484 B.C.E. generated just this kind of large demand for animal products. Flocks enlarged in prevision of the seventh-year ban on sowing would have boosted the production of meat, cheese, wool and leather to feed and equip the large contingents preparing to invade the Delta. Pg's positive assessment of Ishmael reflects the importance of transport logistics provided by Arabian caravaneers, which facilitated the exchanging of animal products for the grain that was not produced in the seventh year. Their active collaboration would also be essential for ensuring that villages are not raided while the men were away from home working on land-clearing projects.

If Pg's depiction of Ishmael fits Xerxes's early reign, does Pg's treatment of Esau also fit? Although Pg stands out as being far more favourably disposed towards Ishmael and Edom than traditions are, Pg insists that Esau moved away from his brother Jacob. How far is hard to decide, but it is obvious that with Esau Pg hits a difficult reality. Pg's non-violence and universalism does not result in a totally irenic world. In a rare outburst of emotions, Rebecca's tantrum over the daughters of Heth (Gen 27:46) prepares the way for Esau's move to his own land tenure away from Jacob's (Gen 36:6–8, 43). The stress upon the distance separating Esau from Canaan suggests that the presence of Edomites in

89. New farmsteads are recorded in the region surrounding Persian Jerusalem; see Carter, *Emergence*, 250.

90. Ibid., 238.

91. P. Crone, "Quraysh and the Roman Army: Making Sense of the Meccan Leather Trade," *BSO(A)S* 70 (2007): 63–88. For instance, one legion (5,000 men) required the hides of some 65,000 goats simply for the tents used on campaigns. This does not include the leather used to make scabbards, shields, covers, bags, horse gears, sandals, water and wine skins, strings, slings, straps and so on. The constant warfare in Northern Syria during the centuries preceding the emergence of Islam depleted the Syrian economy and greatly favoured Arabia.

the Negeb loomed large on Pg's agenda, a presence that Pg was at pains to prove illegitimate. The indirect assertion of the legitimacy of the Bethel cult went hand-in-hand with a critique of the southern neighbours who occupied parts of the land of Canaan shown to Moses. This rhetorical strategy resembles that adopted by Canaanite petty rulers, who are known to have sent numerous declarations of their loyalty to the Amarna Pharaoh, while constantly blaming the ruler of the neighbouring city-state. Pg is nevertheless careful to recognize the presence and the rights of other residents (גרים) in Canaan after the settlement of the sons of Israel there. These גרים are not afforded the personal status of the sons of Israel and do not worship God under the name of YHWH. Yet, the legitimacy of their presence in Canaan is not questioned, since it would have been at loggerheads with the imperial policy of granting land to administrators and soldiers. In fact, Israelites remain גרים in Canaan as much as the other settlers (Lev 25:23). Rather than loudly stating the rights of the Benjaminite population, Pg handed them over to the good-will of Xerxes.

In conclusion, this presentation of Pg's chronology and calendar should refute the claim that "it is possible to discover in the text whatever we wish, for the figures are flexible and can be made to fit all sorts of numerical combinations..."[92] The simple mathematics of the sabbatical calendar offer a level of control for the identification of redactional layers never attained with redactors postulated on the basis of vague theological categories. The discovery of a coherent Pg document recovered intact from the bulk of the Hexateuch impacts directly upon the understanding of the formation of the Pentateuch. It offers an alternative to the Persian date of J and supports the phasing out of J since there is not enough material in the Pentateuch to sustain two separate coherent narratives.

Beyond scholarly debates over the formation the Pentateuch, Pg's presentation of Ishmael and of the peaceful entry of the sons of Israel into the land of Canaan where they later reside harmoniously with non-Israelites is prophetic. Pg has the potential for overcoming the short-comings of the canonical Exodus motif which entails the wiping out of the Canaanites in order to settle the former slaves. With its universalism, its concept of an empty Canaan and its recognition of the legitimate presence of non-Israelites in Canaan, Pg offers a rare scriptural basis for denouncing the use of the Hebrew Bible and the Quran in support of Israelite/Israeli and Islamic terror. Pg's notion of spaceless sanctity

92. Cassuto, *Genesis*, 258.

effectively undercuts all ancient and modern political and religious manipulations of holy space.

These topics require more specialized discussion, but they are enough to point out that the relevance of the study of Pg extends far beyond "continental" critical exegesis.

APPENDIX:
DELIMITATIONS OF THE PRIESTLY NARRATIVE

	Lohfink	Pola	Guillaume
Genesis			
1	1–31	1–28, 31	1–31
2	1–4a	1–4a	1–4a
5	1–27, 28*, 30–32	1–28, 30–32	1–28*, 30–32
6	9–22	9–22	9–22
7	6, 11, 13–16a, 17a, 18–21, 24	6, 11, 13–16a, 17a, 18–21, 24	11–16a, 17–21
8	1, 2a, 3b–5, 13a, 14–19	1, 2a, 3b–5, 13a, 14–19	1–3a, 4–5, 13–19
9	1–3, 7–17, 28–29	1–17, 28–29	1–3, 5–17, 28–29
10	1–7, 20, 22–23, 31–32	1a, 2*–4*, 5*–7, 20, 22–23, 31–32	1–7, 20, 22–23, 31–32
11	10–27, 31–32	10–27, 31–32	10–32
12	4b, 5	4b, 5	4b–5
13	6, 11, 12*	6, 11b, 12*	6, 11b, 12*
16	1, 3, 15–16	1a, 3, 15–16	1, 3, 15–16
17	1–13, 14*, 15–27	1–27	1–27
19	29	29	
21	1b–5	1b–5	2*–5
23	1–20	1–20	1–20
25	7–11a, 12–17, 19–20…26b	7–11a, 12–17, 19–20…26b	7–10, 12–17, 19–21*, 24, 26b
26	34–35	34–35	34–35
27	46	46	46
28	1–9	1–9…	1–9
29			13a, 14a
30			43a
31	…18*	18*	17a, 18
33	18a	18a	18a
35	6a, 9–15, 22b–29	6a, 9*, 10–13, 15, 22b–29	6a, 9–15, 27–29
36	1–2a…6–8, 40–43	1–8	1a, 6–8a, 40–43
37	1–2	1–2a…	1–2a*
41	46a	46a	
46	6–7	6–7	6b–7

47	27b–28	27b–28	27–28
48	3–6	3–7	
49	1a, 28b–33	1a, 28b–32, 33*	1, 29–33
50	12–13	12–13	12–13

Exodus

1	1–5, 7, 13–14	1a, 2–4, 5b–7*, 13–14	7*, 13–14
2	23*, 24–25	23*, 24–25	23*–25
6	2–12	2–9	2–12
7	1–13, 19, 20*, 21b–22	1–7, 19, 20*, 21b–22	1–13, 19–20*, 21*, 22
8	1–3, 11*, 12–15	1–3, 11*, 12–15	1–3, 11*–15
9	8–12	8–12	
11	9–10	9–10	
12	37a, 40–42	1, 3–20, 28, 40–41	1–8*, 11–13, 21–24, 28–31a, 37*, 40–42
13	20		
14	1–4, 8–9, 10*, 15–18, 21*, 22–23, 26, 27*, 28–29	1–4, 8a, 10*, 15–18, 21*, 22–23, 26, 27*, 28–29	5–8a, 15–16, 21–23, 26–29
15	22*, 27		
16	1–3, 6–7, 9–12, 13...14*...16*–18*, 19–21a, 22*, 23–26, 31a, 35b		2–3, 11–12*, 13*–18, 21a, 31a, 35b
17	1*		

	Lohfink	Pola	Frevel[1]	Guillaume
Exodus				
19	1–2a	1	1, 2*	
24	15b–18a	15b–17, 18*	15b–16, 18*	
25	1–2, 8, 9*	1, 8a, 9	1, 2*, 8–9	1–2
26	1–30		1–19*, 30	
29	43–46	45–46	43–44*, 45–46	
31	...18			
34	29–32			
35	4, 5a, 10, 20–22a, 29		1	22–23*, 25
36	2–3a, 8*			8–13
39	32–33a, 42–43		32, 43	
40	17, 33b–35	16, 17a, 33b	17, 33b, 34–35	17, 34b

1. Frevel, *Blick*, only covers the second part of Pg.

	Lohfink	*Frevel*	*Guillaume*
Leviticus			
9	1*, 2–3, 4b–7, 8*, 12a, 15a, 21b–24		
16			2a*, 5a, 7a, 8–10, 21–22, 29*, 34
23			1–6, 23–27, 31a
25			1*–16, 23–31, 44–54
Numbers			
1	1, 2*, 3*, 19b, 21*, 23*, 25*, 27*, 29*, 31*, 33*, 35*, 37*, 39*, 41*, 43*, 46		1*, 2–9, 10*–18, 46
2	1*, 2, 3*, 5*, 7a, 10a, 12*, 14a, 18a, 20a, 22a, 25a, 27*, 29a, 34		
4	1*…2*, 3, 34, *35–36, 37*, 38–40, 41*, 42–44, 45*, 46*, 47–48		
10	11–13	11a, 12a*	11a
12	16b	16	
13	1–3a, 17*, 21, 25, 26*, 32	1–2a, 3*, 17a, 21, 25–26a, 32	1–2, 3b–10, 11*–21a, 23–26a*, 32*
14	1a, 2, 5–7, 10, 26–28, 29*, 35–38	1a, 2, 5–7, 10, 26–29*, 35–38	1–2, 3b–7, 26–29, 35, 38
20	…1*…2, 3b–7, 8*, 10, 11b, 12*…22b… 23*, 25–29	1a, 2, 3*, 4, 6–8, 10, 11b, 22b–23a*, 24*, 25–29	22b, 23*, 25–29
21	4*, 10–11	4*, 10–11	
22	1	1	
26			1*, 2–3*, 51–56, 63*, 64*, 65
27	12–14a, 15–23		12, 15–23
34	1–18		1–2, 5b–6, 7–8a*, 11b–13*
Deuteronomy			
1	3	1, 3a	
32	48–52	48–50, 52	
34	1*…7–9	1*, 5*, 7a, 8	1, 4–5*, 7–8
Josh			
4	…19*		19*
5	10–12		9–12
14	1, 2*		1, 2*
18	1		1*
19	…51		51*

BIBLIOGRAPHY

Abegg, M. G. "The Calendar at Qumran." Pages 145–71 in Neusner and Avery-Peck, eds., *Judaism in Late Antiquity. Part Five, The Judaism of Qumran.*

Abraham, K. "Middle Assyrian Period." Pages 161–222 in Westbrook and Jasnow, eds., *Security for Debt.*

Achenbach, R. "Die Erzählung von der gescheiterten Landnahme von Kadesch Barnea." *ZABR* 9 (2003): 56–123.

Aejmelaeus, A. "Septuagintal Translation Techniques." Pages 116–30 in *On the Trail of Septuagint Translators.* Kampen: Kok Pharos, 1993.

Albani, M. *Astronomie und Schöpfungsglaube.* WMANT 68. Neukirchen–Vluyn: Neukirchener Verlag, 1992.

———. *Der eine Gott und die himmlischen Heerscharen.* Leipzig: Evangelische Verlagsanstalt, 2000.

———. "Die lunaren Zyklen im 364-Tage-Festkalendar van 4QMischmerot/4Qse." *Mitteilungen und Beiträge* 4 (1992): 3–47.

———. "Israels Feste im Herbst und das Problem des Kalenderwechsels in der Exilzeit." Pages 111–56 in Blum and Lux, eds., *Festtraditionen in Israel.*

Albertz, R. "The Canonical Alignment of the Book of Joshua." Pages 287–303 in Lipschits, Knoppers and Albertz, eds., *Judah and the Judeans.*

———. "Der Kampf gegen die Schuldenkrise." Pages 40–60 in Albertz, ed., *Der Mensch als Hüter seiner Welt.*

——— ed. *Der Mensch als Hüter seiner Welt.* Stuttgart: Calwer, 1990.

Altorki, S., and D. Cole. "Land and Identity Among Awlad "Ali Bedouin: Egypt's Northwest Coast." Pages 634–53 in Chatty, ed., *Nomadic Societies.*

Amit, Y. "The Jubilee Law: An Attempt at Instituting Social Justice." Pages 47–59 in *Justice and Righteousness.* Edited by H. G. Reventlow and Y. Hoffman. JSOTSup 137. Sheffield: JSOT Press, 1992.

Amphoux, C.-B., A. Frey and U. Schattner-Rieser, eds. *Études sémitiques et samaritaines offertes à Jean Margain.* Lausanne: Zèbre, 1998.

Andersen, Ø. "The Significance of Writing in Early Greece: A Critical Appraisal." Pages 73–90 in Schousboe and Larsen, eds., *Literacy and Society.*

Andreasen, N.-E. A. *The Old Testament Sabbath.* Missoula: Scholars Press, 1972.

Antoun, R. T. *Arab Village.* Bloomington: Indiana University Press, 1972.

Arambarri, J. M. "Gen. 1,1–2,4a. Ein Prolog und ein Programm für Israel." Pages 65–86 in *Gottes Wege suchend.* Edited by F. Sedlmeier. Würzburg: Echter, 2003.

Archi, A. "The Archives of Ebla." Pages 72–86 in *Cuneiform Archives and Libraries.* Edited by K. R. Veenhof. Leiden: Nederlands historisch-archaeologisch Instituut, 1986.

Arnaud, D. *Emar VI.* Paris: Recherche sur les civilisations, 1986–87.

Assar, G. R. F. "Parthian Calendars at Babylon and Seleucia on the Tigris." *Iran* 41 (2003): 171–91.

Assmann, J. "Zeit und Geschichte in frühen Kulturen." Pages 489–508 in *Time and History.* Edited by F. Stadler and M. Stöltzner. Frankfurt: Ontos, 2006.

Atran, S. "Hamula Organisation and Mashaʾa Tenure in Palestine." *Man* 21 (1986): 271–95.

Atwell, J. E. "An Egyptian Source for Genesis 1." *JTS* 51 (2000): 441–77.

Auld, A. G. *Joshua.* Brill: Leiden, 2005.

Austin, M., and P. Vidal-Naquet. *Economie et société en Grèce ancienne.* Paris: Colin, 1972.

Bacon, B. W. "Calendar of Enoch and Jubilees." *Hebraica* 8 (1891–92): 79–88.

Bailey, L. R. "Biblical Math as Heilsgeschichte?" Pages 84–102 in *A Gift of God in Due Season.* Edited by R. D. Weis and D. M. Carr. JSOTSup 225. Sheffield: JSOT Press, 1996.

Barc, B. "Bible et mathématiques à la période hellénistique." Pages 269–79 in Amphoux, Frey and Schattner-Rieser, eds., *Études sémitiques et samaritaines.*

———. "Du temple à la synagogue." Pages 11–26 in *KATA TOYΣ O' «selon les Septantes» Mélanges offerts en hommage à Marguerite Harl.* Edited by G. Dorival and O. Munnich. Paris: Cerf, 1995.

———. "La chronologie biblique d'Adam à la mort de Moïse." *LTP* 55 (1999): 215–26.

Barnouin, M. "Recherches numériques sur la généalogie de Genèse V." *RB* 77 (1970): 347–65.

Barr, J. *Biblical Words for Time.* London: SCM, 1962.

———. "Was Everything that God Created Really Good?" Pages 55–65 in *God in the Fray.* Edited by T. Linafelt and T. K. Beal. Minneapolis: Fortress, 1998.

Barth, J. *Die Nominalbildung in den semitischen Sprachen.* Hildesheim: Olms, 1967.

Barthélemy, A. *Dictionnaire Arabe–Français.* Paris: Geuthner, 1935.

Bartelmus, R. "Begegnung in der Fremde. Anmerkungen zur theologischen Relevanz der topographischen Verortung der Berufungsvisionen des Mose und des Ezechiel (Ex 3,1–4,17 bzw. Ez 1,1–3,15)." *BN* 78 (1995): 21–38.

Bauks, M. "Die Begriffe מוֹרָשָׁה und אֲחֻזּה in Pg" *ZAW* 116 (2004): 171–88.

———. *Die Welt am Anfang.* WMANT 74. Neukirchen–Vluyn: Neukirchener Verlag, 1997.

———. "La signification de l'espace et du temps dans 'l'historiographie sacerdotale'." Pages 29–45 in Römer, ed., *The Future of the Deuteronomistic History.*

———. "Les notions de 'peuple' et de 'terre' dans l'oeuvre sacerdotale Pg." *Transeuphratène* 30 (2005): 19–36.

———. "'Une histoire sans fin'. L'impasse herméneutique de la notion de 'pays' dans l'Oeuvre sacerdotale Pg. Quelques réflexions suite à la lecture d'un livre récent." *ETR* 78 (2003): 255–68.

Baumgarten, A. I., ed. *Sacrifice in Religious Experience.* Leiden: Brill, 2002.

Beard, L. "From Barefootedness to Sure-footedness: Contrasts Involving Sacred Space and Movement in the Bible." *JS* 14 (2005): 235–60.

Beaulieu, P.-A. "Nabonidus the Mad King." Pages 137–66 in Heinz and Feldman, eds., *Representations.*

Becking, B. "Earliest Samaritan Inscriptions: A Parting of the Ways?" Pages 213–22 in Lipschits, Knoppers and Albertz, eds., *Judah and the Judeans.*

Beckwith, R. T. *Calendar, Chronology and Worship.* Leiden: Brill, 2005.

———. "The Essene Calendar and the Moon." *RQ* 59 (1992): 457–66.

———. "The Qumran Calendar and the Sacrifices of the Essenes." *RQ* 7 (1971): 587–91.

———. "The Qumran Temple Scroll and Its Calendar: Their Character and Purpose." Pages 67–66 in *Calendar, Chronology and Worship.*

———. "The Significance of the 364-day Calendar for the Old Testament Canon." Pages 54–66 in *Calendar, Chronology and Worship.*

Bellis, A. O., and J. S. Kaminsky, eds. *Jews, Christians, and the Theology of the Hebrew Scriptures.* Atlanta: SBL, 2000.

Ben-Dov, J., and W. Horowitz. "The Babylonian Lunar Three in Calendrical Scrolls from Qumran." *ZA* 95 (2005): 104–20.

Ben Zvi, E. "What is New in Yehud? Some Considerations." Pages 32–48 in *Yahwism After the Exile.* Edited by R. Albertz and B. Becking. Assen: Van Gorcum, 2003.

Bergant, D. "Is the Biblical Worldview Anthropocentric?" *NTR* 4 (1991): 5–14.

Bergsma, J. S. "The Jubilee: A Post-exilic Priestly Attempt to Reclaim Lands?" *Biblica* 84 (2003): 225–46.

Berner, C. *Jahre, Jahrwochen und Jubiläen.* BZAW 363. Berlin: de Gruyter, 2006.

Bibb, B. D. "Nadab and Abihu Attempt to Fill a Gap." *JSOT* 96 (2001): 83–99.

Bickerman, E. J. "The 'Zoroastrian' Calendar." *Archív orientální* 35 (1967): 197–207.

Black, J., and A. Green. 'Seven Dots.' Page 162 in *Gods, Demons and Symbols of Ancient Mesopotamia: An Illustrated Dictionary.* London: British Museum Press, 1992.

Blenkinsopp, J. *The Pentateuch: An Introduction to the First Five Books of the Bible.* New York: Doubleday, 1992.

———. "A Post-exilic Lay Source in Genesis 1–11." Pages 49–62 in *Abschied vom Jahwisten.* Edited by J. C. Gertz, K. Schmid and M. Witte. BZAW 315. Berlin: de Gruyter, 2002.

———. "Structure and Meaning in the Sinai–Horeb Narrative." Pages 109–25 in *A Biblical Itinerary in Search of Method, Form and Content.* Edited by E. Carpenter. JSOTSup 240. Sheffield: Sheffield Academic Press, 1997.

———. "The Structure of P." *CBQ* 38 (1976): 276–92.

———. "Was the Pentateuch the Constitution of the Jewish Ethnos?" Pages 41–62 in Watts, ed., *Persia and Torah.*

Blum, E. "Beschneidung und Pesa in Kanaan." Pages 292–322 in *Freiheit und Recht.* Edited by C. Hardmeier, R. Kessler and A. Ruwe. Gütersloh: Kaiser/Gütersloher, 2003.

———. *Die Komposition der Vätergeschichte.* Neukirchen–Vluyn: Neukirchener Verlag, 1984.

———. *Studien zur Komposition des Pentateuch.* BZAW 189. Berlin: de Gruyter, 1990.

Blum, E., and R. Lux, eds. *Festtraditionen in Israel und im Alten Orient.* VWGT 28. Gütersloh: Gütersloher, 2006.

Bogaert, P.-M. "La construction de la tente (Ex 36–40) dans le Monacensis de la plus ancienne version latine." Pages 62–76 in *L'enfance de la Bible hébraïque.* Edited by A. Schenker and P.-M. Bogaert. Geneva: Labor et Fides, 2005.

———. "L'importance de la Septante et du 'Monacensis' de la Vetus Latina pour l'exégèse du livre de l'Exode (chaps. 35–40)." Pages 399–428 in Vervenne, ed., *Studies in the Book of Exodus.*

Bolin, T. M. "The Temple of יהו at Elephantine and Persian Religious Policy." Pages 127–44 in *The Triumph of Elohim*. Edited by D. V. Edelman. Grand Rapids: Eerdmans, 1996.

Borgonovo, G. "Significato numerico delle cronologie bibliche e rilevanza delle varianti testuali (TM–LXX–SAM)." *RSB* 9 (1997): 139–67.

Bork, F. "Zur Chronologie der biblischen Urgeschichte." *ZAW* 47 (1929): 206–22.

Börker-Klähn, J. *Altvorderasiatische Bildstelen und vergleichbare Felsrelief*. Mainz: von Zabern, 1982.

Bosshard-Nepustil, E. *Vor uns die Sinflut*. BWANT 165. Stuttgart: Kohlhammer, 2005.

Bovon, F. "The Suspension of Time in Chapter 18 of Protoevangelium Jacobi." Pages 226–37 in *Studies in Early Christianity*. Tübingen: Mohr Siebeck, 2003.

Bowen, A. C., and R.. Todd. *Cleomedes' Lectures on Astronomy: A Translation of the Heavens*. Berkeley: University of California Press, 2004.

Boyce, M. *History of Zoroastrianism.*3 vols. Leiden: Brill, 1982.

———. *Zoroastrians, Their Religious Beliefs and Practices*. 3d ed. London: Routledge & Kegan Paul, 1985.

Brack-Bernsen, L. "Predictions of Lunar Phenomena in Babylonian Astronomy." Pages 5–19 in Steele and Imhausen, eds., *Under One Sky*.

Braulik, G., W. Gross and S. McEvenue, eds. *Biblische Theologie und gesellschaftlicher Wandel*. Freiburg: Herder, 1993.

Bremmer, J. "Canonical and Alternative Creation Myths in Ancient Greece." Pages 73–96 in van Kooten, ed., *The Creation of Heaven and Earth*.

Bresciani, E. "The Persian Occupation of Egypt." Pages 502–28 in *Cambridge History of Iran*, vol. 2. Edited by I. Gershevitch. Cambridge: Cambridge University Press, 1985.

Briant, P. *Histoire de l'empire perse*. Paris: Fayard, 1996.

———. "Histoire impériale et histoire régionale." Pages 235–45 in *Congress Volume: Oslo, 1998*. Edited by A. Lemaire and M. Sæbø. VTSup 80. Leiden: Brill, 2000.

Britt, B., and P. Creehan. "Chiasmus in Leviticus 16,29–17,11." *ZAW* 112 (2000): 398–400.

Britton, J. P. "Treatments of Annual Phenomena in Cuneiform Sources." Pages 21–78 in Steele and Imhausen, eds., *Under One Sky*.

Brooke, G. "4Q341: An Exercise for Spelling and for Spell." Pages 271–82 in *Writing and Ancient Near Eastern Society*. Edited by P. Bienkowski, C. Mee and E. Slater. LHBOTS 426. London: T&T Clark International, 2005.

———. "4QCommentaries on Genesis A and Genesis D." Pages 198–99 in *Qumran Cave 4, XVII, Parabiblical Texts, Part 3*. Edited by G. J. Brooke et al. DJD 22. Oxford: Clarendon, 2003.

Buck, R. J. "Communalism on the Lipari Islands." *CP* 54 (1959): 35–39.

Cagni, L., G. Fusaro and S. Graziani. "Nutzung des Ackerbodens in Mesopotamien der achaemeniden Zeit." Pages 197–212 in Klengel and Renger, eds., *Landwirtschaft im Alten Orient*.

Calum, C. *Illuminating Leviticus*. Baltimore: The Johns Hopkins University Press, 2006.

Campbell, A. F., and M. A. O'Brien. *Rethinking the Pentateuch*. Louisville: Westminster John Knox, 2005.

———. *Sources of the Pentateuch*. Minneapolis: Fortress, 1993.

Carmichael, C. *Illuminating Leviticus*. Baltimore: The Johns Hopkins University Press, 2006.

————. "The Sabbatical/Jubilee Cycle and the Seven-Year Famine in Egypt." *Biblica* 80 (1999): 224–39.

Carr, D. "BIBLOS GENESEWS Revisited." *ZAW* 110 (1998): 159–72.

————. "The Politics of Textual Subversion: A Diachronic Perspective on the Garden of Eden Story." *JBL* 112 (1993): 577–95.

Carter, C. E. *The Emergence of Yehud in the Persian Period.* JSOTSup 294. Sheffield: Sheffield Academic Press, 1999.

Cassin, E. "Le lion et le roi." Pages 167–213 in *Le semblable et le different: symbolismes du pouvoir dans le Proche Orient ancient.* Paris: La découverte, 1987.

Cassuto, U. *A Commentary on the Book of Genesis.* Jerusalem: Magnes, 1964.

Cazelles, H. "Table des peuples, nations et modes de vie." Pages 67–79 in *Biblica et semitica.* Edited by L. Cagni. Napoli: Istituto universitario orientale, 1999.

Chaney, M. "Bitter Bounty." Pages 250–63 in *The Bible and Liberation.* Edited by N. K. Gottwald and R. A. Horsley. Maryknoll: Orbis, 1993.

Chantraine, P. *Dictionnaire étymologique de la langue grecque.* Paris: Klincksieck, 1968.

Charpin, D. "Chroniques bibliographiques 2." *RA* 96 (2002): 169–91.

————. "Les mois Uwarum et Sebûtum." *NABU* (1989) 93: 66.

Chatty, D., ed. *Nomadic Societies in the Middle East and North Africa: Entering the 21th Century.* HdO 81. Leiden: Brill, 2006.

Chazan, R., W. W. Hallo and L. H. Schiffman, eds. *Ki Baruch Hu: Ancient Near Eastern, biblical, and Judaic Studies in Honor of Baruch A. Levine.* Winona Lake: Eisenbrauns, 1999.

Chirichigno, G. C. *Debt-slavery in Israel and the Ancient Near East.* JSOTSup 141. Sheffield: JSOT Press, 1993.

Cholewiński, A. *Heiligkeitsgesetz und Deuteronomium.* Rome: Biblical Institute, 1976.

Chyutin, M. *Architecture and Utopia in the Temple Area.* LSTS 58; New York: T&T Clark International, 2006.

Cline, D. J. A. "אדם, the Hebrew for Human, Humanity." *VT* 53 (2003): 297–310.

————. "The Evidence for an Autumnal New Year in Pre-Exilic Israel Reconsidered." Pages 371–94 in *On the Way to the Postmodern.*

————. *On the Way to the Postmodern.* JSOTSup 293. Sheffield: Sheffield Academic Press, 1998.

————. "Sacred Space, Holy Places and Suchlike." Pages 542–54 in *On the Way to the Postmodern.*

Cogan, M., B. L. Eichler and J. H. Tigay, eds. *Tehillah le-Moshe: Biblical and Judaic Studies in Honor of Moshe Greenberg.* Winona Lake: Eisenbrauns, 1997.

Cohen, M. E. *The Cultic Calendars of the Ancient Near East.* Bethesda: CDL, 1993.

Collins, J. J. *The Bible After Babel.* Grand Rapids: Eerdmans, 2005.

————. "The Politics of Biblical Interpretation." Pages 195–211 in *Biblical and Near Eastern Essays.* Edited by C. McCarthy and J. F. Healey. JSOTSup 375. London: T&T Clark International, 2004.

Cooper, A., and B. R. Goldstein. "Exodus and Massot in History and Tradition." *Maarav* 8 (1992): 15–37.

Cortese, E. *Josua 13–21: Ein priesterschriftlicher Abschnitt in deuteronomistischen Geschichtswerk.* OBO 94. Fribourg: Universitätsverlag. Göttingen: Vandenhoeck & Ruprecht, 1990.

————. "The Priestly Tent." *Liber Annuus* 48 (1998): 9–30.

Craig, J. L. "Text and Textile in Exodus." *JANES* 29 (2002): 17–30.

Croatto, J. S. "Reading the Pentateuch as a Counter-text." Pages 383–400 in *Congress Volume: Leiden, 2004*. Edited by A. Lemaire. VTSup 109. Leiden: Brill, 2006.

Crone, P. "Quraysh and the Roman Army: Making Sense of the Meccan Leather Trade." *BSO(A)S* 70 (2007): 63–88.

Cross, F. M. *Canaanite Myth and Hebrew Epic.* Cambridge, Mass.: Harvard University Press, 1973.

Cryer, F. H. "The Interrelationships of Gen. 5,32; 11,10–11 and the Chronology of the Flood (Gen. 6–9)." *Biblica* 66 (1985): 241–61.

Currid, J. D. "An Examination of the Egyptian Background of the Genesis Cosmogony." *BZ* 35 (1991): 18–40.

———. *Ancient Egypt and the Old Testament.* Grand Rapids: Baker, 1997.

Dahm, U. *Opferkult und Priestertum in Alt-Israel.* BZAW 327. Berlin: de Gruyter, 2003.

Dalley, S. *Myths from Mesopotamia.* Oxford: Oxford University Press, 1992.

Daniels, D. R., U. Glessmer and M. Rösel, eds. *Ernten, was man sät. Festschrift für Klaus Koch zu seinem 65. Geburtstag.* Neukirchen–Vluyn: Neukirchener Verlag, 1991.

Davies, E. W. "A Mathematical Conundrum: The Problem of the Large Numbers in Numbers i and xxvi." *VT* 45 (1995): 449–69.

Davies, P. C. W. *Space and Time in the Modern Universe.* Cambridge: Cambridge University Press, 1977.

Davies, P. R. "Sons of Cain." Pages 35–56 in *A Word in Season.* Edited by J. D. Martin et al. Sheffield: JSOT Press, 1986.

Denizeau, C. *Dictionaire des parlers arabes de Syrie.* Paris: Geuthner, 1935.

Depuydt, L. "History of the heleq." Pages 79–107 in Steele and Imhausen, eds., *Under One Sky.*

Destro, A., and M. Pesce. "Forgiveness of Sins Without a Victim." Pages 151–73 in Baumgarten, ed., *Sacrifice in Religious Experience.*

Diebner, B. "Die Ehen der Erzväter." *Dielheimer Blätter zum Alten Testament* 8 (1975): 2–10.

Diels, H., and W. Kranz. *Die Fragmente der Vorsokratiker.* Zurich: Weidmann, 1985.

Dietrich, M., and O. Loretz. "Der biblische Azazel und AlT *126." *UF* 25 (1993): 99–117.

Dillmann, A. *Die Bücher Numeri, Deuteronium und Josua.* 2d ed. Leipzig: Hirzel, 1886.

Dohmen, C. "Das Zelt ausserhalb des Lagers." Pages 157–69 in Kiesow and Meurer, eds., *Textarbeit.*

Douglas, M. "The Go-away Goat." Pages 121–41 in Rendtorff and Kugler, eds., *The Book of Leviticus.*

Doumani, B. *Rediscovering Palestine.* Berkeley: University of California Press, 1995.

Dozeman, T. B., and K. Schmid, eds. *A Farewell to the Yahwist?* SBLSS 34. Atlanta: SBL, 2006.

Driel, G. van. "Agricultural Entrepreneurs." Pages 213–23 in Klengel and Renger, eds., *Landwirtschaft im Alten Orient.*

———. *Elusive Silver.* Leiden: Nederlands Instituut voor het Nabije Oosten, 2002.

Driver, S. R. *Introduction to the Literature of the Old Testament.* Edinburgh: T. & T. Clark, 1894.

Durand, J.-M.. *Le culte des pierres et les monuments commémoratifs en Syrie amorrite.* Paris: SEPOA, 2005.

Durand, X. *Des Grecs en Palestine au IIIème siècle avant Jésus-Christ*. Paris: Gabalda, 1997.

Edelman, D. *The Origins of the "Second" Temple*. London: Equinox, 2005.

Eichler, B. L. *Indenture at Nuzi*. New Haven: Yale University Press, 1973.

Eichrodt, W. *Die Quellen der Genesis von neuem untersucht*. Giessen: Töpelmann, 1916.

Eissfeldt, O. "Biblos Geneseōs." Pages 458–70 in *Kleine Schriften*, vol. 3. Tübingen: J. C. B. Mohr, 1966.

———. *Hexateuch-Synopse*. Leipzig: Hinrichs, 1922.

———. "Toledot." Pages 1–7 in *Kleine Schriften*, vol. 4. Tübingen: J. C. B. Mohr, 1968.

Eliav, Y. Z. *God's Mountain: The Temple Mount in Time, Place, and Memory*. Baltimore: The Johns Hopkins University Press, 2005.

Elliger, K. *Leviticus*. Tübingen: Mohr, 1966.

———. "Sinn und Ursprung der priesterlichen Geschichtserzählung." *ZTK* 49 (1952): 121–42.

Emerton, J. A. "When did Terah Die?" Pages 170–81 in *Language, Theology, and the Bible*. Edited by S. E. Balentine and J. Barton. Oxford: Clarendon, 1994.

Eph'al, I. *The Ancient Arabs: Nomads on the Border of the Fertile Crescent, 9th–5th Centuries BC*. Leiden: Brill, 1982.

Etz, D. V. "The Numbers of Genesis V 3–31." *VT* 43 (1993): 171–89.

Eyre, C., and J. Baines. "Interactions between Orality and Literacy in Ancient Egypt." Pages 91–119 in Schousboe and Larsen, eds., *Literacy and Society*.

Fabry, H.-J., and H.-W. Jüngling, ed. *Levitikus als Buch*. BBB 119. Berlin: Philo, 1999.

Fager, J. A. *Land Tenure and the Biblical Jubilee*. JSOTSup 155. Sheffield: JSOT Press, 1993.

Fares, A. "The Cadastral System in Lebanon Comparing to the other International Systems." Online: http://www.fig.net/pub/fig_2002/Ts7–10/TS7_10_fares.pdf.

Finkelstein, J. J. "Ammisaduqa's Edict and the Babylonian 'Law Codes.'" *JCS* 15 (1961): 91–104.

———. *The Ox that Gored*. Philadelphia: American Philosophical Society, 1981.

Firestone, Y. "The Land-equalizing mushâʿ Village." Pages 91–130 in *Ottoman Palestine*. Edited by G. G. Gilbar. Leiden: Brill, 1990.

Fleming, D. E. "A Break in the Line: Reconsidering the Bible's Diverse Festival Calendars." *RB* 106 (1999): 161–74.

———. "Seven-Day Siege of Jericho in Holy War." Pages 211–28 in Chazan, Hallo and Schiffman, eds., *Ki Baruch Hu*.

———. "The Israelite Festival Calendar and Emar's Ritual Archive." *RB* 106 (1999): 8–34.

———. *Time at Emar: The Cultic Calendar and the Rituals from the Diviner's Archive*. Winona Lake: Eisenbrauns, 2000.

Fletcher-Louis, C. H. T. "The Cosmology of P and Theological Anthropology in the Wisdom of Jesus ben Sira." Pages 69–113 in *Of Scribes and Sages*, vol. 1. Edited by A. Craig. London: T&T Clark International, 2004.

Fohrer, G. "Priesterschrift." Pages 568–69 in *Die Religion in Geschichte und Gegenwart*. Edited by K. Galling. Tübingen: Mohr, 1961.

Frankel, D. *The Murmuring Stories of the Priestly School*. VTSup 89. Leiden: Brill, 2002.

———. "Two Priestly Conceptions of Guidance in the Wilderness." *JSOT* 81 (1998): 31–37.

Frei, P. "Persian Imperial Authorization: A Summary." Pages 5–40 in Watts, ed., *Persia and Torah.*

Fretheim, T. E. "The Priestly Document: Anti-Temple?" *VT* 18 (1969): 312–29.

Frevel, C. "Kein Ende in Sicht?" Pages 85–123 in Fabry and Jüngling, eds., *Levitikus als Buch.*

———. *Mit Blick auf das Land die Schöpfung erinnern. Zum Ende der Priestergrundschrift.* HbS 23; Freiburg im Breisgau: Herder, 2000.

Friberg, J. "Mathematics at Ur in the Old Babylonian Period." *RA* 94 (2000): 97–188.

Fritz, V. *Tempel und Zelt.* WMANT 47; Neukirchen–Vluyn: Neukirchener Verlag, 1977.

Fuchs, E. "A Jewish-Feminist Reading of Exodus 1–2." Pages 307–26 in Bellis and Kaminsky, eds., *Jews, Christians.*

Gammie, J. G. *Holiness in Israel.* Minneapolis: Fortress, 1989.

Gane, R. E. *Cult and Character.* Winona Lake: Eisenbrauns, 2005.

———. Review of Jay Sklar, *Sin, Impurity, Sacrifice, Atonement. RBL* (2006). Online: http://www.bookreviews.org.

———. *Ritual Dynamic Structure.* Piscataway, N.J.: Gorgias, 2004.

García Martínez, F. *Qumranica Minora*, vol. 2. Leiden: Brill, 2007.

Gardner, B. *The Genesis Calendar: The Synchronistic Tradition in Genesis 1–11.* Lanham: University Press of America, 2001.

Gerhards, M. *Die Aussetzungsgeschichte des Mose.* WMANT 109; Neukirchen–Vluyn: Neukirchener Verlag, 2006.

Gerleman, G. "Nutzrecht und Wohnrecht: zur Bedeutung von ʿḥzh und nḥlh." *ZAW* 89 (1977): 316–17.

Gerstenberger, E. S. *Das dritte Buch Mose: Leviticus.* Göttingen: Vandenhoeck & Ruprecht, 1993.

———. *Israel in der Perserzeit.* Stuttgart: Kohlhammer, 2005.

Gertz, J. C. *Tradition und Redaktion in der Exoduserzählung.* FRLANT 186. Göttingen: Vandenhoeck & Ruprecht, 2000.

Gertz, J. C., K. Schmid and M. Witte, eds. *Abschied vom Jahwisten.* BZAW 315. Berlin: de Gruyter, 2002.

Gesche, P. D. *Schulunterricht in Babylonien im ersten Jahrtausend v. Chr.* AOAT 275. Münster: Ugarit Verlag, 2000.

Gilders, W. K. *Blood Ritual in the Hebrew Bible.* Baltimore: The Johns Hopkins University Press, 2004.

Glass, Z. G. "Land, Slave Labor and Law." *JSOT* 91 (2000): 27–39.

Glessmer, U. "Calendars in the Qumran Scrolls." Pages 213–78 in *The Dead Sea Scrolls After Fifty Years.* Edited by P. W. Flint and J. VanderKam. Leiden: Brill, 1999.

———. "Der 364-Tage Kalendar und die Sabbatstruktur seiner Schaltungen in ihrer Bedeutung für den Kult." Pages 379–98 in Daniels, Glessmer and Rösel, eds., *Ernten, was man sät.*

———. "Horizontal Measuring in the Babylonian Astronomical Compendium MUL.APIN and in the Astronomical Book of 1En." *Henoch* 18 (1996): 259–82.

———. "The Otot Texts (4Q319) and the Problem of Intercalations in the Context of the 364-Day Calendar." Pages 125–64 in *Qumranstudien.* Edited by H.-J. Fabry, A. Lange and H. Lichtenberger. Göttingen: Vandenhoeck & Ruprecht, 1996.

Gmirkin, R. E. *Berossus and Genesis, Manetho and Exodus.* LHBOTS 433. London: T&T Clark International, 2006.

Goldstein, B. R., and A. Cooper. "The Festivals of Israel and Judah and the Literary History of the Pentateuch." *JAOS* 110 (1990): 19–31.

Gomes, J. F. *The Sanctuary of Bethel and the Configuration of Israelite Religion.* BZAW 368. Berlin: de Gruyter, 2006.

Gooding, D. W. *The Account of the Tabernacle.* Cambridge: Cambridge University Press, 1959.

Gordon, C. H. "The Seventh Day." *UF* 11 (1979): 299–302.

Görg, M. "Beobachtungen zum sogenannten Azazel-Ritus." *BN* 33 (1986): 10–16.

———. "Das Menschenbild der Priesterschrift." *BK* 42 (1987): 21–29.

Gowan, D. E. *Theology in Exodus.* Louisville: Westminster John Knox, 1994.

Grabbe, L. L. *A History of the Jews and Judaism in the Second Temple Period*, Volume 1. LSTS 47. London: T&T Clark International, 2004.

———. "The Priests in Leviticus." Pages 207–24 in Rendtorff and Kugler, eds., *The Book of Leviticus.*

Grayson, A. K. *Assyrian and Babylonian Chronicles.* TCS 5. Locust Valley, N.Y.: J. J. Augustin, 1975.

———. "Königslisten und Chroniken." Pages 89–101 in vol. 6 of *Reallexikon der Assyriologie.* Edited by E. Ebeling and B. Meissner. Berlin: de Gruyter, 1980.

Groneberg, B. "Die Tage des šigû." *NABU* (1989) 9: 7–10.

Gropp, D. M. *The Samaria Papyri from Wadi Daliyeh.* DJD 28. Oxford: Clarendon, 2001.

Gross, W. "Die Gottebenbildlichkeit des Menchen im Kontext der Priesterschrift." *TQ* (1981): 244–64.

———. "Die Gottebenbildlichkeit des Menchen nach Gen. 1,26.27 in der Diskussion des letzen Jahrzehnts." *BN* 68 (1993): 35–48.

———. "Die Wolkensäule und die Feuersäule in Ex 13 + 14." Pages 142–65 in Braulik, Gross and McEvenue, eds., *Biblische Theologie.*

———. "Ex 12,10: Satzbau und Redaktionskritik." Pages 217–26 in Kiesow and Meurer, eds., *Textarbeit.*

———. "Syntaktische Erscheinungen am Anfang althebräischer Erzählungen: Hintergrund und Vordergrund." Pages 131–45 in *Congress Volume: Vienna, 1980.* Edited by J. A. Emerton. Leiden: Brill, 1981.

Grünwaldt, K. *Das Heiligkeitsgesetz Leviticus 17–26.* BZAW 271. Berlin: de Gruyter, 1999.

———. *Exil und Identität.* BBB 85. Frankfurt: Hain, 1992.

Gunkel, H. *Genesis.* Göttingen: Vandenhoeck & Ruprecht, 1910.

Haag, H. "Priesterschrift." Pages 1365–66 in *Bibel-Lexikon.* Einsiedeln: Benzinger, 1956.

Habel, N. C. "The Challenges of an Ecojustice Hermeneutic." Pages 290–306 in *Relating to the Text.* Edited by T. J. Sandoval and C. Mandolfo. JSOTSup 384. London: T&T Clark International, 2003.

———. *The Land is Mine.* Minneapolis: Fortress, 1995.

Hallo, W. W. "New Moons and Sabbaths." *HUCA* 48 (1977): 1–18.

Halpern, B. "The Assyrian Astronomy of Genesis 1." *Eretz-Israel* 27 (2003): 74*–83*.

———. "Assyrian and pre-Socratic Astronomies and the Location of the Book of Job." Pages 255–64 in *Kein Land für sich allein. Studien zum Kulturkontakt in Kanaan, Israel/Palästina und Ebirnâri für Manfred Weippert zum 65. Geburtstag.* Edited by U. Hübner and E. A. Knauf. Fribourg: Universitätsverlag. Göttingen: Vandenhoeck & Ruprecht, 2002.

————. "Biblical versus Greek Historiography." Pages 101–27 in *Das Alte Testament— ein Geschichtsbuch?* Edited by E. Blum, W. Johnstone and C. Markschies. Münster: Lit, 2005.

————. "Late Israelite Astronomies and the Early Greeks." Pages 323–52 in *Symbiosis, Symbolism, and the Power of the Past.* Winona Lake: Eisenbrauns, 2003.

Haran, M. "Ezekiel, P, and the Priestly School." *VT* 58 (2008): 211–18.

Harrington, D. J. "The 'Holy Land' in Pseudo-Philo, 4 Ezra, and 2 Baruch." *Emanuel* (2003): 661–72.

Harris, R. *Ancient Sippar.* Leiden: Nederlands Historisch-Archaeologisch Instituut, 1975.

Harvey, J. E. *Retelling the Torah: The Deuteronomistic Historian's Use of Tetrateuchal Narratives.* JSOTSup 403. London: T&T Clark International, 2004.

Hayward, C. T. R. "The Assyrian Astronomy of Genesis 1." *Eretz-Israel* 27 (2003): 74*– 83*.

Hayward, R. "The Sanctification of Time in the Second Temple Period: Case Studies in the Septuagint and Jubilees." Pages 141–67 in *Holiness Past and Present.* Edited by S. C. Barton. London: T&T Clark International, 2003.

Hawley, R. "On the Alphabetic Scribal Curriculum at Ugarit." Pages 57–68 in *Proceedings of the 51st Rencontre assyriologique internationale.* Edited by R. D. Biggs, J. Myers and M. T. Roth. Chicago: Oriental Institute, 2008.

Heinz, M., and M. H. Feldman, eds. *Representations of Political Power.* Winona Lake: Eisenbrauns, 2007.

Heinzerling, R. "Bileams Rätsel: Die Zählung der Wehrfähigen in Numeri 1 und 26." *ZAW* 111 (1999): 404–15.

————. "'Einweihung' durch Henoch? Die Bedeutung der Altersangaben in Genesis 5." *ZAW* 110 (1998): 581–89.

————. "On the Interpretation of the Census Lists by C. J. Humphreys and G. E. Mendenhall." *VT* 50 (2000): 250–52.

Hendel, R. S. "4Q252 and the Flood Chronology of Genesis 7–8." *DSD* 2 (1995): 72–79.

————. *The Epic of the Patriarch.* Atlanta: Scholars Press, 1987.

Henkelman, W. F. M. "Animal Sacrifice and 'External' Exchange in the Persepolis Fortification Tablets." Pages 137–66 in *Approaching the Babylonian Economy.* Edited by H. D. Baker and M. Jursa. AOAT 330. Münster: Ugarit-Verlag, 2005.

Hepner, G. "Israelites Should Conquer Israel." *RB* 113 (2006): 161–80.

————. "The Morrow of the Sabbath is the First Day of the Festival of Unleavened Bread (Lev. 23,15–17)." *ZAW* 118 (2006): 389–404.

Hertog, G. den. "Jos 5,4–6 in der griechischen Übersetzung." *ZAW* 110 (1998): 601–6.

Hess, R. S. "The Book of Joshua as a Land Grant." *Biblica* 83 (2002): 493–506.

————. "Lamech in the Genealogies of Genesis." *BBR* 1 (1991): 21–25.

Hieke, T. *Die Genealogien der Genesis.* HbS 39. Freiburg im Breisgau: Herder, 2003.

Hjelm, I. *Jerusalem's Rise to Sovereignty.* JSOTSup 404. London: T&T Clark International, 2004.

Hoch, J. *Semitic Words in Egyptian Texts of the New Kingdom and Third Intermediary Period.* Princeton: Princeton University Press, 1994.

Hoenig, S. B. "Sabbatical Years and the Year of Jubilee." *JQR* 59 (1969): 222–36.

Hoffmann, D. *Das Buch Leviticus 1–11.* Berlin: 1905–1906.

Hoglund, K. G. *Achaemenid Imperial Administration in Syria-Palestine and the Missions of Ezra and Nehemiah.* Atlanta: SBL, 1992.

Holmstedt, R. "The Restrictive Syntax of Genesis i 1." *VT* 58 (2008): 56–67.

Holzinger, H. *Das Buch Josua.* Tübingen/Leipzig: Mohr: 1901.

Horowitz, W. "The 360 and 364 Day Year in Ancient Mesopotamia." *JANES* 24 (1996): 35–41.

———. "The 364 Day Year in Mesopotamia, Again." *NABU* (1998–99) 49. Online http://www.achemenet.com/recherche/textes/babyloniens/nabu/nabu.htm.

Houston, W. J. "Towards an Integrated Reading of the Dietary Laws of Leviticus." Pages 142–61 in Rendtorff and Kugler, eds., *The Book of Leviticus.*

Hughes, J. *Secrets of the Times.* JSOTSup 66. Sheffield: JSOT Press, 1990.

Hunger, H., and D. Pingree. *MUL.APIN, an Astronomical Compendium in Cuneiform.* AfOB 24. Horn: F. Bergern & Söhne, 1989.

Hurowitz, V. "The Priestly Account of Building the Tabernacle." *JAOS* 105 (1985): 21–30.

Hurowitz, W., and V. A. Hurowitz. "Urim and Thummim in Light of a Psephomancy Ritual from Assur (*LKA* 137)." *JANES* 21 (1992): 95–115.

Husser, J. M. "Entre mythe et philosophie. La relecture sapientielle de Genèse 2–3." *RB* 107 (2000): 232–59.

Isawy, C. *An Economic History of the Middle East and North Africa.* New York: Columbia University Press, 1982.

Jacobus, H. "The Curse of Cain (Jub. 8.1–5): Genealogies in Genesis 5 and Genesis 11 and a Mathematical Pattern," *JSP* 18 (2009): 207–32.

Janowski, B. "Azazel." *DDD*, 128–31.

Janzen, D. *The Social Meanings of Sacrifice in the Hebrew Bible.* BZAW 344. Berlin: de Gruyter, 2004.

Jaubert, A. "The Calendar of Qumran and the Passion Narrative in John." Pages 62–75 in *John and Qumran.* Edited by J. A. Charlesworth. London: Chapman, 1972.

———. *The Date of the Last Supper.* Translated by Isaac Rafferty. New York: Alba House, 1965.

———. *La date de la cène.* Paris: Gabalda, 1957.

Jenson, P. P. *Graded Holiness.* JSOTSup 106. Sheffield: JSOT Press, 1992.

Jepsen, A. "Zur Chronologie des Priesterkodex." *ZAW* 47 (1929): 252–55.

Jericke, D. *Abraham in Mamre.* CHANE 17. Leiden: Brill, 2003.

Joannès, F. "Pouvoirs locaux et organisation du territoire en Babylonie achéménide." *Transeuphratène* 3 (1990): 173–89.

Johnstone, W. "The Use of Leviticus in Chronicles." Pages 243–55 in Sawyer, ed., *Reading Leviticus.*

Jong, A. de. "Animal Sacrifice in Zoroastrianism." Pages 127–48 in Baumgarten, ed., *Sacrifice in Religious Experience.*

Joosten, J. *People and Land in the Holiness Code.* VTSup 67. Leiden: Brill, 1996.

Jursa, M. "From the Neo-Babylonian Empire to Achaemenid Rule." Pages 73–94 in *Regime Change in the Ancient Near East and Egypt.* Edited by H. Crawford. Oxford: Oxford University Press, 2007.

Kaiser, O. *Einleitung in das Alte Testament.* Gütersloh: Mohn, 1969.

Kalisch, M. M. *A Historical and Critical Commentary on the Old Testament: Leviticus.* London: Longman, Green, Reader & Dyer, 1867–72.

Kapelrud, A. S. "The Mythological Features in Genesis Chapter I and the Author's Intentions." *VT* 24 (1974): 178–86.

Kaufmann, Y. *The Religion of Israel.* Chicago: University of Chicago Press, 1960.

Kawashima, R. S. "The Jubilee, Every 49 of 50 Years?" *VT* 53 (2003): 117–20.

————. "The Jubilee Year and the Return of Cosmic Purity." *CBQ* 65 (2003): 370–89.

Kearney, P. J. "Creation and Liturgy." *ZAW* 89 (1977): 375–87.

Keenan, D. K. *The Question of Sacrifice.* Bloomington: Indiana University Press, 2005.

Kellermann, D. *Die Priesterschrift von Numeri 1:1 bis 10:10.* BZAW 120. Berlin: de Gruyter, 1970.

Kellogg, S. *The Book of Leviticus.* New York: Funk & Wagnalls, 1900.

Kiesow, K., and T. Meurer, eds. *Textarbeit.* Münster: Ugarit-Verlag, 2003.

Kilian, R. "Die Hoffnung auf Heimkehr in der Priesterschrift." *Bibel und Leben* 7 (1966): 39–51.

————. "Die Priesterschrift: Hoffnung auf Heimkehr." *Wort und Botschaft* (1967): 226–43.

————. *Literarkritische und formgeschichtliche Untersuchung des Heiligkeitsgesetzes.* BBB 19. Bonn: Hanstein, 1963.

Kilzi, J. Online: http://www.geometre-expert.fr/content/file/liban5.pdf.

Klein, R. W. "Archaic Chronologies and the Textual History of the Old Testament." *HTR* 67 (1974): 255–63.

Klengel, H., and J. Renger, eds. *Landwirtschaft im Alten Orient.* Berlin: Dietrich Reimer, 1999.

Klinkott, H. "Xerxes in Aegypten. Gedanken zum negativen Perserbild in der Satrapenstele." Pages 34–53 in *Aegypten unter fremden Herrschern zwischen persischer Satrapie und roemischer Provinz.* Edited by S. Pfeiffer. Frankfurt am Main: Antike, 2007.

Knauf, E. A. "Der Exodus zwischen Mythos und Geschichte." Pages 73–84 in *Schriftauslegung in der Schrift.* Edited by R. G. Kratz, T. Krüger and K. Schmid. BZAW 300. Berlin: de Gruyter, 2000.

————. "Die Priesterschrift und die Geschichten der Deuteronomisten." Pages 101–18 in Römer, ed., *The Future of the Deuteronomistic History.*

————. "Does 'Deuteronomistic historiography' (DtrH) Exist?" Pages 388–98 in *Israel Constructs Its History.* Edited by A. de Pury, T. Römer and J.-D. Macchi. JSOTSup 306. Sheffield: Sheffield Academic Press, 2000.

————. "Genesis 36,1–43." Pages 291–300 in *Jacob.* Edited by J.-D. Macchi and T. Römer. Geneva: Labor et Fides, 2001.

————. "Grenzen der Toleranz in der Priesterschaft." *BK* 58 (2003): 224–27.

————. *Ismael.* Wiesbaden: Harrassowitz, 1989.

————. "Seine Arbeit, die Gott geschaffen hat, um sie auszuführen." *BN* 111 (2002): 24–27.

————. "Supplemanta Ismaelitica 14." *BN* 61 (1992): 22–26.

Knauth, R. J. D. "Debt Release: Cancelled, Suspended or Completed?" *ZABR* forthcoming.

Knipping, B. R. *Die Kundschaftergeschichte Numeri 13–14.* Hamburg: Kovac, 2000.

Knohl, I. "Two Aspects of the Tent of Meeting." Pages 73–79 in Cogan, Eichler and Tigay, eds., *Tehillah le-Moshe.*

Knoppers, G. N. *1 Chronicles 10—29.* AB 12A. Garden City: Doubleday, 2004.

Koch, K. *Die Priesterschrift von Exodus 25 bis Levitikus 16.* FRLANT 71. Göttingen: Vandenhoeck & Ruprecht, 1959.

Köckert, M. "Das Land in der priesterlichen Komposition des Pentateuch." Pages 147–62 in *Von Gott reden.* Edited by D. Vieweger and E.-J. Waschke. Neukirchen–Vluyn: Neukirchener Verlag, 1995.

————. *Leben in Gottes Gegenwart*. FAT 43. Tübingen: Mohr Siebeck, 2004.

Kohata, F. *Jahwist und Priesterschrift in Exodus 3–14*. BZAW 166. Berlin: de Gruyter, 1986.

Kooten, G. H. van, ed. *The Creation of Heaven and Earth. Re-interpretations of Genesis 1 in the Context of Judaism, Ancient Philosophy, Christianity, and Modern Physics*. Leiden: Brill, 2005.

Körting, C. "Gottes Gegenwart am Jom Kippur." Pages 221–58 in Blum and Lux, eds., *Festtraditionen in Israel*.

Kramer, C. *Village Ethnoarchaeology*. London: Academic Press, 1982.

Kratz, R. G. *The Composition of the Old Testament*. London: T&T Clark International, 2005.

Kraus, F. *Königliche Verfügungen in altbabylonischer Zeit*. Leiden: Brill, 1984.

Krüger, T. "Das menschliche Herz und die Weisung Gottes." Pages 65–92 in *Rezeption und Auslegung im Alten Testament und in seinem Umfeld*. Edited by R. G. Kratz and T. Krüger. OBO 153. Fribourg: Universitätsverlag. Göttingen: Vandenhoeck & Ruprecht, 1997.

Kuenen, A. *Historisch-kritische Einleitung in die Bücher des Alten Testaments hinsichtlich ihrer Entstehung und Sammlung* I.1. Leipzig, 1887.

Kuhrt, A. "The Cyrus Cylinder and Achaemenid Imperial Policy." *JSOT* 25 (1983): 83–97.

————. "Cyrus the Great of Persia: Images and Realities." Pages 169–92 in Heinz and Feldman, eds., *Representations*.

Kurtz, J. H. *Sacrificial Worship of the Old Testament*. Minneapolis: Klock & Klock, 1980.

Kutsch, E. "Der Sabbat—ursprünglich Vollmondtag?" Pages 71–77 in *Kleine Schriften zum Alten Testament*. Edited by L. Schmidt. BZAW 168. Berlin: de Gruyter, 1986.

————. "Der Kalender des Jubiläenbuches und das Alte und das Neue Testament." *VT* (1961): 39–47.

Laaf, P. *Die Pascha-Feier Israels*. BBB 36. Bonn: Hanstein, 1970.

Labat, R. *Nouveaux textes hémérologiques d'Assur*. Paris, 1957.

Labuschagne, C. J. "The Life Span of the Patriarchs." Pages 121–27 in *New Avenues in the Study of the Old Testament*. Edited by A. S. van der Woude. OTS 25. Leiden: Brill, 1989.

Lafont, S. "Fief et féodalité dans le Proche-Orient ancien." Pages 515–644 in *Les féodalités*. Edited by E. Bournazel and J. Poly. Paris: Presses universitaires de France, 1998.

Lambert, W. G. *Babylonian Wisdom Literature*. Oxford: Clarendon, 1960.

Lambert, W. G., and A. R. Millard. *Atra-hasis*. Oxford: Clarendon, 1969.

Landsberger, B., and J. V. K. Wilson. "The Fifth Tablet of Enuma Elish." *JNES* 20 (1961): 154–79.

Lang, B. "The Social Organization of Peasant Poverty in Biblical Israel." Pages 83–99 in *Anthropological Approaches to the Old Testament*. Edited by B. Lang. Sheffield: Almond, 1985.

Larsson, G. "The Chronology of the Pentateuch." *JBL* (1983): 401–9.

————. "Septuagint versus Massoretic Chronology." *ZAW* 114 (2002): 511–21.

Latron, A. *La vie rurale en Syrie et au Liban*. Beyrouth: Institut français de Damas, 1936.

Launderville, D. "Ezekiel's Cherub: A Promising Symbol or Dangerous Idol?" *CBQ* 65 (2003): 165–83.

Leaney, A. R. C. *The Rule of Qumran and Its Meaning.* London: SCM, 1966.

Lecoq, P. *Les inscriptions de la Perse achéménide.* Paris: Gallimard, 1997.

Lefebvre, J.-F. *Le jubilé biblique.* OBO 194. Fribourg: Editions universitaires, 2003.

Leibowitz, Y. *Peuple. Terre. Etat.* Paris: Plon, 1995.

Lemaire, A. "Histoire et administration de la Palestine à l'époque perse." Pages 11–53 in *La Palestine à l'époque perse.* Edited by E.-M. Laperrousaz. Paris: Cerf, 1994.

———. "Le Sabbat à l'époque royale israélite." *RB* 80 (1973): 161–85.

———. "Populations et territoires de la Palestine à l'époque perse." *Transeuphratène* 3 (1990): 31–74.

Levenson, J. D. *Creation and the Persistence of Evil.* San Francisco: Harper & Row, 1988.

———. "The Hebrew Bible, the Old Testament, and Historical Criticism." Pages 19–59 in *The Future of Biblical Studies: The Hebrew Scriptures.* Edited by R. E. Friedman and H. G. M. Williamson. Atlanta: Scholars Press, 1987.

———. "The Perils of Engaged Scholarship: A Rejoinder to Jorge Pixley." Pages 239–46 in Bellis and Kaminsky, eds., *Jews, Christians.*

Levin, C. *Der Jahwist.* FRLANT 157. Tübingen: Vandenhoeck & Ruprecht, 1993.

Levine, B. A. *In the Presence of the Lord.* Leiden: Brill, 1974.

———. "On the Semantics of Land Tenure in Biblical Literature." Pages 134–93 in *The Tablet and the Scroll.* Edited by M. E. Cohen, D. C. Snell and D. B. Weisberg. Bethesda: CDL, 1993.

Levinson, B. M. "The Case for Revision and Interpolation within the Biblical Legal Corpora." Pages 55–56 in Levinson, ed., *Theory and Method.*

———. "The Right Chorale." Pages 129–53 in *Not in Heaven.* Edited by J. Rosenberg and J. C. Sitterson Jr. Bloomington: Indiana University Press, 1991.

———, ed. *Theory and Method in Biblical and Cuneiform Law.* Sheffield: Sheffield Academic Press, 1994.

Lewy, H., and J. Lewy. "The Origin of the Week and the Oldest West Asiatic Calendar." *HUCA* 17 (1942–43): 1–152.

Lim, T. H. "The Chronology of the Flood Story in a Qumran Text (4Q252)." *JJS* 43 (1992): 288–98.

Lipiński, E. "Traditions juridiques des Sémites de l'Ouest à l'époque préhellénistique." *Transeuphratène* 8 (1994): 121–35.

Lipschits, O. "Achaemenid Imperial Policy, Settlement Processes and the Status of Jerusalem in the Middle of the Fifth Century BCE." Pages 19–52 in Lipschits and Oeming, eds., *Judah and the Judeans in the Persian Period.*

———. "The Rural Settlement in Judah in the Sixth Century B.C.E.: A Rejoinder." *PEQ* 136 (2004): 99–107.

Lipschits, O., G. Knoppers and R. Albertz, eds. *Judah and the Judeans in the Fourth Century BCE.* Winona Lake: Eisenbrauns, 2007.

Lipschits, O., and M. Oeming, eds. *Judah and the Judeans in the Persian Period.* Winona Lake: Eisenbrauns, 2006.

Lipschits, O., and D. Vanderhooft. "Yehud Stamp Impressions in the Fourth Century BCE: A Time of Administrative Consolidation?" Pages 75–93 in Lipschits, Knoppers and Albertz, eds., *Judah and the Judeans.*

Liss, H. "'Describe the Temple to the House of Israel.'" Pages 122–43 in *Utopia and Dystopia in Prophetic Literature.* Edited by E. Ben Zvi. Helsinki: Finnish Exegetical Society. Göttingen: Vandenhoeck & Ruprecht, 2006.

———. "The Imaginary Sanctuary: The Priestly Code as an Example of Fictionality in the Hebrew Bible." Pages 663–90 in Lipschits and Oeming, eds., *Judah and the Judeans in the Persian Period.*

Lissovsky, N., and N. Naʾaman, "A New Outlook on the Boundary System of the Twelve Tribes." *UF* 35 (2003): 291–332.

Lohfink, N. "Die Abänderung der Theologie des priesterlichen Geschichtswerks im Segen des Heiligkeitsgesetzes." Pages 129–36 in *Wort und Geschichte*. Edited by H. Gese and H. Rüger. Kevelaer: Butzon & Berker, 1973.

———. "Die Priesterschrift und die Geschichte." Pages 213–53 in *Studien zum Pentateuch*. Stuttgart: Katholisches Bibelwerk, 1988 (= "The Priestly Narrative and History." Pages 136–72 in *Theology of the Old Testament*. Minneapolis: Fortress, 1994.)

———. "Original Sins in the Priestly Historical Narrative." Pages 106–10 in *Theology of the Pentateuch*. Minneapolis: Fortress, 1994.

Lyotard, J.-F. *The Postmodern Condition*. Manchester: Manchester University Press, 1984.

Maccoby, H. "Holiness and Purity." Pages 153–70 in Sawyer, ed., *Reading Leviticus*.

Magen, Y. "The Dating of the First Phase of the Samaritan Temple." Pages 157–211 in Lipschits, Knoppers and Albertz, eds., *Judah and the Judeans*.

Márquez Rowe, I. "How Can Someone Sell His Own Fellow to the Egyptians?" *VT* 54 (2004): 335–43.

———. "The King's Men at Ugarit." *JESHO* 41 (2002): 1–19.

Marx, A. *Les systèmes sacrificiels de l'Ancien Testament*. VTSup 105. Leiden: Brill, 2005.

Marx, E. "The Political Economy of Middle Eastern and North African Pastoral Nomads." Pages in 78–97 in Chatty, ed., *Nomadic Societies*.

McEvenue, S. E. *The Narrative Style of the Priestly Writer*. Rome: Biblical Institute, 1971.

———. "Word and Fulfilment." *Semitics* 1 (1970): 104–10.

Medan, Y. "A Temporary Weeping and a Weeping for Generations: The Sin of the Spies." *Megadim* 10 (1990): 21–37.

Middlemas, J. *The Troubles of Templeless Judah*. Oxford: Oxford University Press, 2005.

Milgrom, J. "Concerning Jeremiah's Repudiation of Sacrifice." Pages 119–21 in *Studies in Cultic Theology and Terminology*. Leiden: Brill, 1983.

———. "The Firstfruits Festivals of Grain and the Composition of Leviticus 23:9–21." Pages 81–89 in Cogan, Eichler and Tigay, eds., *Tehillah le-Moshe*.

———. "Jubilee: A Rallying Cry for Today's Oppressed." *Bible Review* 13, no. 2 (1997): 16, 48.

———. *Leviticus: A Continental Commentary*. Minneapolis: Fortress, 2004.

———. *Leviticus: A New Translation with Introduction and Commentary*. AB 3. New York: Doubleday, 1991–2000.

———. *Numbers*. Philadelphia: Jewish Publication Society, 1990.

———. "On Decoding very Large Numbers." *VT* 49 (1999): 131–32.

———. "Priestly 'P' Source." *ABD* 5:454–61.

———. "A Response to Rolf Rendtorff." *JSOT* 60 (1993): 82–85.

Miller, P. E. "Karaite Perspectives on Yôm Terûâ." Pages 537–41 in Chazan, Hallo and Schiffman, eds., *Ki Baruch Hu*.

Mills, G. *Finance for Trade*. Geneva: International Trade Centre UNCTAD/WTO, 2005.

Morfino, M. M. "Il corno del clamore" che annuncia liberazione." *Theologia and Historica* 9 (2000): 9–75.

Mowinckel, S. *Tetrateuch–Pentateuch–Hexateuch*. Berlin: Töpelmann, 1964.

Muilenburg, J. "The Biblical View of Time." *HTR* 54 (1961): 225–53.

Mundy, M. "Village Land and Individual Title: *Musha* and Ottoman Land Registration in the ʿAjlun District." Pages 58–79 in *Village, Steppe and State*. Edited by E. Rogan and T. Tell. London: British Academic Press, 1994.

Naʾaman, N. "From Conscription of Forced Labor to a Symbol of Bondage." Pages 746–58 in *"An Experienced Scribe who Neglects Nothing."* Edited by Y. Sefati et al. Bethesda: CDL, 2005.

———. "Lebo-Hamath, Ṣubat-Hamath, and the Northern Boundary of the Land of Canaan." *UF* 31 (1999): 417–41.

Nadan, A. "Colonial Misunderstanding of an Efficient Peasant Institution." *JESHO* 46 (2003): 320–54.

———. "The Competitive Advantage of Moneylenders over Banks in Rural Palestine." *JESHO* 48 (2005): 1–39.

Nehmé, A. *Al-Mounjid*. Beyrouth: Dar el-Machreq, 1975.

Neumann-Gorsolke, U. *Herrschen in den Grenzen der Schöpfung*. WMANT 101. Neukirchen–Vluyn: Neukirchener Verlag, 2004.

Neusner, J., and A. J. Avery-Peck, eds. *Judaism in Late Antiquity*. Part Five, *The Judaism of Qumran: A Systemic Reading of the Dead Sea Scrolls*. Vol. 1, *Theory of Israel*. HdO 1/56. Leiden: Brill, 2001.

Nicholson, E. W. *The Pentateuch in the Twentieth Century: The Legacy of Julius Wellhausen*. Oxford: Clarendon, 1998.

Niehoff, M. R. "Creatio ex nihilo Theology in Genesis Rabbah in Light of Christian Exegesis." *HTR* 99 (2006): 37–64.

Nihan, C. *From Priestly Torah to Pentateuch: A Study in the Composition of the Book of Leviticus*. Tübingen: Mohr Siebeck, 2007.

Nöldeke, T. "Die sogennante Grundschicht des Pentateuch." Pages 1–144 in *Untersuchungen zur Kritik des Alten Testaments*. Kiel, 1869.

Noort, E. "The Disgrace of Egypt." Pages 3–19 in *The Wisdom of Egypt*. Edited by A. Hilhorst and G. H. van Kooten. Leiden: Brill, 2005.

North, R. *Sociology of the Biblical Jubilee*. Rome: Pontifical Biblical Institute, 1954.

Northcote, J. "The Schematic Development of Old Testament Chronography: Towards an Integrated Model." *JSOT* 29 (2004): 3–36.

Noth, M. *Das dritte Buch Mose: Leviticus*. Göttingen: Vandenhoeck & Ruprecht, 1962.

———. *Exodus, a Commentary*. Philadelphia: Westminster, 1962.

———. *Leviticus*. Translated by J. E. Anderson. London, SCM, 1965.

———. *Numeri*. Göttingen: Vandenhoeck & Ruprecht, 1966.

———. *Überlieferungsgeschichte des Pentateuch*. Stuttgart: Kohlhammer, 1948.

———. *Überlieferungsgeschichtliche Studien*. Tübingen: Niemeyer, 1967.

Nyberg, H. S. "Questions de cosmogonie et de cosmologie mazdéennes." *JA* 219 (1931): 1–134.

Olivier, J. P. J. "Restitution as Economic Redress." *ZABR* 3 (1997): 12–25.

Olson, D. T. *The Death of the Old and the Birth of the New*. Chico, Calif.: Scholars Press, 1985.

Olyan, S. M. "Ben Sira's Relationship to the Priesthood." *HTR* 80 (1987): 261–86.

———. *Rites and Rank*. Princeton: Princeton University Press, 2000.

Oppert, J. "Chronology." Pages 64–68 in *Jewish Encyclopedia*, vol. 4. New York: Funk & Wagnells, 1901–16.

Otto, E. "Der Ackerbau in Juda im Spiegel der alttestamentlichen Rechtsüberlieferungen." Pages 229–36 in Klengel and Renger, eds., *Landwirtschaft im Alten Orient*.

———. "Die nachpriesterschriftliche Pentateuch Redaktion." Pages 63–111 in Vervenne, ed., *Studies in the Book of Exodus*.

———. "Die Paradieserzählung Genesis 2–3. Eine nachpriesterschriftliche Lehrerzaehlung in ihrem religions-historischen Kontext." Pages 167–92 in *"Jedes Ding hat seine Zeit..."* Edited by A. A. Diesel et al. BZAW 241. Berlin: de Gruyter, 1996.

———. "Forschungen zur Priesterschrift." *TRu* 62 (1997): 1–50.

———. "Programme der sozialen Gerechtigkeit." *ZABR* 3 (1997): 26–65.

Panaino, A. "Calendars I: Pre-Islamic." Pages 658–68 in *Encyclopaedia Iranica*, vol 4. Edited by E. Yarshater. London: Routledge & Kegan Paul, 1990.

Payne Smith, J. *A Compendious Syriac Dictionary*. Winona Lake: Eisenbrauns, 1998.

Perlitt, L. "Priesterschrift im Deuteronomium?" *ZAW* 100 (1988): 65–88 (= pages 123–43 in *Deuteronomium-Studien*. FAT 8. Tübingen: J. C. B. Mohr, 1994.)

Petersen, D. L. "The Ambiguous Role of Moses as Prophet." Pages 311–24 in *Israel's Prophets and Israel's Past*. Edited by B. E. Kelle and M. Bishop Moore. LHBOTS 446. London: T&T Clark International, 2006.

Petit, T. *Satrapes et satrapies dans l'empire achéménide de Cyrus le Grand à Xerxès I.* Paris: Belles Lettres, 1990.

Pettinato, G. *The Archives of Ebla*. Garden City: Doubleday, 1981.

Pinker, A. "A Goat to Go to Azazel." *JHS* 7 (2007). Online: http://www.arts.ualberta.ca/JHS/abstracts-articles.html#A69.

Pola, T. *Die ursprüngliche Priesterschrift*. WMANT 70. Neukirchen–Vluyn: Neukirchener Verlag, 1995.

Porten, B. "The Calendar of Aramaic Texts from Achaemenid and Ptolemaic Egypt." Pages 13–32 in *Irano-Judaica*, vol. 2. Edited by S. Shaked and A. Netzer. Jerusalem: Ben Zvi Institute, 1990.

Porten, B., et al. *The Elephantine Papyri in English*. Leiden: Brill, 1996.

Porten, B., and A. Yardeni. *Textbook of Aramaic Documents from Ancient Egypt*. Winona Lake: Eisenbrauns, 1986.

Powels, S. "The Samaritan Calendar." Pages 681–742 in *The Samaritans*. Edited by A. D. Crown. Tübingen: J. C. B. Mohr, 1989.

Pralon, D. "Le style de Léviticus des Septantes." Pages 47–81 in *La Bible d'Alexandrie 3*. Edited by Harlé and D. Pralon. Paris: Cerf, 1988.

Prémare, A.-L. de, et al. *Dictionaire Arabe–Français*. Paris: L'Harmattan, 1996.

Propp, W. H. C. *Exodus 1–18*. AB 2. New York: Doubleday, 1998.

Puech, E. "Requête d'un moissonneur du sud-judéen à la fin du VIIème siècle av. J.-C." *RB* 110 (2003): 5–16.

Pury, A. de. "Abraham. The Priestly Writer's 'Ecumenical' Ancestor." Pages 163–81 in *Rethinking the Foundations*. Edited by S. L. McKenzie, T. Römer and H. H. Schmid. BZAW 294. Berlin: de Gruyter, 2000.

————. "The Jacob Story and the Beginning of the Formation of the Pentateuch." Pages 51–72 in Dozeman and Schmid, eds., *A Farewell to the Yahwist?*

————. "Pg as the Absolute Beginning." Pages 99–128 in *Les dernières rédactions du Pentateuque, de l'Hexateuque et de l'Ennéateuque.* Edited by T. Römer and K. Schmid. Leuven: Leuven University Press, 2007.

Rabe, N. *Vom Gerücht zum Gericht.* Tübingen: Francke, 1994.

Rad, G. von. *Theology of the Old Testament*, vol. 2. Louisville: Westminster John Knox, 2001.

Radner, K. "The Neo-Assyrian Period." Pages 265–88 in Westbrook and Jasnow, eds., *Security for Debt.*

Rainer, A. "Der Kampf gegen die Schuldenkrise—das Jobeljahrgesetz Levitikus 25." Pages 40–60 in Albertz, ed., *Der Mensch als Hüter seiner Welt.*

Renaud, B. "Les généalogies et la structure de l'histoire sacerdotale dans le livre de la Genèse." *RB* 97 (1990): 5–30.

Rendsburg, G. A. "The Vegeterian Ideal in the Bible." Pages 319–33 in *Food and Judaism.* Edited by L. J. Greenspoon, R. A. Simskins and G. Shapiro. Omaha: Craighton University Press, 2005.

Rendtorff, R. *Das überlieferungsgeschichtliche Problem des Pentateuch.* BZAW 147. Berlin: de Gruyter, 1977.

————. "Is it Possible to Read Leviticus as a Separate Book?" Pages 22–35 in Sawyer, ed., *Reading Leviticus.*

————. "Leviticus 16 als Mitte der Tora." *BibInt* 11 (2003): 252–58.

Rendtorff, R., and R. A. Kugler, eds. *The Book of Leviticus.* VTSup 93. Leiden: Brill, 2003.

Rezetko, R., T. H. Lim and W. B. Aucker, eds. *Reflection and Refraction: Studies in Biblical Historiography in Honour of A. Graeme Auld.* VTSup 113. Leiden: Brill, 2007.

Robinson, G. "Das Jobel-Jahr." Pages 471–94 in Daniels, Glessmer and Rösel, eds., *Ernten, was man sät.*

————. "The Idea of Rest in the Old Testament and the Search for the Basic Character of the Sabbath." *ZAW* 92 (1980): 32–42.

————. *The Origin and Development of the Old Testament Sabbath.* Frankfurt: Peter Lang, 1988.

Rodríguez, A. *Substitution in the Hebrew Cultus.* Berrien Springs: Andrews University Press, 1979.

Roeder, G. *Die ägyptische Götterwelt.* Zürich: Artemis, 1959.

Rogan, E. L. *Frontiers of the State in the Late Ottoman Empire.* Cambridge: Cambridge University Press, 1999.

Römer, T., ed. *The Future of the Deuteronomistic History.* BETL 147. Leuven: Peeters, 2000.

————. "Israel's Sojourn in the Wilderness and the Construction of the Book of Numbers." Pages 419–46 in Rezetko, Lim and Aucker, eds., *Reflection and Refraction.*

————. "Le Pentateuque toujours en question." Pages 343–74 in *Congress Volume: Basel, 2001.* Edited by A. Lemaire. VTSup 92; Leiden: Brill, 2002.

————. *The So-called Deuteronomistic History.* London: T&T Clark International, 2005.

Roo, J. C. R. de. "Was the Goat for Azazel Destined for the Wrath of God?" *Biblica* 81 (2000): 233–42.

Rösel, M. "Die Chronologie der Flut in Gen. 7–8." *ZAW* 110 (1998): 590–93.

Ruiten, J. T. A. G. M. van. *Primaeval History Interpreted*. Leiden: Brill, 2000.

Ruwe, A. *"Heiligkeitsgesetz" und "Priesterschrift."* FAT 26. Tübingen: Mohr Siebeck, 1999.

———. "The Structure of the Book of Leviticus in the Narrative Outline of the Priestly Sinai Story (Exod 19:1–Num. 10:10*)." Pages 55–78 in Rendtorff and Kugler, eds., *The Book of Leviticus*.

Sacchi, P. "Measuring Time Among the Jews: The Zadokite Priesthood, Enochism, and the Lay Tendencies of the Maccabean Period." Pages 95–118 in *The Early Enoch Literature*. Edited by G. Boccaccini and J. J. Collins. SJSJ 121. Leiden: Brill, 2007.

Sadka, Y. "*Hinne* in Biblical Hebrew." *UF* 33 (2001): 479–93.

Sallaberger, W. *Der kultische Kalender der Ur III-Zeit*. Berlin: de Gruyter, 1993.

Sasson, J. M. "'The mother of all…' Etiologies." Pages 205–20 in *"A Wise and Discerning Mind." Essays in Honour of Burke O. Long*. Edited by S. M. Olyan and R. C. Culley. Brown Judaic Studies 325. Providence, RI: Brown University Press, 2000.

———. "Time…to Begin." Pages 183–94 in *"Sha'arei Talmon": Studies in the Bible, Qumran, and the Ancient Near East*. Edited by M. Fishbane. Winona Lake: Eisenbrauns, 1992.

Sawyer, J. F. A., ed. *Reading Leviticus*. JSOTSup 227. Sheffield: Sheffield Academic Press, 1996.

Schacht, J. *An Introduction to Islamic Law*. Oxford: Clarendon, 1964.

Schaebler, B. "Practicing Musha: Common Land and Common Good in Southern Syria under the Ottomans and the French." Pages 241–311 in *New Perspectives on Property and Land in the Middle East*. Edited by R. Owen. Cambridge, Mass.: Harvard University Press, 2001.

Schaper, J. *Priester und Leviten im achämenidischen Juda*. FAT 31. Tübingen: Mohr Siebeck, 2000.

Scharbert, J. "Priesterschrift." *LTK* 7 (1963): 753.

Schenker, A. "The Biblical Legislation on the Release of Slaves." *JSOT* 78 (1988): 23–41.

———. "Der Boden und seine Produktivität im Sabbat und Jubeljahr." Pages 123–33 in *Recht und Kult im Alten Testament*. Edited by A. Schenker. OBO 172. Fribourg: Universitätsverlag. Göttingen: Vandenhoeck & Ruprecht, 2000.

———. "What Connects the Incest Prohibitions with the Other Prohibitions Listed in Leviticus 18 and 20?" Pages 162–85 in Rendtorff and Kugler, eds., *The Book of Leviticus*.

Schloen, D. *The House of the Father as Fact and Symbol: Patrimony in Ugarit and in the Ancient Near East*. Winona Lake: Eisenbrauns, 2001.

Schmid, K. "Die Unteilbarkeit der Weisheit." *ZAW* 114 (2002): 21–39.

———. "The Late Persian Formation of the Torah: Observations on Deuteronomy 34." Pages 237–51 in Lipschits, Knoppers and Albertz, eds., *Judah and the Judeans*.

———. "The So-called Yahwist and the Literary Gap Between Genesis and Exodus." Pages 29–50 in Dozeman and Schmid, eds., *A Farewell to the Yahwist?*

Schmidt, L. *Studien zur Priesterschrift*. BZAW 214. Berlin: de Gruyter, 1993.

Schmidt, W. H. *Die Schöpfungsgeschichte der Priesterschrift*. WMANT 17. Neukirchen–Vluyn: Neukirchener Verlag, 1964.

————. *Einführung in das Alte Testament*. Berlin: de Gruyter, 1985.

————. *Exodus*. BKAT 2. Neukirchen–Vluyn: Neukirchener Verlag, 1974.

————. *Exodus, Sinai und Mose*. Darmstadt: Wissenschaftliche Buchgesellschaft, 1990.

Schousboe, K., and M. T. Larsen, eds. *Literacy and Society*. Copenhagen: Akademisk Forlag, 1989.

Schrader, L. "Kommentierende Redaktion im Noah–Sintflut–Komplex der Genesis." *ZAW* 110 (1998): 489–502.

Seale, A. S. "Numbers 13:32." *Expository Times* 68 (1956): 28.

Seebass, H. "Die Ankündigung des Mosetodes." Pages 457–67 in Kiesow and Meurer, eds., *Textarbeit*.

————. "'Holy' Land in the Old Testament: Numbers and Joshua." *VT* 56 (2006): 92–104.

————. "Pentateuch." Pages 185–209 in *Theologische Realenzyklopädie*, vol. 26. Edited by G. Krause. Berlin: de Gruyter, 1996.

Seidl, T. "Levitikus 16—'schlussstein' des priesterlichen Systems der Sündenvergebung." Pages 219–48 in Fabry and Jüngling, eds., *Levitikus als Buch*.

Sérandour, A. "A propos des calendriers des livres d'Esdras et de Néhémie." Pages 281–89 in Amphoux, Frey and Schattner-Rieser, eds., *Études sémitiques et samaritaines*.

Sider, D. *The Fragments of Anaxagoras: Introduction, Text, and Commentary*. 2d ed. Sankt Augustine: Academia, 2005.

Simonetti, C. "Die Nachlassedikte in Mesopotamien und im antiken Syrien." Pages 5–54 in *Das Jobeljahr im Wandel*. Edited by G. Scheuermann. Würzburg: Echter, 2000.

Ska, J.-L. "De la relative indépendance de l'écrit sacerdotal." *Biblica* 76 (1995): 396–415.

————. *Introduction à la lecture du Pentateuque*. Bruxelles: Lessius, 2002.

Skaist, A. "Emar." Pages 237–50 in Westbrook and Jasnow, eds., *Security for Debt*.

Skinner, J. *A Critical and Exegetical Commentary on Genesis*. Edinburgh, 1910.

Sklar, J. *Sin, Impurity, Sacrifice, Atonement*. Sheffield: Sheffield Phoenix, 2005.

Smelik, K. A. D. "The Creation of the Sabbath (Gen. 1.1–2.3)." Pages 9–11 in *Unless Some One Guide Me...* Edited by J. W. Dyk et al. Maastricht: Shaker, 2001.

Smend, R. Jr. *Die Entstehung des Alten Testaments*. Stuttgart: Kohlhammer, 1978.

Smend R. Sr. *Die Erzählung des Hexateuch auf ihre Quellen untersucht*. Berlin: Reimer, 1912.

Smith M. S. *The Pilgrimage Pattern in Exodus*. JSOTSup 239. Sheffield: Sheffield Academic Press, 1997.

Spencer, J. R. "PQD, the Levites, and Numbers 1–4." *ZAW* 110 (1998): 535–46.

Stackert, J. *Rewriting the Torah*. FAT 2/52. Tübingen: Mohr Siebeck, 2007.

Staubli, T. "Verortungen im Weltganzen." *BK* 58 (2003): 20–29.

Steck, O. H. "Aufbauprobleme in der Priesterschrift." Pages 287–308 in Daniels, Glessmer and Rösel, eds., *Ernten, was man sät*.

————. "Der Mensch und die Todesstrafe." *TZ* 53 (1997): 323–34.

————. *Der Schöpfungsbericht der Priesterschrift*. FRLANT 115. Göttingen: Vandenhoeck & Ruprecht, 1975.

Steele, J. M., and A. Imhausen, eds. *Under One Sky*. AOAT 297. Münster: Ugarit-Verlag, 2002.

Stein, K. W. "Rural Changes and Peasant Destitution: Contributing Causes to the Arab Revolt in Palestine, 1936–1939." Pages 143–70 in *Peasants and Politics in the Modern Middle East*. Edited by F. Kazemi and J. Waterbury. Miami: Florida International University Press, 1991.

Steiner, M. "Two Popular Cult Sites of Ancient Palestine. Cave 1 in Jerusalem and E 207 in Samaria." *SJOT* 11 (1997): 16–28.

Stenring, K. *The Enclosed Garden*. Stockholm: Almqvist & Wiksell, 1966.

Stern, M. *Greek and Latin Authors on Jews and Judaism*, vol. 1. Jerusalem: Israel Academy of Science and Humanities, 1976.

Stern, S. "The Babylonian Calendar at Elephantine." *ZPE* 130 (2000): 159–71.

————. *Time and Process in Ancient Judaism*. Oxford: Littman Library of Jewish Civilization, 2003.

Steuernagel, C. *Das Buch Josua*. Göttingen, 1899.

Stipp, H.-J. "Alles Fleisch hatte seinen Wandel auf der Erde verdorben." *ZAW* 111 (1999): 167–86.

————. "Gedalja und die Kolonie von Mizpa." *ZABR* 6 (2000): 155–71.

Stolper, M. W. *Entrepreneurs and Empire*. Istanbul: Nederlands historisch-archaeologisch instituut te Istanbul, 1985.

Stordalen, T. "Genesis 2,4: Restudying a Locus Classicus." *ZAW* 104 (1992): 163–77.

Sweet, L. E. *Tell Ṭoqaan*. Ann Arbor: University of Michigan Press, 1960.

Syrén, R. *The Forsaken Firstborn*. JSOTSup 133. Sheffield: Sheffield Academic Press, 1993).

Taggar-Cohen, A. "Law and Family in the Book of Numbers." *VT* 48 (1998): 74–94.

Tal, A. *A Dictionary of Samaritan Aramaic*. HdO 1/50. 2 vols. Leiden: Brill, 2000.

Tal, O. "Some Remarks on the Coastal Plain of Palestine under Achaemenid Rule." Pages 71–93 in *L'archéologie de l'empire achéménide*. Paris: de Boccard, 2005.

Talmon, S. "Calendars and Mishmarot." Pages 108–17 in vol. 1 of *Encyclopedia of the Dead Sea Scrolls*. Edited by L. H. Schiffman and J. C. VanderKam. 2 vols. Oxford: Oxford University Press, 2000.

————. "The Desert Motive." Pages 31–63 in *Biblical Motifs*. Edited by A. Altmann. Cambridge, Mass.: Harvard University Press, 1966.

————. "Qumran Studies: Past, Present and Future." *JQR* 85 (1994): 1–35.

Taubenschlag, R. "Citizens and Non-citizens in the Papyri." Pages 211–22 in *Opera Minora*. Warsawa: Państwowe wydawnictwo naukowe, 1959.

Tengström, S. *Die Toledotformel*. Uppsala: C. W. K. Gleerup, 1981.

Testuz, M. *Les idées religieuses du livre des Jubilés*. Geneva: Droz, 1960.

Tiemeyer, L. S. *Priestly Rites and Prophetic Rage*. FAT 2/19. Tübingen: Mohr Siebeck, 2006.

Tigay, J. H. "לא נסלחה 'He Had not Become Wrinkled' (Deuteronomy 34.7)." Pages 345–50 in Zevit, Gitin and Sokoloff, eds., *Solving Riddles*.

————. *The Evolution of the Gilgamesh Epic*. Philadelphia: University of Pennsylvania Press, 1982.

Tigchelaar, E. J. C. "Bare Feet and Holy Ground." Pages 17–36 in *The Revelation of the Name YHWH to Moses*. Edited by G. H. van Kooten. Leiden: Brill, 2006.

————. "Lights Serving as Signs for Festivals" (Genesis 1.14b) in Enuma eliš and Early Judaism." Pages 31–48 in van Kooten, ed., *The Creation of Heaven and Earth*.

Tsumura, D. *Creation and Destruction*. Winona Lake: Eisenbrauns, 2005.

Uehlinger, C., and S. Müller Trufaut. "Ezekiel 1, Babylonian Cosmological Scholarship and Iconography: Attempts at Further Refinement." *TZ* 57 (2001): 140–71.

Ulfgard, H. *The Story of Sukkot*. BGbE 34. Tübingen: Mohr Siebeck, 1998.

Ulrich, E. "The Bible in the Making." Pages 51–66 in P *The Bible at Qumran*. Edited by P. W. Flint. Grand Rapids: Eerdmans, 2001.

Utzschneider, H. *Das Heiligtum und das Gesetz*. Fribourg: Universitätsverlag. Göttingen: Vandenhoeck & Ruprecht, 1988.

VanderKam, J. C. "2 Maccabees 6,7a and Calendrical Change in Jerusalem." *JSJ* 12 (1981): 52–74 (= pages 105–27 in *From Revelation to Canon*).

———. *The Book of Jubilees*. Sheffield: Sheffield Academic Press, 2001.

———. *From Joshua to Caiaphas*. Minneapolis: Fortress, 2004.

———. *From Revelation to Canon*. SJSJ 62. Leiden: Brill, 2002.

———. "The Origin, Character, and Early History of the 364-Day Calendar: A Reassessment of Jaubert's Hypotheses." *CBQ* 41 (1979): 390–411 (= pages 81–104 in *From Revelation to Canon*. SJSJ 62. Leiden: Brill, 1994–2000).

Van Seters, J. *Prologue to History: The Yahwist as Historian in Genesis*. Zürich: Theologischer Verlag, 1992.

———. "The Report of the Yahwist's Demise has been Greatly Exaggerated!" Pages 143–57 in Dozeman and Schmid, eds., *A Farewell to the Yahwist?*

Veenhof, K. R. "Old Assyrian Period." Pages 93–160 in Westbrook and Jasnow, eds., *Security for Debt*.

———. "Redemption of Houses in Assur and Sippar." Pages 599–616 in *Munuscula Mesopotamica*. Edited by B. Böck, E. Cancik-Kirschbaum and T. Richter. Münster: Ugarit-Verlag, 1999.

Vervenne, M. "The Cultic and Civil Calendars of the Fourth Day of Creation (Gen. 1,14b)." *SJOT* 11 (1997): 163–80.

———. "The 'P' Tradition in the Pentateuch: Document and/or Redaction?" Pages 67–90 in *Pentateuchal and Deuteronomistic Studies*. Edited by C. Brekelmans and J. Lust. BETL 94. Leuven: Leuven University Press, 1990.

———. "The Patriarchs and the Exodus." Pages 1–16 in *The Interpretation of Exodus*. Edited by R. Roukema. CBET 44. Leuven: Peeters, 2006.

Vervenne, M., ed. *Studies in the Book of Exodus*. BETL 126. Leuven: University Press, 1996.

Vogels, W. "The Cultic and Civil Calendars of the Fourth Day of Creation (Gen. 1,14b)." *SJOT* 11 (1997): 163–80.

———. "Nos origines: Genèse 1–11." Pages 44–47 in *L'horizon du croyant*. Ottawa, 1992.

Vries, S. J. de. "God's Provision for the Well-being of Living Creatures in Genesis 9." Pages 87–105 in *Literary Encounters with the Reign of God*. Edited by S. H. Ringe and H. C. Kim. London: T&T Clark International, 2004.

Wachholder, B. Z., and S. Wacholder. "Patterns of Biblical Dates and Qumran's Calendar: The Fallacy of Jaubert's Hypothesis." *HUCA* 66 (1995): 1–40.

Waerzeggers, C. "Endogamy in Mesopotamia in the Neo-Babylonia Period." Pages 319–42 in *Mining the Archives*. Edited by C. Wunch. Dresden: ISLET, 2002.

Wagenaar, J. A. "The Cessation of Manna. Editorial Frames for the Wilderness Wandering in Exodus 16,35 and Joshua 5,10–12." *ZAW* 112 (2000): 192–209.

———. *Origin and Transformation of the Ancient Israelite Festival Calendar*. BZABR 6. Wiesbaden: Harrassowitz, 2005.

————. "The Priestly Festival Calendar and the Babylonian New Year Festivals." Pages 218–52 in *The Old Testament in Its World*. Edited by R. Gordon and J. C. de Moor. OTS 52. Leiden: Brill, 2005.

Wagner, V. "Zur Existenz des sogennanten 'Heiligkeitsgesetzes.'" *ZAW* 86 (1974): 307–16.

Warburton, D. "Before the IMF." *JESHO* 43 (2000): 65–131.

Warriner, D. *Land Reform and Development in the Middle East*. London: Royal Institute of International Affairs, 1957.

————. "Land Tenure in the Fertile Crescent in the Nineteenth and Twentieth Centuries." Pages 71–78 in *The Economic History of the Middle East 1800–1914*. Edited by C. Issawi. Chicago: University of Chicago Press, 1975.

Waters, M. "Cyrus and the Achaemenids." *Iran* 42 (2004): 91–102.

Watson, R. S. *Chaos Uncreated*. BZAW 341. Berlin: de Gruyter, 2005.

Watts, James W. *Ritual and Rhetoric in Leviticus: From Sacrifice to Scripture*. Cambridge: Cambridge University Press, 2007.

Watts, J. W., ed. *Persia and Torah: The Theory of Imperial Authorization of the Pentateuch*. Atlanta: Society of Biblical Literature, 2001.

Weimar, P. "Chaos und Kosmos." Pages 196–211 in *Mythos im Alten Testament und seiner Umwelt*. Edited by A. Lange, H. Lichtenberger and D. Römheld. BZAW 278. Berlin: de Gruyter, 1999.

————. "Der Tod Aarons und das Schicksal Israels." Pages 345–58 in Braulik, Gross and McEvenue, eds., *Biblische Theologie*.

————. *Die Meerwundererzählung*. Wiesbaden: Harrassowitz, 1985.

————. "Die Toledot-Formel in der priesterschriftlichen Geschichtsdarstellung." *BZ* 18 (1974): 65–93.

————. "Gen. 37—Eine vielschichtige literarische Komposition." *ZAW* 118 (2006): 485–512.

————. "Sinai und Schöpfung." *RB* 95 (1988): 337–85.

————. "Struktur und Komposition der priesterschriftlichen Geschichtsdarstellung." *BN* 23 (1984): 81–134.

Weinberg, J. P. "The Word ndb in the Bible." Pages 365–75 in Zevit, Gitin and Sokoloff, eds., *Solving Riddles*.

Weinfeld, M. *Deuteronomy and the Deuteronomist School*. Oxford: Clarendon, 1972.

————. *The Place of the Law in the Religion of Ancient Israel*. VTSup 100. Leiden: Brill, 2004.

————. "Sabbath, Temple and the Enthronement of the Lord." Pages 501–12 in *Mélanges bibliques et orientaux en l'honneur de M. Henri Cazelles*. Edited by A. Caquot and M. Delcor. AOAT 212. Kevelaer: Butzon & Bercker, 1981.

————. *Social Justice in Ancient Israel*. Jerusalem: Magnes, 1995.

Wellhausen, J. *Prolegomena to the History of Ancient Israel*. Translated by J. S. Black and A. Menzies; Cleveland: Meridian, 1957.

Wenham, G. *Numbers*. Leicester: Inter-Varsity, 1981.

Westbrook, R. "Cuneiform Law Codes and the Origin of Legislation." *ZA* 79 (1989): 201–22.

————. "The Old Babylonian Period." Pages 63–92 in Westbrook and Jasnow, eds., *Security for Debt*.

————. "Patronage in the Ancient Near East." *JESHO* 48 (2005): 210–33.

———. *Property and the Family in Biblical Law*. JSOTSup 113. Sheffield: Sheffield Academic Press, 1991.

———. "Social Justice and Creative Jurisprudence in Late Bronze Syria." *JESHO* 44 (2001): 24–7.

———. "What is the Covenant Code?" Pages 15–36 in Levinson, ed., *Theory and Method*.

Westermann, C. *Genesis*. Minneapolis: Fortress, 1984.

Weulersse, J. *Paysans de Syrie et du Proche-Orient*. Paris: Gallimard, 1946.

Wevers, J. W. *Notes on the Greek Text of Leviticus*. Atlanta: Scholars Press, 1997.

Weyde, K. W. *The Appointed Festivals of YHWH*. FAT 2/4. Tübingen: Mohr Siebeck, 2004.

Wiesenhofer, J. "Kontinuität oder Zäsur? Babylon unter den Achämeniden." Pages 167–88 in *Babylon: Focus mesopotamischer Geschichte, Wiege früher Gelehrsamkeit, Mythos in der Moderne*. Edited by J. Renger. Saarbrücken: SDV, Saarbrücker, 1999.

Wilhem, G. *Grundzüge der Geschichte und Kultur der Hurriter*. Darmstadt: Wissenschaftliche, 1982.

Willi-Plein, I. "Am Anfang einer Geschichte der Zeit." *TZ* 53 (1997): 152–64.

Williamson, H. G. M. "Comments on Oded Lipschits, The Fall and Rise of Jerusalem." In *Conversation with Oded Lipschits: The Fall and Rise of Jerusalem*. Edited by D. Vanderhooft. Winona Lake: Eisenbrauns, 2005. (= *JHS* 7 [2007]: article 2. Online: http://www.arts.ualberta.ca/JHS/abstracts-articles.html#A63.)

———. "Once upon a time…?" Pages 517–28 in Rezetko, Lim and Aucker, eds., *Reflection and Refraction*.

Wojciechowski, M. "Certains aspects algébriques de quelques nombres symboliques de la Bible." *BN* 23 (1984): 29–31.

Wright, B. G. III. "The Letter of Aristeas and the Reception History of the Septuagint." *BIOSCS* 39 (2006): 47–67.

Wright, D. P. *The Disposal of Impurity*. Atlanta: Scholars Press, 1987.

———. "The Fallacies of Chiasmus." *ZABR* 10 (2004): 143–68.

Wright, R. M. *Linguistic Evidence for the Pre-Exilic Date of the Yahwistic Source*. LHBOTS 419. London: T&T Clark International, 2005.

Yon, M. "La stele de Sargon II à Chypre." Pages 161–68 in *Khorsabad, le plais de Sargon II, roi d'Assyrie*. Edited by A. Caubet. Paris, 1995.

Young, D. W. "The Influence of Babylonian Algebra on Longevity among the Antediluvians." *ZAW* 102 (1990): 321–35.

———. "The Sexagesimal Basis for the Total Years of the Antediluvian and Postdiluvian Epochs." *ZAW* 116 (2004): 502–27.

———. "The Step-down to Two Hundred in Genesis 11,10–25." *ZAW* 116 (2004): 323–33.

Zaccagnini, C. "Land Tenure and Transfer of Land at Nuzi." Pages 79–96 in *Land Tenure and Social Transformation in the Middle East*. Edited by T. Khalidi. Beirut: American University Press, 1984.

———. "War and Famine at Emar." *Orientalia* 64 (1995): 96–100.

Zatelli, I. "The Origin of the Biblical Scapegoat Ritual." *VT* 48 (1998): 254–56.

Ze'evi, D. *An Ottoman Century*. Albany: State University of New York Press, 1996.

Zenger, E. "Priesterschrift." Pages 578–89 in *LTK*. Freiburg: Herder, 1999.

Zerubavel, E. *The Seven Day Circle*. London: The Free Press, 1985.

Zevit, Z. "Dating Ruth." *ZAW* 117 (2005): 574–600.

————. "The Priestly Redaction and Interpretation of the Plague Narrative in Exodus." *JQR* 66 (1975–76): 193–211.

Zevit, Z., S. Gitin and M. Sokoloff, eds. *Solving Riddles and Untying Knots*. Winona Lake: Eisenbrauns, 1995.

Ziemer, B. *Abram–Abraham*. BZAW 350. Berlin: de Gruyter, 2005.

————. "Erklärung der Zahlen von Gen 5 aus ihrem kompositionellen Zusammenhang," ZAW 121 (2009): 1–18.

Zorn, J. R., J. Yellin and J. Hayes. "The *m-(w)-ṣ-h* Stamp Impressions." *IEJ* 44 (1994): 161–83.

Indexes

Index of References

INDEX OF AUTHORS